California Slim

California Slim

The Music, the Magic, and the Madness

Andrew J. Bernstein

To order additional copies of this book, contact:
Xlibris Corporation
1-888-795-4274
www.Xlibris.com
Orders@Xlibris.com
127048

For Teo, Katie, and Kim

In the Beginning

It was March 1962 when I invested in a hundred-dollar banjo and began lessons on Tuesday nights at Dana Morgan Studio Music Shop in downtown Palo Alto. A young guy with a shock of black hair, a goatee, and black horn-rimmed glasses on his nose came out to meet me when I checked in for my first lesson.

"Are you my seven o'clock?"

"Yeah."

"What's your name?"

"Andy Bernstein."

"I'm Jerry Garcia. Follow me."

He led me back to a small musty-smelling practice room with a couple of stools.

"Take your banjo out. Have you ever played an instrument before?"

"Just the drums."

"Do you have any rhythm?"

"Yup."

"Well, you're gonna need it with the banjo."

"No problem. Hey, do you know Kreutzmann?"

"Yeah, I know Bill. He teaches here. But you won't be learning any rock 'n' roll from me. I teach folk and blue grass."

"That's fine."

"By the way, since I'm missing the middle finger on my picking hand, do as I say, not as I do."

"Yes, sir."

(When I was fourteen, I was very respectful.)

The first lesson consisted of: (1) Jerry telling me to watch and listen as he demonstrated how to double thumbpick; (2) Jerry playing "Pig in a Pen"; (3) Jerry playing more; and (4) more.

After forty-five minutes, he took me out to the front, asked to get paid, and told me to practice and come back next week.

Somehow, maybe by osmosis, I was able to half-ass play by the following week. The next five or six lessons went down well; and by the second month, I was fingerpicking.

A. Bernstein Archives

Jerry Garcia, 1962

One evening, I came to the store a little early, and Jerry was jamming up front, playing a type of jug band blues, with Ron McKernan on harmonica and jug. I had known Ron back in junior high school, but I had no idea he was a musician—and a damn good one.

A. Bernstein Archives

Ron McKernan, 1960

Without missing a lick, Jerry looked over at me and said, "Can you come back later? I'm busy now."

"Can I listen?"

"Sure."

They sounded and looked like a couple of Appalachian hillbillies, but, unbeknownst to me, they were already playing professionally as Mother McCree's Uptown Jug Champions.

Jerry's limited patience as a teacher made it difficult

for me to learn chord structure. He much preferred hanging out with his girlfriend, Sara Ruppenthal, at St. Michael's Alley, a nearby coffee shop. Pretty soon, he began asking me to come get him at St. Mike's before my lessons. I did that once or twice, and then decided he wasn't into it. The money wasn't worth it to him, even though he and Sara had a baby on the way.

But that would not be the last I saw of Jerry.

When Bill Kreutzmann returned from private school for junior year, he rekindled his friendship with my pal Tom McCarthy. While Bill was away, he had learned some things about life and matured. He looked like a damn cowboy and was pretty determined to be one. McCarthy was having none of that. He berated Bill, reminding him that the drums were his calling.

One afternoon, after some drinking, Tom confronted Bill, telling him to get in his room and get busy with the up-until-now ignored drum kit. Bill resisted, at first gently, then with a temper. It bordered on physical as Tom herded Bill into his room and figured out how to lock him in. Bill played for two hours behind the door. Although cowboying was not discussed again as a possible life commitment, Bill favored cowboy hats for many years.

By the end of junior year, he was drumming with The Legends. Fronted by Jay Price, one of the few black guys around Palo Alto, The Legends were the premier dance band on the Peninsula—for a while.

A. Bernstein Archives

Bill Kreutzmann,
1962

By senior year, Kreutzmann and McCarthy were both emancipated and sharing an apartment, perfecting their skills at being bachelors. Bill still taught drums at Dana Morgan's, but was taking jazz lessons and hanging out with some older guys over on the west side of Menlo Park. There was a scene going down there with musicians, artists, and writers. Jerry Garcia and Bob Weir (another Dana Morgan prodigy) were part of it, as well as Ron McKernan, who was now known as Pigpen. They were way into jug band music, and had a strong local following among the folk set. Drums were not required, but Bill liked this crowd, who were worlds away from his high school buddies. He was often gone a day or two at a time.

Not surprisingly, Bill turned on to pot in Menlo Park and introduced it to McCarthy. No one else knew about it. I had no idea what it was, other than from the crappy movies they showed us in health class. That year, 1965, a very colorful, bright, and high-spirited Palo Alto High School grad named Gordie Howe was busted with pot in Los Altos Hills. It made front-page news, with serious charges and possible time, ensuring that those who smoked pot kept it to themselves.

Warlocks Emerge

A. Bernstein Archives
The Only Known Warlocks Poster

While I was busy living a fast-paced life as a senior and speculating about marijuana, Bill Kreutzmann got more and more involved with the Menlo Park crowd. The jug band was also affected by the British invasion and all that excitement. Something was going on at Dana Morgan's, where jam sessions in the front room of the shop had become more rock-oriented. Now they needed a drummer. The next thing I knew, Bill came to school one day and told us his new band, named The Warlocks, would be playing at Magoo's Pizza Parlor in Menlo Park. Aside from Bill on drums, Jerry was on guitar and vocals, Bob Weir was on rhythm guitar and vocals, Ron McKernan was on keyboard, harp, and vocals, and Dana Morgan, the studio owner's son, was on bass.

We didn't know what to expect, but it turned out to be *great*. They did covers of Beatles, Rolling Stones, and Chuck Berry songs, and some blues. We were sure Bill's new band had a future. After that first gig, they were invited back to play at Magoo's every Wednesday night for a month. I never missed a show.

Palo Alto Historical Society
The Warlocks, with Phil Lesh on Bass (ca. 1965)

In its issue of September 2, 1993, *Rolling Stone* quoted Jerry describing this first foray into public performance:

> [The] first time we played in public, we had a huge crowd of people from the high school, and they went fuckin' nuts. The next time we played, it was packed to the rafters. It was a pizza place. We said, "Hey, can we play here on Wednesday nights? We won't bother anybody. Just let us set up in the corner." It was pandemonium immediately.

Critical to Bill's life at that time was his relationship with his girlfriend, Brenda Bass, a redhead who had graduated from Cubberly High and lived in South Palo Alto. She loved Bill and was at every show The Warlocks played around the Bay Area. When Brenda became pregnant, Bill was a father before he had graduated from high school. Their daughter, Stacy, was a beauty. Brenda and I had gone out as friends a few times when she and Bill were not getting along, before the baby was born. Once the baby came, Bill and Brenda lived with Bill's parents for a while until he graduated. The Warlocks were playing bars in San Francisco at that point, and Bill and Bobby were under age. Bill couldn't play a few of the clubs because he looked too young, so he forged an ID, using the name Bill Sommers—which is how he is identified on the first Grateful Dead album.

Near the end of my senior year, I heard that my favorite band in the world would be coming to San Francisco in two months. The Beatles would be playing at the Cow Palace on August 31, 1965.

One week before that, I read in the paper that the band would be staying at the Cabana in Palo Alto, the only high-rise hotel on the Peninsula at the time. And then it happened: My friend Rudy Cambra found out that his brother-in-law was the security director for the Cabana, and needed some extra bodies as security guards while the Beatles were there. We were hired over the phone.

When Rudy and I showed up at the Cabana for our training the next day, we were given floor plans of the hotel. The Beatles would occupy the entire top floor and would only enter and exit the hotel together, with their security detail. When they were moving, we were to stay in our assigned positions and maintain our perimeter. It sounded like a military operation.

Awesome!

They gave us security credentials that were to be worn with our sports coats and slacks, white shirt, and tie. The security badges were rectangular, with "THE BEATLES" across the top, our names in the middle, and a yellow ribbon at the bottom, which said in gold print, "Welcome The Beatles." It was as if fate had chosen me.

The Boys were scheduled to arrive at the hotel sometime between 3:00 and 6:00 P.M. on the Thursday before their Friday performance. Thursday afternoon around the Cabana was electric. Outside, the fans were massing on the sidewalks along El Camino Real. Inside, the lobby was packed with reporters, photographers, and cops.

I got a plum assignment. Only one elevator car would be in service for the top floor from 3:00 till 6:00, and I would be guarding the elevator entrance at the top. That meant I was certain to see my idols up close!

While I was at my post, several "VIPs" tried to bluff their way in. One

A. Bernstein Archives

persistent woman showed up time and again in the elevator. It became a joke between us, with her trying to get in, and me saying it wasn't gonna happen. I recognized her right away. She was a local folk singer with long black hair and a new album out—Joan Baez. Although she didn't get past me, she eventually did get through and managed to bed John, as I recall from her biography.

Robert Altman Archives
Joan Baez

Thirty minutes before the Beatles arrived, my bubble was burst. For some reason, I was relieved of my duty on the top floor and repositioned on the floor below, again at the elevator entrance. If the elevator accidentally stopped on my floor, I was to keep people away. I had a two-way radio, so I knew when the elevator would move, with The Beatles inside. As the car whizzed past my floor, I pressed my ear to the doors, but I only heard laughter. So very close, and yet so far away.

The next big event was the Rolling Stones' visit to San Jose, scheduled for December 4, 1965. I was going to see them, no matter what it took. After all, they were the *bad* boys, the loose ones—yes, the dangerous ones. But they would be in the Bay Area for only one night.

When Stones tickets went on sale, Rudy and I were in line at 8:00 A.M. We were cool. First row balcony.

I already had my wardrobe planned. Just one problem: I didn't own it; my friend Todd Nimitz did. Fortunately, Todd was a rhythm and blues guy, so he didn't know that the suit he had bought, a year before the Beatles hit America, was the exact outfit that the band later wore on the cover of their first album, *Meet The Beatles*—right down to the velvet ring around

A. Bernstein Archives

the neck, where the collar would normally be. Pegged, no cuffs. And it was a perfect fit. Todd was amazed when I offered him seventy-five dollars for it, a lot of money in 1965. Since I already had the boots, I was in.

The Stones arrived in the Bay Area on a Thursday night before the Saturday show in San Jose. Rudy and I drove to the airport to see them. They were on the other side of the glass, right in front of us. We were able to say "hi" to each band member as he passed by, and give a thumbs up. Mick looked me right in the eyes, smiled, and gave a thumbs up back through the glass. Rudy and I jabbered all the way home.

When the Stones came out onstage on Saturday night, it was pandemonium from the first notes. The band did a lot of old American blues standards, like "Red Rooster." Mick fashioned himself Sonny Boy Williamson, playing the harp and screeching out the vocals in his best Liverpool blues affectation. It was raw and beautiful. The crowd was rowdy—chairs were flying on the floor level. I had on the Beatles suit and boots, and rocked my ass off all night.

In the Center of a Changing World

S hortly before Tom McCarthy went into the Marines, he and I were hanging out when Bill Kreutzmann called, asking us to meet him at T. C. Christies, a haberdashery in downtown Palo Alto. Bill was there with the rest of the Warlocks—Jerry Garcia, Bob Weir, and Dana Morgan—all getting measured for Beatles suits. Someone's parents thought it would be a good idea and was paying for it. The only one who refused to be there was Pigpen. Potential success was not enough to get him into one of those suits.

When Tom and I got down there, it was hysterical watching Jerry getting fitted for slacks. He hated having some guy running a tape measure from his crotch down to his ankle. As it turned out, Jerry was a Levis and sneakers guy, and the group never did wear those Beatles suits.

About this same time, the Warlocks were performing on the Peninsula at places like The Embers, in Redwood City. They soon replaced Dana Morgan with Phil Lesh, a very accomplished local musician from the Menlo Park scene, via Berkeley, to play bass. They also developed a relationship at that time with Augustus Owsley Stanley III, a Berkeley chemistry dropout, LSD cook *par excellence*, and budding sound expert. He was a most extraordinary fellow, who would play a role in my musical life a few years down the line.

A. Bernstein Archives
Augustus Owsley Stanley III

The next time I saw Jerry was just before the band moved to Los Angeles for a while, partly funded with Owsley's money. At the time, I had just quit a job as a delivery truck driver and taken a new one as a cook (with no experience) at Foster's Freeze on El Camino Real.

One afternoon at Foster's, just as the lunch crowd was booming and I was up to my ass in burgers on the grill, I noticed a couple of familiar faces tapping on the window of the parking lot side of the little building. It was Jerry and Pig.

I shrugged, as if to say, "What? I'm busy!"

Jerry pantomimed eating a burger, and then pulled out the pocket of his Levis to indicate that he had no money. He and Pig looked like a couple of boxcar drifters. How could I refuse them? I fixed up two double cheeseburgers, two extra large fries, and two giant strawberry shakes, and quickly hustled them out the back door. The boys disappeared into the old wreck of a car they were driving and headed north on El Camino with smoke billowing out the back.

They would return to the Bay Area one year later, after a few acid tests, as The Grateful Dead.

Before McCarthy left for Camp Pendleton, we had one last breakfast together at Bennington Café on University Avenue, where we had breakfasted, off and on, over the past year. Tom had come to know some of Kreutzmann's friends from Menlo Park. I was looking at a newspaper that morning, reading Tom parts of a review of a book by a Menlo Park author, Ken Kesey, who had just published *One Flew Over the Cuckoo's Nest*.

At some point, Tom looked over my shoulder, as if someone were behind me. I turned and saw a bear of a man smiling down at me.

"Please, read on," he said. "I haven't read the review." Then he let out a big barrel of a laugh.

Tom had recognized the man as one of Bill's Menlo Park friends. Not knowing who he was, I read the entire review out loud. The big man slapped my back and loudly proclaimed, "Sounds like a great read. I think I'll go buy me a copy!"

It was Kesey himself.

Around this time, I was taking a weight-training class at Foothill College. The instructor was a guy named Jim Fairchild, a former Palo Alto High School football coach and PE instructor. I was skinny, *very* skinny, but there was a kid even skinnier in this class named Gregg Rolie. Because of our lack of muscle mass, Coach Fairchild used to give both of us grief, particularly Gregg, who had a lot of long hair in a rock star style. A cocky wise guy, Gregg gave it right back to the coach. I often saw Gregg on campus, hanging around with the other longhaired musicians. We didn't talk a lot, except to commiserate over bearing the brunt of Fairchild's jabs.

My social life at that time focused on the Bay Area club scene, which produced some great talent. The East Bay focused on blues and R&B, and the West Bay more on rock and pop. One of the regular acts at a Sunnyvale club called The Bold Knight was a copycat of Paul Revere and the Raiders, which went by the name of William Penn and His Pals. Most of the musicians were from the Palo Alto area.

A. Bernstein Archives
Foothill College Campus

One night, after a dance where William Penn and His Pals had played, Rudy and I were heading out the door, when someone yelled, "Hey, Rudy, what's happenin'?"

It was Gregg from weight training. It turned out that he was "William Penn," the keyboard player and lead singer. We looked at each other and chuckled, since we had been in Fairchild's class ten hours earlier, sweating and building up our pathetic bodies. If Fairchild had seen him in his big plume hat, embroidered vest, and topcoat, Gregg would have had to quit the morning weight-training class or be subjected to a slow, painful death. Gregg went on to become part of the musical legend of the San Francisco sound.

By September 1966, it was full speed ahead in San Francisco. Hippiedom had blossomed, and Bill Graham was in the business of fueling the fire. The

Fillmore was rocking every week, from Thursday to Sunday. There were clubs throughout the Bay Area, including the Matrix in San Francisco, which featured up-and-coming rock bands like the Doors, and the Embers in Redwood City, where the house band was a soul-inspired group named Sly and the Family Stone.

A. Bernstein Archives

The Original Fillmore Auditorium Today, at the Corner of Fillmore and Geary

My friends and I piled into cars to go to the Fillmore almost every weekend. Bill Graham had an eclectic taste in music—Thelonius Monk to Chuck Berry. The Grateful Dead were now leading the pack, along with the Jefferson Airplane, Big Brother and the Holding Company, Quicksilver Messenger Service, Blue Cheer, Moby Grape, and a throng of others. We smoked so much weed on the way to the Fillmore that we were cosmic pilgrims by the time we hit the steps up to the auditorium. I had a favorite spot, house left, under the dressing rooms of this grand old place, where I could trip and expand the world between my ears to my heart's content.

Psychedelic Cowboys

Chris Newell Archives
A Boy and His Bus

As 1966 turned into 1967, I was becoming less and less interested in Foothill College, and more and more interested in getting out and around. To do that, I bought a '61 VW microbus, tore out the rear seats, built a bed and cabinets in back, and insulated the roof with carpet scraps. I spent many nights sleeping in that bus on some of my favorite streets in Palo Alto.

On weekends in those days, I often used to head down to Big Sur to camp, take LSD, and have fun with my friends. When the weekend finally arrived for the Monterey Pop Festival, we loaded up our gear and drugs (but no tickets), and headed down the coast like a band of gypsies. I was the head of the caravan most of the way in my hot rod bus, which now had a 914 Porsche engine. No girls on this trip, just the Palo Alto psychedelic cowboys. Added to our regular assortment of acid, weed, and shrooms, we also had a new addition, pure THC in oil form. It was a big mistake to bring it, but we had no idea at the time.

We arrived at the Ventana Campground just as the sun was setting on Thursday night. It's frightening to think back that I was driving the curves of Highway 1, along a 300-foot drop to the Pacific Ocean, in a fog (the real kind), as I was seeing dragons floating across the road.

The next morning, several of us went up to Monterey to get tickets, but when we saw that the line was two blocks long, we decided it made sense to leave a couple of guys there, and the rest of us would head back down to Big Sur. We arrived back at the camp around 4:00 P.M., synched up the eight-track car stereos in a couple of vehicles, and turned up the Dead doing "Little School Girl."

I was the master joint roller, so it was up to me to carefully coat a Zig Zag on one side with the brown THC oil from that little bottle, like painting with honey. I had to open the van door, since the pungent odor was quickly taking over the air in the bus.

This shit is STRONG!

With the Dead blaring under the giant redwoods and the fog from the Pacific swirling around the camp, we partook of the Oil of Herbs of Fire. By the time the two guys we left behind returned with tickets for the Saturday night show, it was obvious to them that there was another, far more explorative reason we had come south that weekend. Although we all had tickets, only three of the eight went to the show. The rest of us stayed at the mother camp, allowing the combination of the oil and the LSD to take us on as yet unexplored journeys.

Our friends who made it to the Saturday night show at the festival raved about the magic of a new talent, Jimi Hendrix. They said it was as though no one else had played. No one else at all.

"You guys missed something," one of them said. "But he's doing the Fillmore in two nights, with the Jefferson Airplane opening. If you can get in, you *gotta* go."

Hoping that tickets were available at the door, my friend Herb and I drove like mad to make the show. It turned out that we could have taken our time, because Hendrix was still unknown, so there was only half a house. But the Airplane had played Monterey, and were so intimidated by Hendrix that they refused to open. Thus, the third band on the bill, Gabor Szabo, opened instead.

I was dumbfounded by what followed. Whatever I had seen previously, and I had seen quite a few bands in the years leading up to that night, this guy blew the socks off all of it. He made the guitar talk, shout, scream, and then cry actual musical tears.

He was a wonder unto himself and otherworldly.

One fateful Friday evening around this time, I was enjoying a hot fudge Sunday at the Peninsula Creamery in downtown Palo Alto when a young Polynesian woman came up to me, and said, "I really like your poncho. The embroidery's beautiful."

I took one look at her pretty face and well-endowed chest, and replied, "Thank you very much. May I buy you an ice cream?"

I soon found out that Alicia was from Hawaii and only seventeen. I was nineteen, and had no business even talking to her. But I had a hormonal drive, and she was very impressionable. So we began to meet downtown from time to time and eventually ended up in the back of my bus, where we smoked joints and rolled around on the bed. She wasn't a virgin, but I was reluctant to take things all the way, considering her age.

She told me she lived with her brother and widower father in Menlo Park. After a couple of weeks, I began to sneak in her window once in a while on Friday nights after her father went to work, and she knew her brother wasn't coming home. Like a fool, I started to take this arrangement for granted, and it became a regular thing—although I kept the contact to heavy petting.

On one particular Friday night, I had taken some acid early in the evening and was decked out in my wire rim glasses, poncho, and knee-high leather moccasins, with my long hair and muttonchop sideburns. I parked my bus around the corner from her house, and in I went. Off came the clothes. Although it was difficult, I was once again able to restrain myself, but just barely.

All of a sudden, the lights came on, blinding us. Standing in the entrance of Alicia's bedroom was the most evil sight I had ever seen: her father. He wasn't tall, maybe five-foot-nine, with greasy jet black hair that hadn't seen a comb or a brush in months. His bottom front teeth protruded up and over his top lip, and his eyes were as dark as coal. In his right hand, he was holding a knife, with a leather strap attached to it, wrapped around his wrist.

"Get out of that bed, Alicia!" he ordered. "Go in your brother's room and get some clothes on!"

She ran past him into the hallway, screaming, "Daddy, no, no, no!"

He looked at me and said, with a thick pidgin accent, "I gonna cut you fuckin' heart out, hippie!"

I threw off the covers and stood up on the bed, still erect. He stared at me.

Behind him, his daughter was screaming, "Don't kill him! Don't kill him!"

"Shuddup!" he said, and then moved toward me.

I was shaking.

"Killing me isn't worth going to jail for the rest of your life," I begged.

I was still stoned on acid, this guy was the meanest looking SOB I had ever seen, and he was preparing to butcher me.

Just as I was thinking of making a run for it, the doorbell rang, and I heard men yelling, "Sheriff's Department, open the door!"

"Open the door!" he commanded his daughter.

When I realized I was going to live, I began to cry.

A moment later, two deputy sheriffs appeared in the hallway. One of them said to the pissed father, "Make way, and put down that knife!"

The other deputy said to me, "Get your clothes on."

While I was getting dressed, I could hear the deputies talking to the father, who gave his name as Manuel.

"Do you want to press charges?"

"Yes."

At this point, the deputies were my saviors, and I was grateful to be going to jail and not to the morgue. They handcuffed me and escorted me out of the house. As I walked by Manuel and his daughter, I felt shame and remorse. I also realized that he probably never intended to kill me, but just wanted to scare some sense into me—which he did.

The LSD seemed to have been shocked out of me. The deputies in the front seat were having their little laughs at my expense, referring to me as Buffalo Bill. I guess they were pretty close to the proper comparison.

At the county jail in Redwood City, I had my mugs taken, and they impounded my wallet, keys, and belt.

The officer who booked me said, "You're not as yet being charged with any crime, but we're holding you on suspicion of statutory rape, pending hospital tests on the girl."

They put me in a small holding room that had benches on four sides.

I was alone, but I could hear the sounds from the nearby cells. The men sounded like caged animals. That scared the shit out of me.

Through a small window to his office, the jailer said, "If you're charged tonight, you'll put on that orange jumpsuit that's in that cardboard box right in front of you, along with some shower slippers, and you'll be held for the weekend for a hearing on Monday morning."

I'm pretty much fucked.... Except I'm fairly sure I didn't come in her.

Because I was on acid, I couldn't swear to anything.

Three hours later, a deputy unlocked the door and looked at me with a serious expression.

"I've got bad news for you," he said.

My heart sank.

"Buffalo Bill..., you're gonna have to spend the night at home. We so hoped you would be joining us for the weekend."

When he saw the look of relief on my face, he burst out laughing. He had been fucking with me.

"The test results from Stanford Hospital came back negative," he said. "You're free to go."

The jailer led me out to the booking desk, where they returned my property. I had no money in my pocket, not a dime. It was now 2:00 A.M. I was too ashamed to call anybody to pick me up. The deputies said if they caught me hitchhiking, they would bring me back in. So I walked.

It took me an hour to get back to her house, where my bus was still sitting around the corner. It was very dark there, without any streetlights. This was not a safe neighborhood, and I knew it—but I had been blinded by pussy.

What if her dad knows this is my bus? What if he's waiting for me? What if his friends are?

I crept up slowly, unlocked the door as quietly as I could, and got in. Locking the door, I said a little prayer and turned the key. The bus started right up. I jammed it into first and roared away.

Early the next morning, I drove down to Pfeiffer Beach in Big Sur, my sanctuary on the Monterey coast.

I parked the bus and walked the two miles out to the beach, where I meditated on life and death for hours. When it got cold later in the day, I built a small fire out of driftwood and just sat there, taking in the beauty. I swore to myself I would never be so stupid again. It was the longest twenty-four hours I had ever spent, and it wasn't even twenty-four hours yet.

The Hairiest, Scariest Bus Driver Ever

A. Bernstein Archives

I had been fascinated with trucks and buses ever since I was a baby. My poor parents must have been driven crazy by my addiction. By the time I was eighteen, I could identify any number of large vehicles by year, make, and model: Peterbilts, White Freightliners, Internationals, Autocar Diesels, Macks—all of them. I had to find some outlet to be a road dude—other than my VW bus. The logical choice was to drive a *big* bus, and the school buses of the day were just fine with me.

Crown Coaches and Gilligs dominated the west coast market. These were not plastic Blue Birds but solidly built behemoths that were all steel and customized to the specs of the school district. The biggest were tandem axle, 91-passenger monsters, almost forty feet long. Mostly built for rural districts, there were only a few around the Bay Area. Like everything else I desired in this life, I wanted to drive one of those buses *so* bad. I also decided I wouldn't cut my hair; they had to take me as I was.

The Palo Alto Unified School District operated a fleet of Gillig 79-passenger diesel-powered transit buses, which were hunky, flat-nosed beauties. In the late summer of 1967, I strolled past the buses lined up and sparkling in the sun at the district's utility yard and walked into the office, all six-foot-seven of me—seven feet, if you counted the hair and the cowboy boots. In a clean shirt and Levis, with the manners my mom had taught me, I felt assured they would not be put off.

A pleasant woman sitting at a typewriter greeted me with a smile. When I said I was interested in becoming a bus driver, she called to someone named Ray in the next office. Out walked an elderly gentleman, maybe sixty-three or sixty-four, with an easy grin and gentle manner. After a brief chat, he hired me, pending the paperwork and getting my class B learner's permit. We went out into the yard, where he introduced me to the driving instructor, John Tipton, a fellow from Missouri, who had a crew cut and a laid back manner. Over the years, we became good friends.

A few days later, once the paperwork was in order and I had my permit in hand, I headed over to the bus yard, where John familiarized me with the dashboard controls and the shifting pattern. After a few minutes, I was driving out of the yard for my first on-the-road training.

I took to it immediately. John was quite surprised. I had been born to drive this mammoth. Sitting high on the driver's seat, I could see everything in front, around, and below me. As I made sweeping right turns, facing head-on traffic, I saw the looks on the faces of the drivers in their little cars.

A. Bernstein Archives

Cockpit of a Gillig

"He's driving our children?!"

Yup, I was fixin' to—the hairiest, scariest bus driver ever, complete with dark granny glasses.

The day before school started, I showed up for my first drivers' meeting. It was a friendly group of about twenty men and women, black, white, all ages. Ray welcomed the new drivers with "another school year" speech. I felt part of a close-knit group that was committed to providing safe and friendly service to the children of Palo Alto. I drew the best runs, the scenic hills west of town. That was the perfect job for me.

Before sunrise on my first day, I checked out all the systems on the bus, then headed up Page Mill Road. About the time the sun rose over the bay, I reached the narrow part of the route that climbs into the foothills of the Coast Range, which separates the bay from the Pacific Ocean. When I reached Foothills Park, the morning sun was bathing the horizon in a golden glow. I greeted my charges with a smile as they marched up the stairs, giving each one a warm "Good morning!" I shared the best part of my day with these bright, energetic kids, and over time became friends with each one of them.

Sometime in my second week on the job, I turned on the radio and set the dial to KSAN, one of the first alternative FM rock stations in the country. The kids and I enjoyed the music as we rolled. My route took me along the switchbacks on Arastradero Road, with its open pasture land and horses grazing on both sides. Finally, I made a left turn in front of Zots Beer Garden onto Alpine Road, and then drove a few miles to my final stop in Portola Valley. After dropping the kids off at Gunn High School in Palo Alto, I took a ten-minute break.

I repeated the same run for the younger kids who went to Nixon Elementary. (Not *that* Nixon!) At first, the little kids were a bit alarmed at my appearance, but soon realized I was a big pussycat. The mothers of the kindergarteners greeted me each morning and afternoon. I became the guardian of their youngsters, whom they trusted to get them down the hill and back up each day. I was always sober and straight when I climbed into bus number six.

I could go on about how important that job was to me, but I only want to mention one other thing. Just about every morning, as I drove down the mountain, at a particularly narrow turn in the road, I came face to face with another big Gillig, this one from the Los Altos School District. As we passed within a few feet of each other, I could tell the other driver was also tall, with long hair, a pork pie hat, a fuzzy face, and cool shades. Each morning, we nodded to each other, our mirrors almost rubbing.

A road brother.

Tom and Jim George were longhaired redheaded twin brothers, who also drove school buses—Jim for Los Altos and Tom for Palo Alto. They were a couple of characters, who shared my love of big vehicles. Both of them were bright guys, who loved to hang out and smoke weed at the cottage I had recently rented in a redwood grove in Los Altos. They studied

The Urantia Book, something about flying saucers and a hotel in Chicago in the '30 s that had mystical powers. At some point, they came to believe that giving away their possessions would lead to a higher level of spirituality. Therefore, I became the recipient of a 1941 Chevrolet rescue firetruck (a gigantic panel truck with dual rear wheels) and a four-cylinder Honda motorcycle. Eventually, I gave the motorcycle back, but kept the cool panel truck, with "Castro Valley" written on the side, from the city it had served for so many years.

A. Bernstein Archives

The Round Table Pizza parlor on California Avenue in Palo Alto was our regular meeting place. After work one night, the brothers told me we would be joined by the bus driver I passed every morning at the hairpin curve on Page Mill Road.

"His name's Maynard Lutts," Jim said.

"What the fuck kinda name is *that*?"

"He's one of a kind, Andy. You'll like him."

After a short wait, Maynard walked through the door. He was quite a sight. Probably 6'4", with a black leather motorcycle jacket, Levis, and old-school motorcycle boots like the ones Marlon Brando wore in *The Wild One*. Maynard's hair was a white-guy fro that hung down and out at the same time. When I stood up to shake hands, I noticed, after his shades came off, that he had a very calm and peaceful face with a warm smile. He also had very light blue eyes, the color of my dad's.

We had heard about each other, and of course I saw him each morning on the turn. I knew from Tom and Jim that Maynard's parents were eccentric Socialists from the '50s, who had raised Maynard and his two younger brothers as vegetarians. His father was a pharmacist, and his mother was a head nurse at Stanford Hospital.

In the course of the evening, I learned that Maynard and I shared the same tastes in cars, trucks, motorcycles, music, and, of course, the road.

"Andy," he asked, "you ever drive one of those midship Hall-Scott–powered Gilligs from the mid-Fifties?"

"No, but I sure as hell hear that one you drive bellowing as you pass me every morning. Love the sound! Palo Alto's only got one left…, a Fifty-three…bus number ten, driven by that Nazi press photographer, Chuck."

"Yeah, I see him around town once in a while."

This was the start of a friendship that would eventually change my life. After that night, Maynard regularly joined the three of us at my cottage, yakking about trucks, getting high, and listening to a shitload of Leon Russell records, among others.

Tom and Jim eventually became long-distance Greyhound bus drivers, and moved on, but Maynard and I remained close. The money was better in Palo Alto, so he eventually came over to my district. We were the two best drivers they had, so we always got the plum runs and field trips, not to mention the first choice of new buses when they were delivered from Gillig.

Crimson and Other Madness

Jake Pierre Archives

By early '68, the music scene in Palo Alto had moved beyond The Grateful Dead, who were now part of the San Francisco scene. The remnants of Gregg Rolie's band, William Penn and His Pals, were among the local musicians. There were some great bar bands that played the Bay Area club circuit. The Poppycock, a local club in downtown Palo Alto, booked some wonderful old blues guys like Lightnin' Hopkins, Hound Dog Taylor, and John Lee Hooker. Young rock bands, like The Gollywogs, out of El Cerrito, just north of Berkeley, were regulars there. Within a year, the Wogs would change their name to Credence Clearwater Revival and release their first chart-busting album. Other brilliant bands, like The Charlatans, Mother Earth, and scores of others kept Palo Alto rockin'.

Most of the bands were as yet unrecorded. Of course, we remained big fans of the Dead, who still played college gigs. My friends Pete Kelley, Tom Haid, and I followed them around to some of their Bay Area gigs. Bill Kreutzmann was cool (for a while) with the backstage passes for us "original fans." At a college show in Santa Clara one Friday afternoon, Jerry walked up to us backstage, smiled, and proclaimed, "You guys are our biggest fans."

Yes, Jerry, the guys from the local high school were—and still are—your biggest fans.

It was a magic time in Palo Alto. The establishment was losing its grip, and the streets were more and more becoming the property of young people. Music and dope and antiwar fervor dominated. Music defined us more than the media attention and the hype. It was everywhere. The songs and lyrics were ours, and spoke to our feelings of discontent, of love for mankind, and of new possibilities. We had a language, we had a dress code (anything not done before), and we had causes.

In the summer of 1968, my friend from high school, Rollie Grogan, received a general discharge from the Marines after a court martial for selling pot. He and Tom McCarthy had become jarheads right after graduation. Rollie was the stepson of a downtown Palo Alto jeweler. With a perfect swimmer's body, he had a real future in swimming, but preferred to party and smoke. He was an outrageous fellow, smart, but full of himself and his need to be the center of attention. Back in school, he had always wanted to get the laughs, believing that a good sense of humor was a chick magnet. He could never pull it off, but it was hilarious watching him try.

Rollie and I had stayed close while he was in the Marines, and now he was bursting at the seams to get back to Palo Alto. While he was still in the Corps, living in Oceanside, he had formed a plan to be part of the music scene in the Bay Area, and had successfully spun his special brand of bullshit to some of his Marine buddies about how to take San Francisco by storm. His relationship with the Dead was the sealer. His buddies bought it—hook, line, and sinker.

He brought two of them "straight out of the crotch" to Palo Alto once they were all discharged. Within a week, they had rented a second-floor two-bedroom apartment in an old house on Addison Street, right next to the Mormon Church.

So here were Rollie and his buddies, Larry and Jerry, far from being part of the local scene, but ready for action. Another Marine, David, returned to New York after being discharged, but joined them later on.

Robert Altman Archives
Bill Graham Being Bill Graham

By this time, Bill Graham wouldn't put on a concert in his San Francisco venues (Fillmore and Winterland) without a light show. Producing those in a ballroom setting was new territory. Bill Ham, who operated a company called Headlights, was the first to come up with the techniques that set the standard. With big plans to form their own light show venture, Rollie, Larry, and Jerry pooled their money to live cheaply and invest in the equipment needed to get started. Rollie also had a rich grandfather in

Stockton, who was an easy tap. As for my role in all this, I had the local connections, and didn't look like a recently released Marine, something that enabled me to move within the "community" easily. As the resident freak, I was now onboard.

We all went to work at the apartment on Addison to create our light show company, which we christened "Crimson Madness" from some idea Rollie got when we were all high one night. I divided my day between school bus driving and putting plans together for the show. Larry and Jerry, both bright guys, enrolled in classes at Foothill on the G.I. Bill, studying to become something other than light artists. Rollie also went to Foothill, but he had no intention of becoming a serious student, although he did have intentions: He knew the college had a vast audio-visual and filmmaking department, so the goods were there to borrow for an alert student who also had a light show in his future. He checked out 16mm Hasselblad motion picture cameras, classroom overhead projectors, and Kodak carousel slide projectors. Soon Addison House was overrun with gear, art supplies, and old junk from Army surplus depots.

Herb Pemberton, another of my buddies from high school days, who could figure out just about any mechanical challenge, was brought in as a technical adviser and tweak monger. He, Rollie, and I were doing most of the footwork, and my VW bus came in handy as the work vehicle. Larry and Jerry attended class and kept money coming in from their GI Bill. They also contributed on the artistic side, painting slides and becoming proficient at creating liquid overhead projections. This involved placing one Petri dish on top of another, with colored mineral oil in between, and then manipulating the top dish to create floating pulsating images. We practiced on white sheets hung in the apartment living room. Pot smoking was continuous, and ideas flowed like water.

Rollie also made connections with local Palo Alto musicians, putting himself out there as a booking agent/manager. We soon got to know a band named Together, a soul/rock group that featured two black singers, Ron and Gary, and a keyboard player named Cory. A band named Blue Mountain was also making a name for itself around town, with a few horns and a female lead singer with chops, giving it a bigger sound. Before long, Rollie was representing the interests of Blue Mountain and Together. He named the whole family of ventures Vortex Productions.

South of the Border, Down Mexico Way

A. Bernstein Archives

My friend Steve, who had originally suggested that I take banjo lessons with his own teacher, Jerry Garcia, went on to build a sailboat and become a sailor. At some point, he got some experience in Europe on a smuggling operation. I never heard the whole story, but bales of pot in waterproof wrap washed up on the shores of Scotland, many miles in the opposite direction from where they were supposed to land. I think some of the Europeans in that venture got caught, but Steve came home.

At some point, he introduced me to one of the characters involved in the European operation—a bright, clean-cut guy from Santa Cruz named Chris, who fashioned himself an international drug smuggler of the first order. He even had a name for his operation, IDS, International Drug Smugglers. Chris claimed to have completed ten successful operations from Mexico to California, through Arizona, and was planning another one as soon as he found a partner and a vehicle.

The "Most Gullible Guy" in the Palo Alto High School class of 1965—*me*—was looking for adventure and had a souped-up VW microbus. Chris let me know that I was privileged to be on trip Number 11.

When I told Rollie what I was about to do, he said, "You're fuckin' crazy! We'll never see you again."

"But I can make five grand and have a hell of an adventure."

"Good luck, pal!"

Obviously, my gullible moniker was well deserved, because I wasn't the least bit concerned about getting caught, spending time in a Mexican jail, or being shot by banditos.

The journey began on the late afternoon of Halloween, October 31, 1968. Chris planned to follow the same blueprint he had used on the ten previous trips, first traveling down to Culiacán, in the state of Sinaloa. He also made it clear there was to be no dope on us while en route.

"We'll be passing through several states," he said, "and I want us clean…, both in Mexico and here."

Yes, sir, El Comandante, Señor IDS.

So no dope it was.

Since we would be entering Mexico through Tucson, I called my old Paly friend Jon to ask if we could crash at his place for the night. After meeting Jon at his little southwest-style bungalow, we went to dinner and later on got stoned on his dope. Jon was a little put off by Chris. Although he thought I was taking a big risk, he saw the ship had already sailed, and it was too late for a lecture.

The next morning, we got an early start and cleared the border around 10:00 A.M. No searches going into Mexico, just bring your pesos and have a good time. We were now on the four-lane Pan-American Highway, which had recently been given a face-lift in preparation for the upcoming Olympics in Mexico City.

The southern Arizona desert scenery changed shortly after we crossed the border. Now there were beautiful rolling hills, with farmers walking alongside the highway to their fields, and women and children waiting for buses. I was aware that I was in a different country. If anything went wrong, I was a long way from home.

About noon, we crossed the border from the state of Sonora into Sinaloa. As I pulled up to the lowered border gate, I saw my first Federales, with very large weapons strung over their shoulders. Several others milled around, looking at us suspiciously. They had seen VW microbuses in the past, with longhairs driving. Although I had my hair tied in a ponytail and tucked up in my straw cowboy hat, my long mutton chops were in plain sight. Chris spoke some Spanish to them, and we were waved through.

Twenty miles down the road, while Chris was napping on the bed in back, the throttle cable broke, and I had no power. As I quickly pulled the bus off to the side of the road, Chris woke up and freaked out, thinking we had been stopped by the police. I assured him everything was okay—except for the fact that we lost the throttle cable and couldn't go anywhere. I hopped out and opened the engine cover on the back of the bus, as locals walked by in their casual white garb, checking us out. Sure enough, the cable was sprung and couldn't be fixed. It was time for Plan B.

Our destination, Culiacán, was about a hundred miles away. We figured it would have a VW shop, but what to do now? It was time for good old American ingenuity. As Chris talked with a few of the locals in Spanish, I rigged up a throttle "cable" out of two shoelaces, connected one end to the lever on the carburetor, and ran it up through the open hatchback door. My plan was that both the engine cover and the hatchback door would be partially open, so that one guy could hang out the back and operate the throttle while the other drove.

From talking to the locals, Chris discovered that there was a shop up the road in the next small town. He got directions, and off we went. With Steve hanging out the back and me at the wheel, all of Mexico heard me screaming, "Let off a little!" when I wanted to stop, and "Give me a little more!" when I wanted to shift.

I'm glad this isn't happening with two hundred pounds of weed under the bed.

The "shop" turned out to be a tin shack on the outskirts of a very small village, with a mechanic who was, at most, fifteen. The expression on his face as we limped up said, "Customers! Gringo customers!"

There was no way the shoelace rig was going to get us to Culiacán, so we were at his mercy. He understood the problem immediately, and told us he would have a temporary fix within thirty minutes, after he got some parts. As he rode off on his bicycle, Chris and I looked at each other. We had no options.

The kid returned ten minutes later with a sack full of wire, string, little springs, and fasteners. We had a throttle cable in thirty minutes, and it worked! He was a clever young man who saved our asses, and was mighty pleased with the fifty dollars Chris paid him for his work. I've never forgotten that kid.

We rolled into Culiacán about 2:00 P.M. The parts guy at the VW dealership said he could get us a new cable and have it installed by the next morning. So we booked two rooms next to each other at a nearby hotel. The place was dirty, but not filthy. As we climbed the stairs to our rooms, the bellboy spat on the carpet. Not a good sign.

I rested for a while, and then told Chris I was going out for a walk.

"Put your hair up and keep a low profile," he said.

No problem. At six-foot-seven, a hundred and eighty pounds, and hairy, I'll fit right in.

Every person who saw me—man, woman, and child—stared. I just smiled back.

Chris knocked on my door around 6:00 P.M., looking in control and refreshed, except that his eyes were a little droopy.

Later on, we went back downstairs and met his contact, Carlos, in front of the hotel. He was a tall young man, very well dressed, a college student in his early twenties, working on an advanced degree, who spoke perfect English. In fact, he looked so preppy that even my mother would have loved him. His big brown eyes and smile, which would have melted any señorita's heart, reminded me of Tom McCarthy.

We hopped in a cab to begin a journey deep into the barrio of Culiacán. The streets were dark, the houses not much more than shacks, and the smells got worse the deeper into the barrio we traveled. It seemed like we were driving in circles. But wherever we were going, our lives were in Carlos's hands.

Finally, we stopped. There were no streetlights, only the dark rutted dirt road we had been on for half an hour. When we got out, the taxi took off in a cloud of dust. We knocked on the door of one of the shacks. It opened slightly, words were exchanged in Spanish, and we were soon standing in someone's combination kitchen and living room—actually, just walls and a roof with a dirt floor. Dinner was cooking in a pot suspended over an open fire in a small pit in the middle of the room. A couple of women were tending to the meal, while yelling at some kids who were running around.

There was a large table along the far wall, with small homemade wooden chairs scattered about.

Carlos went into another room to check up on the whereabouts of his friends, and soon returned with two guys in their mid-forties. They didn't look friendly, but they didn't look dangerous, either. One was carrying a knapsack.

Soon, out came two small bricks, wrapped in red cellophane over grey construction paper. I really didn't want to get stoned, followed by blazing paranoia and confusion, topped off by a panic attack.

But Chris said, "I don't smoke pot, Andy. It's up to you. Your thumbs up or down will decide."

SHIT FUCK!!

I rolled a fatty and did my job. It was immediately obvious to me from the taste that the weed was from Michoacán, and that it was fresh. Instead of getting paranoid, I was able to relax and give a two-thumbs-up seal of approval.

Big smiles all around. Glasses and a bottle of tequila appeared, and the mood lightened considerably, with laughing, backslapping, and good wishes exchanged.

As we left, the same taxi and driver were waiting for us, with the engine running. I asked Chris what the plan was. He said we would meet these guys in three nights at a prescribed location outside of town.

Early, the next morning, Chris knocked on my door.

"Pack up, Andy, we're going to Mazatlán," he said with a big grin on his face. He had made reservations for a bungalow on the beach at a secluded little vacation spot that was a favorite for American and Canadian smugglers.

But first, of course, we had to pick up my microbus at the shop. A hundred and fifty U.S. dollars later, we were on our way.

We rolled into Mazatlán sometime after 8:00 P.M. The owners of the small resort at the end of a beach road greeted Chris like an old family member. For the next couple of days, I hung out on the beach, body-surfed, and chased little crabs that ran sideways along the sand.

The last night we were there, when I returned to our bungalow after a walk on the beach, Chris was sitting at the small kitchen table. I looked at him, expecting to hear "Hi!" but was shocked into silence. He was leaning on the table with a small tie-off around his bicep and a needle in his arm. I gulped, unable to get out any words.

After a moment, I asked, "What the hell is this? What's going on? Are you a junkie?"

Chris just looked at me. "Yeah, I'm a junkie. Do you have a problem with that?"

"No. Not if I was in California and had never met you," I said. "Fuck, man, we're in Mexico, getting ready to risk everything. I had a right to know in advance that I was with a junkie."

"Yeah, I suppose you're right."

What a prick! We've been a rolling felony WITHOUT the pot.

I was fucked, and about to get even more fucked when we brought two hundred pounds of marijuana into the States. I would now face heroin charges as well as pot charges if we got caught. I would never see sunlight again.

The next morning, when we drove back to Culiacán, Chris acted as if nothing had changed. After dinner, we drove to the meeting site a few minutes before 7:00. It was off the road in the bush. I didn't want to wait long. If they didn't show up, it was a sign we shouldn't proceed.

At 7:05, the same damned taxi drove up, with Carlos and his two associates. Chris got into the taxi and did the money exchange. After that, Carlos's two buddies opened the trunk of the taxi and started carrying large burlap sacks over to me to stash under the bed in the back of my van. The opening under the bed was barely big enough to accept the sacks. Then we were on our way.

I drove north out of Culiacán on a pitch black highway. Chris climbed into the back to sleep. When we were ten kilometers from the Sonora border, I woke him up. He told me to sit in the passenger seat, put my hair up into my hat, and keep my mouth shut.

The border crossing was manned with heavily armed Federales, who peered into the bus while Chris went into the office. Within sixty seconds, we were on the road again. Whether he paid off the head guy or just took a piss, I'm not sure—but he seemed to know just about every Federale along the route.

After we crossed the border, I climbed in back and got into bed. Several hours later, when I opened one of the window curtains, the sun was rising, and we were on a two-lane road in the mountains. It was clear we were no longer on the Pan-American Highway.

"Where the hell are we?" I asked Chris.

"We're going back a different way," he said. "At the moment, we're in the northeast sector of Sonora state. It's a very poor area, sparsely populated…, mostly by Indians."

As we drove along, I saw levels of poverty I had never imagined. Eventually, we crossed over the crest of the mountains. Below us stretched the vast Sonoran desert in every direction—an inhospitable expanse.

"If you look carefully," Chris said, "you can see Arizona."

When we got down to the desert floor, it was dry and hot, with the wind blowing up the dust. By mid-afternoon, we reached Agua Prieta, a shit hole town just south of the Arizona border.

I really want this to be over.

As we sat down at a sleazy restaurant in town, I glanced at a headline on an American newspaper nearby:

AMERICANS GO TO THE POLLS TODAY

Holy shit, it's election day!

On the day Nixon got elected for his first term, I was somewhere on the Sonoran desert, smuggling weed into the States.

That's something to tell the grandkids!

"Alright," Chris said, "here's the plan. You're gonna drive me back into the desert at four thirty this afternoon. Just after sundown, you'll drop me and the sacks off."

When I realized I wasn't going to be with the weed when I crossed the border, I was relieved.

"Then you'll drive all the way back to Hermosillo," he said, "about a hundred and fifty miles to the south, pick up the Pan-American Highway, and head north back up to Nogales. You won't have any contraband, so you can pass the intensive border check on the Arizona side. It'll take you about eight hours to drive down to Hermosillo and back up to Tucson, clear U.S. customs, and then drive east along the border on the U.S. side to meet me in Douglas, just across from Agua Prieta."

A. Bernstein Archives
Richard Nixon

"So that's the plan," I said, "except for one thing. How are you and the bags going to get across the desert?"

"I'm gonna carry 'em on my back, in two trips."

This guy has some balls. He's gonna have to carry a bag about four miles..., *and then walk four miles back to get the next one.*

"I'll meet you at 2:00 A.M., sharp," he said, "at the back left corner of the student parking lot at Cochise Junior College, in Douglas. It's on the highway on the left as you pass through town."

As we left Agua Prieta, there was next to no traffic on the road to the drop-off point, so when two cars came up on us, one from the front and the other from the back, I knew something was wrong—especially when the red lights started flashing.

"Federales," said Chris. "Stay cool."

Oh, okay. No problem.

They were upon us within seconds. I stopped the bus. Two big boys approached, holding rifles. Fearsome-looking would be putting it mildly. They walked up to both sides of the bus, and then, in Spanish, told us to open the window curtains in back. The Federale on my side asked me in English if we had seen anybody on the road while we were driving. I said we hadn't, but we had only been on the road for a short time. He asked our business, and I said we had just crossed the border and were miners headed for our stake outside Hermosillo.

"You need to be very careful, Señor," he said. "Two armed and very dangerous criminals escaped from a local prison. Keep your eyes open and don't pick up anyone."

With that, they walked back to their patrol cars and sped off.

Within one hour, the sun was down and Chris was ready to go. Together we pulled the sacks out, and I split. Around 9:00 P.M., I pulled up to the border crossing at Nogales. The bus was a mess, and I was a mess. On the U.S. side, an immigration officer directed me straight to the vehicle inspection station. When I got there, another officer showed me where to park and pointed to an office.

Inside a little room, a man in uniform asked me where I had been, and why my bus was so dusty. I gave him an explanation that was eighty percent true, leaving out the part about the Sonora desert and the two hundred pounds of pot. He told me I could leave and go have a bite to eat if I wanted while they searched my bus, which would be ready in an hour.

I headed out to the main street and walked back into Mexico, where I was approached by a couple of street venders who were selling gum. They were just kids, maybe ten years old. I could see they were hungry, so I asked the one who spoke English if they would like to have dinner with me. They accepted my invitation with great enthusiasm.

We ate at a taqueria, laughing and telling stories and becoming amigos. This was the first relaxation I had had in days.

After dinner, we strolled back towards the border, where we shook hands and said goodbye. Then off they went to pester more tourists.

When I got back to the vehicle inspection station, my bus was parked in the general parking lot, a good sign. Before I left, one of the inspectors asked where I was going. I knew this was a trick question, so I said I was going to Tucson to my friend's house.

I was pretty sure they would be following me to see if I took the highway east to Bisbee, or stayed on the main route to Tucson. In fact, there was a tail, but I spotted it immediately. They stayed with me for fifteen miles, and then pulled off. Since I had passed the Bisbee exit, pretending to be going to Tucson, I had to double back to head east to Bisbee, then Douglas, where I hoped to find Chris waiting for me at the college.

It was now around 10:30 P.M., and I had three and a half hours to cover a hundred and ninety-five miles. Driving across the desert gets spooky, but after a while I just settled in.

Why hurry?

Ten miles out of Douglas, I stopped at a roadside all-night diner to get a snack. As soon as I walked out of the rest room, two cops came in. When I looked at them, I knew they had seen my bus, with its California plates. That produced a bad feeling in my stomach. I was alone, with a bus, near Douglas, a known smuggling point. Ignoring the cops, I sat down at the counter, ordered coffee and a piece of apple pie à la mode, and made small talk with the waitress. Hoping that Chris was waiting, I needed to get going, but didn't want to leave before the police. When they finally got out of there, off I went. I figured there were so many points where this thing could turn to shit, I might as well just keep moving.

Cochise Community College was easy to find, right where Chris said it would be, and I had no trouble finding the student parking lot. Within thirty seconds, he was at my window, and we loaded the bundles into the bus. Chris was exhausted, but looked pretty good. I was impressed.

We drove up to my friend Jon's house in Tucson, where we spent the rest of the night and most of the next day sleeping.

Chris wanted to hit the road late that afternoon and head up to Lake Tahoe.

"Lake Tahoe?!" I was flabbergasted. "That's bullshit! I don't wanna go to Tahoe. I wanna go to Palo Alto, *now!* I want this fucking thing over and done!"

But he said he had a customer waiting for him in Tahoe, so in the end he won. Looking back on it now, I'm sure the detour had something to do with heroin. So off we were again, this time on our way to Phoenix, Las Vegas, and points north.

Chris agreed to take the wheel all the way to Vegas, so I crawled into the back and went to sleep.

Several hours later, I realized that the bus was coming to a stop. When I looked out one of the windows, I could see lights in the distance and a great canyon of some sort off to the side of the road. Chris pulled open the curtain between the front and the back.

"We've lost power," he said, looking very upset.

"Where the hell are we?"

"On top of Hoover Fucking Dam, buddy. We gotta push the bus off the road."

We were blocking the right lane of a two-lane highway over the top of the dam.

With two hundred pounds of weed sitting under me! Is this whole thing a dream, or what?

I got out and pushed while Chris steered.

At the far end of the dam, there was a light from what looked like a gas station. We decided that I would stay with the bus while Chris went to look for a payphone. Luckily he found one and called AAA.

By the grace of God, no cops showed up before the tow truck arrived from Boulder City to haul us into the Las Vegas VW dealership. By now it was around 5:00 A.M., so the place wasn't open yet. We decided to go to a hotel/casino across the street for an all-you-can-eat buffet breakfast. Then Chris checked into the hotel, and I went back to bed in the bus to wait for the dealership to open at 7:00.

I sure needed that hour of sleep. The service rep said that the bus needed a minor clutch repair, but it should only take a couple of hours.

I went back across the street to hang out at the casino so Chris could sleep for a while. Around 9:30, I called the dealership from a payphone, and was glad to hear that the bus was ready. Soon, Chris and I were back on the road, headed due north to Tahoe, with me at the wheel.

As I drove along, I started thinking of all the trouble we could get into if anything went wrong in this state.

When it comes to pot, Nevada's a hang 'em high state.

In Tonopah, we stopped to eat at a wild west restaurant, where the bartender entertained us with stories about UFO sightings in the area.

When we got back to the bus, Chris took the wheel, and I took to my bed, praying that this nightmare would be over within the next twenty-four hours.

Maybe UFOs will carry us off to their planet. Anything to be done with this madness.

Unfortunately, Chris had another agenda. When I got back into the passenger seat, a few hours later, he started talking about this favorite girl he had at the Moonlight Ranch, the whorehouse just outside of Carson City. At first, I thought he was just talking. But then it became clear that he planned to make a pussy stop.

"Listen, Chris," I said, "this is my bus, and there's no way you're stopping before we reach Tahoe."

He didn't say anything, but I sensed that the fucker was going to do what he wanted, and I was too tired to argue with him, so I just climbed back into bed.

Sure enough, sometime after midnight, I felt the bus make a right turn onto a dirt road with rocks and ruts, and then park.

When Chris turned off the engine, I thought, *Dare I look?*

I peeked out the curtain and saw that we were parked in front of the Moonlight Ranch. It was no longer the bunch of house trailers that I had visited five years before, but a well-lit mansion with fifteen cars in the parking lot—a few of them police cruisers.

Just taking a coffee break with the girls, I suspect.

"Hey, Chris," I said, "don't you think this is a little bit risky, with cop cars right over there?"

"Relax, Andy. Stopping here is an IDS tradition. We gotta keep the good karma rollin' along, man."

You fuckhead imbecile moron!

I decided that one of us had to stay with the pot, so I went back to sleep on top of it, while Chris got on top of his favorite whore.

Around 2:00 A.M., when the asshole, now drunk on pussy and tequila, came back out, I surrendered the bed to him and took over the wheel. Once I got the dirt driveway behind me, the two-lane northbound highway went straight through downtown Carson City. The only cars around were cops, and there seemed to be a stoplight at every corner.

About an hour later, I pulled into South Shore Lake Tahoe, just as the sun was coming up.

I woke Chris up and asked as politely as I could, "Where am I going? I need an address and directions."

"Where the fuck are we?" he snorted from under the covers.

"In South Shore. It's fucking below zero. Get your fat ass up here."

By this point, I had had all I could take from this junkhead motherfucker.

He climbed up front and directed me to a neighborhood on the lake side of Highway 50. After we pulled into a driveway somewhere, he got out and knocked on the front door. When a guy appeared, Chris signaled for me to come over, which I did in short order.

Chris introduced me to Ken, who seemed nice enough. His house was clean and tidy and warm. I soon discovered that the reason for this was his wife, who showed me to a guest room. At least for the moment, I felt safe.

After a long and completely relaxing hot shower, my first in days, I dressed and went to talk to Chris, who was drinking coffee with Ken in the kitchen.

"Can we talk?" I said.

Chris followed me into my room. Not wanting to make a scene, I closed the door.

"The party's over, my friend," I said. "I'll be happy to leave you with your cut, and I'll take mine, but I'm going home now."

He seemed confused.

"Hey, man," he said, "let's spend a day or two here and relax. Then we can go back. I need to see some other people."

I'm sure you do.

"Since Mazatlán, Chris, I've lost all faith in you. I'm outta here, with or without you, no later than eight tomorrow morning."

"I understand, man. I'll be ready."

A few minutes later, after washing up, he said, "I'll be back in a few hours." Then he left the house with Ken.

"You wanna have some breakfast?" Mrs. Ken asked.

"If it isn't too much trouble, ma'am, I'm pretty hungry."

As I sat there, eating her delicious bacon and eggs, I said to myself, *Fuck it! I'm gone. I can be in Palo Alto in four hours if the weather holds.*

Having some homemade hot food in me made me feel like Superman. One more pit stop, and I was at the door.

"Please tell Chris," I said to the kind lady, "he can find me at Addison House with all our souvenirs from Mexico."

It actually took me closer to five hours to get back to Palo Alto, thanks to the snow on the road. When I walked in, the guys were amazed to see me. Rollie literally dropped his jaw. I'm not sure what they were thinking—probably that I had cooked my goose and was sitting in a jail somewhere, getting a crash course in Español.

Chris showed up a few days later to get his share. I was cordial to him, and we parted company without any drama.

IDS trip number twelve, a few months later, was Chris's last. He got busted in his new motor home, on the Douglas side of the border, shortly after being followed out of the Cochise College parking lot. He ended up spending three years in a federal penitentiary in southern California. Someone told me that Chris was reading books on how teletransportation could get him out of prison.

Apparently, it didn't work.

The Vortex Spins On

Jake Pierre Archives

After my excursion to Mexico, I was certain that smuggling dope was not the life for me, so I plunged back into developing the light show with my friends. Crimson Madness was becoming an art form in need of an audience. Since none of us played music, the natural progression was to start promoting music. We produced our first concert and light show at the

Addison Elementary School auditorium in Palo Alto, which held about two hundred people. That was our first show under the name Vortex Productions. It featured Blue Mountain, for whom Rollie was acting as booking agent. The musicians were excited, since they had never played in front of a light show before. We made up some funky posters and passed them around town, used Foothill College's lighting equipment, which we had checked out for the weekend, and rented a PA system for the sound. Primitive, but a start. The business plan at this point was to get up to speed on the light show, manage a few bands, and produce local concerts.

A. Bernstein Archives

Venue for Our First Gig

I was the trucker for the light show as well as an artist, which was easy this first time, since we didn't have a lot of gear. Larry found enough pieces of white fabric to string together a "projection screen" thirty feet wide by eight feet high at the back of the stage. We set up the lighting gear on a scaffold. Larry's girlfriend, Missy, ran a refreshment table near the front—mostly apple juice and brownies.

As a crowd gathered outside, waiting for the doors to open, we felt a rush, knowing that we would be in the entertainment business within minutes. Herb was outside, selling tickets at two bucks a pop.

The crowd was pleased with the music, but really got off on the lights. Everything came together, with Army surplus rheostat motors creating swirling wheels of color.

After that initial dive, we promoted a few shows at a church on Hamilton Avenue in Palo Alto and got permission to do shows at Foothill College. Crimson Madness was coming together nicely, a thing of beauty when we pulled it off right.

I had my old running buddy Doug Blenio, an excellent artist, do a Crimson Madness logo on each side of my VW bus. It featured a madman from the mid-chest up holding a flashlight in his hand, which gave off a crimson light shining on his crazy face. "CRIMSON MADNESS LIGHTS" circled the logo in red. Awesome.

After Bill Graham closed down the original Fillmore Auditorium at Geary and Fillmore Streets, he moved to the Carousel Ballroom (originally designed to look like the inside of a sheik's harem) on the corner of Market and Van Ness, naming it Fillmore West. Our next goal: get an audition with Mr. Graham to perform with major acts. But first, an unexpected opportunity came knocking.

Steve Virello Archives

Jerry Garcia, El Camino Park in Palo Alto, 1967

Neal Cassady died on February 4, 1968. He had been a close friend of the Dead's, drawn to them like a moth to a flame, so Jerry and company decided to put on a wake/acid test for him at the old Fillmore, which was now sitting empty. The owners rented the place to them for one night. Bill Graham had nothing to do with this. I called the Dead's office to see if they had booked a light show. They hadn't, so we landed the gig to send Neal on his way. It was by invitation only, and the one time I dropped acid and did a light show with the Dead. I don't remember an awful lot about that night, other than the laughing and hysterical time we had celebrating Neal's far-fetched life. Long live the memory of that crazy SOB.

Cab Cova Archives

We had a wonderful opportunity to perform two more shows at the old Fillmore with the Dead on November 7 and 8, 1968, for yet another small-time producer before the doors of the old place were locked for ten years. The "Holy Man Jam" at The Family Dog venue on the Great Highway across the street from the Pacific Ocean was our next San Francisco show. It was another "one off" event that went on for several nights, this time featuring Ali Akbar Khan, Big Brother and the Holding Company, Timothy Leary, Allen Ginsberg, and other "holy men" and rock bands. There was also a light show competition, which we won hands down. It was the first time Crimson Madness ever did rear-screen projection, which was very cool. I wanted to look holy that night, so I wore white suede loafers, pink pants, and a bright red slinky cowboy shirt. My hair was big time out, a perfect Jewfro. Mirrored aviators finished the look. I kept those suede loafers around for special "spiritual" occasions, should another arise.

Ron Rakow Archives

Pig and Janice, Cut from the Same Cloth (1968)

My Friend Al

Those suede loafers bring up an important topic in this tale: my personal haberdashery. Although I probably wouldn't have owned up to it then, I was very particular about what I draped over my six-foot-seven frame. Against my strong objections, my mother had always insisted on approving my clothes until I was seventeen. Once I was out from under her watchful eye, my hair grew long and fashion got risky. By the time I was nineteen, mom barely recognized me.

A used clothing store on Emerson Street in downtown Palo Alto was originally called Moe's, and then at some point became Stanford Clothing Store. I'd bought a few things there for Halloween one year in high school, but never considered it for everyday wear. That changed one day when I walked by a short elderly man, who was standing in front of the place. He threw his head back as if he were staring up at a cloud, and looked me in the eye.

"How the hell tall *are* you, son?" he asked.

Since I had boots on, I probably seemed seven feet tall to him. He was wearing a well-pressed suit with a blue tie, and looked very dapper. When I told him my height, he stuck out his hand and said, "I'm Al. Come on in, let's talk."

That was the beginning of a fifteen-year friendship with Al Newhouse.

Al was in his early sixties when I met him and had been around Palo Alto for most of his life. Very few sixty-year-olds wanted anything to do with me and my scraggly friends. "God awful hippies!" was the general tone of the senior set. But Al looked beyond my appearance and was eager to dress such an eccentric character.

He gets it!

Al went out of his way to find whatever I asked for, in my size, even making outrageous suggestions from time to time. On every visit, I made sure I had thirty to sixty minutes to spend with him and his pals. He always welcomed me with a big smile and a shot of whiskey. I hated the stuff, but for Al I made the sacrifice, just to hang with his crew. I think I turned a few of them around about the war and hippies. They loved to dress me, and I always thanked them. They got a real kick out of it.

When bell-bottoms first came in, Levi Strauss wasn't making them. The first bell-bottoms were Navy surplus denims from World War II. You had to be connected to find the real deal, and I was. Al found them, along with a Navy pea coat in my size. As I went through various phases, he always came up with the prize, never letting me down. Even 1940s tweed trousers. Al also found just the right hat to go with them. When I wanted extra long western shirts with pearly buttons, he provided them in both embroidered and unembroidered styles. I used to freak my poor mother out. Her Ivy League expectations for me had long since flown out the window.

The countless hours spent with Al are among my most precious memories. I knew how lucky I was to have him every time someone praised a '40s coat, pinstriped pants with triple pleats, or blue suede shoes. Al accepted me for who I was, and I did the same with him. It was as though our ages met somewhere in the middle, say forty-five. His son was Dave Newhouse, sportswriter for the *Oakland Tribune* in its heyday. He made his father so proud.

Sadly, Al had a drinking problem, which got worse with age. Eventually, his daughter ran the store, and Al didn't come in much. I tried to keep up with him, but finally accepted the fact that I wouldn't be seeing him anymore. His daughter called one day to tell me that Al had passed on. My walking, talking freak show wardrobe was courtesy of Al Newhouse, and he did a spectacular job of keeping me among the best-dressed dropouts on the Peninsula.

Thank you, Al.

Madness and Mayhem

A. Bernstein Archives

On Saturday, December 6, 1969, a free concert was planned at Altamont Speedway, forty miles east of San Francisco in Altamont Pass. Before the show, I kept up with various incarnations that the concert went through during its planning over two or three weeks, with updates every day, then eventually every hour. The Rolling Stones, who had missed Woodstock, would be headlining. Some of the information was alarming to me. The first was Sam Cutler's frantic face on TV as the spokesman for the show. I would later meet Sam when he worked for The Grateful Dead. At this time, he was the Rolling Stones' tour manager, a most unglamorous job, since it mostly involved making sure everyone got on the plane on time.

I was just a regular Joe Schmoe who happened to do a bit of promoting, worked in a light show, and knew some of the parties I saw on TV, who seemed to be the brains behind the concert. Grateful Dead people, mostly. I knew how much cocaine was around a few of the people showing up on TV as part of the production team. However, being the fan I was of the Stones, there was no way I was not going to that concert, so off I went in the VW bus with Herb Pemberton in tow.

We headed out very early that Saturday morning, having no idea what the parking or seating would be like. As we drove through the fields of the East Bay, I realized this place was way the hell out of the city. As we approached the Altamont Speedway, around 7:30 A.M., cars were parked all along the side of the road, telling us there wouldn't be any parking at the concert itself. So we hoofed it for about two miles until we reached the entrance, which was pretty much total chaos.

Herb wanted to go up the slope and mingle with the crowd. I wanted to stay close to the stage, where they were setting up sound gear and lights. A great deal of work was obviously still required, and I was sure I could help in some way. A combination of production and security people were working on and around the stage. Being tall and looking like I belonged, I walked up to security, made the right kind of noises, and I was backstage. I could see that no area was designated as an office or central meeting place. A flatbed truck pulled up, loaded with portable fencing, which some guy said needed to be set up to secure a backstage area. About twenty of us started rolling it out. It had to be staked up every ten feet to create a perimeter a hundred feet out from each side of the stage.

Once the fence was completed, two of the guys invited me onto the Family Dog bus, an old blue school bus owned by Chet Helms, a key promoter in San Francisco who, with his group, Family Dog Productions, put on shows at the Avalon Ballroom and The Great Highway. The bus was parked right behind and above the stage on a little knoll. Since there was no backdrop, I could see everything. For better or worse, this was about as formal an office as there was. A tiny trailer about fifty yards to the rear would be the Stones' dressing room, whenever they arrived. The speedway office was also being used. Since I'd helped with the fence, I got a backstage pass from one of the Family Dog lieutenants. If things got crazy, however, it was splitzville for me.

By now, it was about 9:30 A.M., and dear old Owsley was tossing handfuls of orange sunshine tabs of acid out to the audience from the stage. Handful after handful got distributed; there were early morning casualties everywhere. He was on and off the bus all day, stoned, as were most of the other people onboard. I was not. The most stoned was Chet himself. He sat comatose in the lotus position all day, never leaving the back of the bus.

A. Bernstein Archives
My Sanctuary in the Madness

Since the single clear head on that old bus was mine, I made it my business that it stayed safe and sane. My size and the fact that I knew my way around a school bus convinced most people that if I said I was running the show, that was the end of the story.

Chet couldn't talk. I brought him food and water from the front of the bus throughout the day, but he only took a little. His old lady was as badly off as he was. I controlled the door to the bus and kept it locked for most of the day. No one got on without my approval. When folks came looking for Chet, the same answer worked all day: "He's comatose in the back." I would let them take a look if they pressed the matter, and then they would split to find someone else in charge. When Sam Cutler stopped by, I expressed concern that Owsley was last seen dosing the crowd from the stage. I could see the fear in his eyes.

The bands were flown in by helicopter one at a time, as at Woodstock. But this was no Woodstock, not even close. I forget the order of the bands, but Crosby, Stills, Nash, and Young played fairly early, when things were still in the "Let's see how this plays out" phase. The crowd pushed and shoved to be up next to the small stage. Security, or more accurately, guys acting like they were security, carried broken-off pool sticks. No one got hit in the early stages, but these guys were drinking steadily. It looked like it could get ugly.

The Jefferson Airplane played during the early afternoon. Marty Balin and Grace Slick tried to keep order on the stage, since the set change had been a long one, and the waiting, wasted crowd was getting restless. By this time, people were pressing right up against the stage. From my vantage point on the bus, it looked like more people had shown up than the place could hold. Harleys were blasting up the hill, scattering people in all directions.

Midway through the Airplane's set, the violence began in earnest. The pool stick guys roamed the stage, swinging at audience members who got too close: Swing, swig more booze, and find someone else to go after. At one point, Marty tried to stop them from making things worse. In the middle of a song, he grabbed the shoulder of one of them and got a pool stick across his forehead for his efforts. The Airplane left, with Marty dazed and bleeding. Things were getting out of hand, and it was only 2:00 P.M.

Just about this time, I looked out the bus window and saw George Hurst, an old friend from high school, who had once jumped off a roof and impaled himself on a bamboo shoot, but lived to tell the tale. He was another classmate who had joined the Marines. Recognizing me at once, he tapped on the window.

Shit!

He was carrying a long, stout walking stick.

Crazed ex-marine with a weapon…, who's most likely sampled some of Owsley's candy. Great!

I told one of the guys on the bus that I'd be right back and not to let anyone else on while I was gone.

George rambled at me, incoherent, and most assuredly was stoned on LSD.

"How many hits have you had, George?"

"Maybe five or six…. I'm comin' on the bus with ya."

"Not now, George, maybe later. Why don't you just go home?"

I headed for the bus door.

Now that he knew where I was, I wouldn't be able to shake him. I don't know how he got backstage, but I was certain security would make a mess of him if he threatened them with that stick.

His eyes were the size of Eskimo Pies, and I doubt he even heard me.

After I made my way back onto the bus, I checked on Chet. No response. His girlfriend had come around, but was freaked by the attack on Marty. I should have taken the advice I had just given George, but I still wanted to see the Stones.

Robert Altman Archives

Chet Helms at Altamont Before Owsley's LSD Sidelined Him

From my blue cocoon on the bus, it was getting very strange outside.

The Dead management had their fingers in this mess, and they should have known better. The Stones wanted something too much, and used their influence, along with Sam Cutler as a stooge, to stage this evolving nightmare.

Helicopters flew in and out all afternoon. The bands wanted out as soon as they were done. The Stones arrived about 4:15. When their chopper landed, they were hustled over to the small trailer behind the bus. All their equipment was being loaded onto the stage over the next hour or so. Chet was now semiconscious, and people were coming onto the bus to try to talk to him. I was still the self-appointed screener, along with one of Chet's partners.

As I was waiting for the next person to request a meeting with Chet, George Hurst showed up outside the window. I could see madness on his face. He started banging on the bus with his big stick, screaming my name and demanding to be allowed on.

Fifty feet away, Keith Richards was approaching the bus, eyes intense, without a chaperone. He was clearly agitated.

Shit, there's George swinging away, and here comes Keith!

In a flash, two security guys who were trying to catch up with Keith saw George and dragged him away behind the bus.

I opened the bus door for Keith. He asked if Sam Cutler or Chet Helms were around. I told him Chet was, but I hadn't seen Sam for a few hours. Keith wanted to talk to Chet, so I let him in, explaining that Chet had been out of it all day, so he might not have anything helpful to say. Then I led him to the back, where Chet was now mumbling to some blond, but was obviously still out of it.

Keith went up to Chet, and said, "What the fuck's goin' on, mate?"

But Chet just smiled and pointed out the window.

Keith was very concerned. Turning to me, he asked, "How long you been on the bus?"

"All day."

"If you see Sam Cutler, tell him I'll be at the trailer. I need to see that bugger, *now!*"

He looked out at the crowd in a way that made me think he was wondering what the hell he was doing here. I'm sure the thought of canceling the show went through his mind, but that could only lead to further pandemonium—or worse.

Robert Altman Archives
Keith Richards, 1969

About this time, someone showed up who I thought was "Scoop" Nisker, the alternative news broadcaster for KSAN radio in the city, though I wasn't a hundred percent sure it was him. He told me he had just arrived, so I brought him up to speed on the events of the day and the general bad vibes. We agreed that this was not representative of anything that had gone on in our experience with Bay Area concerts. How could this happen?

As the sun set behind the Altamont hills on this winter evening, the wind died and the temperature dropped fifteen degrees. Pretty soon, huge bonfires sprang up all over the fields. The crowd began chanting that they wanted the Stones. I heard a few gunshots.

If the Stones don't play soon, this place will explode!

Sometime around 6:00 o'clock, the Stones hit the stage. They looked very tense: stiff bodies, unsmiling faces.

The crowd roared, the stage lights went red, and the band kicked off with one of their hits.

"Scoop" and I climbed onto the roof of the bus to watch the show. We were perhaps sixty feet from the band, with a clear shot of the events as they unfolded. Security stalked the stage. It was hard to tell whether they would be eager or restrained with their pool cues. I believed they were trying to use restraint.

During "Sympathy for the Devil" (probably not a wise choice), there was a big commotion right in front of Mick. We couldn't see exactly what happened, but someone went down. "Scoop" and I looked at each other and said, "Oh, fuck!" at the same time. Mick called for people to calm down. He and the rest of the band were clearly freaked.

What "Scoop" and I didn't realize at the time was that we had just witnessed a homicide.

The victim got carried off—as the Stones played on.

I had had enough. Saying goodnight to "Scoop," I got my things from the bus and started the long trek back to the real world, walking away from Dante's inferno.

Even the highway was crazy when I reached it, choked with traffic. As the Stones played in the background, a flatbed truck hauling old cars stacked on a trailer crept by, hemmed in by the concert traffic. People had climbed onto the trailer, taking over the empty cars, looking out like ghosts foreshadowing disaster. I kept on walking. It felt like hours before I recognized my VW bus on the other side of the road. Mentally and physically exhausted, I crashed in the back. Herb actually showed up a little later. I was glad to see him. He offered to drive home; I didn't argue.

A lot of the dream died that day. The concert had been marred by violence and chaos from the minute I arrived. I didn't try to understand it and didn't want to think about it.

Crimson Glow at Fillmore West

By now, Crimson Madness had been designing and operating various pieces of lighting equipment for over a year. Because we needed a studio, we moved into a large house on Waverley Street, which had a basement we could use for that purpose.

Somehow Rollie got us the much anticipated audition at the Fillmore West.

The fucker made it happen! I swear he can talk circles around anyone I've ever known.... Not that we don't deserve the shot.

It was time to get busy, and we worked our tails off.

David O'Neil soon joined us from New York when he got the news about the Fillmore gig. He was very smart, with an intensity that made his eyes shine. He had a quick temper, but an equally sharp wit and sense of humor. David wanted to build an "infinity" machine for the light show that would not produce the same image twice. We were full of so many ideas on how to make this production phantasmagorical that we were bursting at the seams.

Among the final touches to our show, we incorporated film into the media mix, looping sections of 16mm footage with graphics, then firing the whole montage with spinning color wheels, thus creating several layers of pulsating, almost three-dimensional colored images. When projected from the back of the Fillmore West auditorium, the moving collage would be a perfect centerpiece for a rotation, or segment of music. We placed our hand-painted 35mm glass slides on homemade light boxes so we could quickly identify the slides that most effectively worked for the music being played. On top of all this action, we overlaid liquid projections with colored mineral oils, gently (and not so gently) moving the Petri dishes to create visual rhythms that matched the tempos of the music. It was truly a pioneering art form, and we were all Davy Crocketts. However, this was just happening in our basement for the moment. The true test was coming up.

Rollie and I had made contact with other light artists who were not too uptight to talk about what they did. Jerry Abrams, Bill Ham's partner from the original Headlights, was a very nice guy and shared many things with us, including his Fillmore West "secrets" about how to project below the low-hanging, billowing cloth ceiling that made the place look like a harem.

By this time, Rollie had a steady girlfriend, an Italian chick from Redwood City. Gail was tall with long black hair and bangs, beautiful green eyes, and olive skin. Very striking, to be sure. She loved a good party, and with us that was 24-7. Gail became a permanent member of the Crimson Madness family. To put up with Rollie's consuming interest in Rollie Inc. took a special kind of gal, and Gail fit the bill.

On the day of our audition, we arrived at the Fillmore West at 3:00 P.M. to load in. Three bands were also auditioning that night, hoping for real gigs as well: Black Oak Arkansas, Mason Proffit, and Mendelbaum. Black Oak was a Deep Southern bunch of hell-raising rockers led by James "Jim Dandy" Mangrum. They released ten albums in the 1970s with moderate success. Mason Proffit was an as yet unrecorded band from the Midwest; their brand of music was the folk rock genre, like Crosby, Stills, and Nash, or Pure Prairie League. Mendelbaum was a rock band out of Marin County.

A. Bernstein Archives

Black Oak Arkansas

By soundcheck late in the afternoon, everybody was ready to try to impress the hell out of Bill Graham. The front doors opened at 6:30 P.M., and the first band came on at 7:30 sharp. The members of Crimson Madness worked collectively, stuck to the game plan, and the show looked beautiful that evening. Since the music was incredibly diverse, from full-on head-banging, to mellow sounds, to light rock, we got to show what we could do. The light show was an important part of the experience for the mostly stoned audience members. We left with smiles, and hoped for the best.

The big news from the Fillmore didn't come until a month later. It came in the form of a phone call and a follow-up letter. We were to perform lights for a four-night run: May 22, 23, 24, and 25, 1970. Within a week, we learned that the band line-up was B. B. King, Albert King, and Mendelbaum. It was a momentous event, as these two blues giants with the same last name had never appeared together before. Both claimed to be the "King" of the blues guitar. But Mendelbaum was the sentimental favorite, our audition buddies from Marin County.

B. B. had an enormous hit with "The Thrill Is Gone," which appealed to a whole new audience of young people, while Albert provided a much sharper and more traditional rendition of the electrified Delta blues. We could not have been more excited for our first performance as light artists at the best-known music venue in America at the time.

We were also invited to play in the pre-show traditional basketball game against the Fillmore staff, with Bill Graham at point guard. Hell, yes, we accepted. This was part of becoming a member of the Fillmore family, something we all wanted to be. For me, however, it was initiation by fire—the giant who was all left feet on the court.

Every show at Fillmore West had a poster, some probably worth over a million dollars today. Ron Rakovitch, a friend who lived across the street from my house, and worked at a music store, told me that all the music shops in the Bay Area got advance copies of those posters. Since they were also outlets for BASS Tickets, it was free eye candy advertising for the windows. "Record Store" Ron said he would grab one of the posters for me when this show's pouch arrived from Bill Graham Productions.

With only three weeks to prepare for the Fillmore, we were crazy busy in the basement, so we decided to bring onboard another artist/animator to brighten things up. This was no ordinary character. On the Foothill campus, there were a couple of unique guys who defied description, which was not easy to do in 1970. They made their own clothes out of old leather patches worked into mountain man–looking attire, head to toe. Their pants were bell-bottomed with silver conchos sewn up the sides. They wore moccasins and carried their money and such in leather pouches attached to homemade leather belts. One of these guys was quite tan and had long sun-bleached hair. The other was a classic square-jawed, good-looking guy, pale with dark brown hair down his back. I often saw him playing his guitar with the "jammers" at the Foothill student union.

One morning, when I climbed the front porch steps of Waverley House, the screen door opened and Rollie walked out with one of the leather-clad mountain men, the tan one with the sun-bleached hair.

"This is Jake Pierre," he said. "Jake the Snake. Jake's an illustrator, Andy. He's gonna spruce up the graphics for our upcoming Fillmore show."

We did the "Bro" handshake and commented that we'd seen each other at Foothill. Jake was somewhat quiet, a warm guy with great talent, who specialized in fantasy characters that were a mix of "animal people," Knights of the Round Table, and landscapes from Hobbitland.

A. Bernstein Archives
Waverley House

Jake's leather-clad friend, Jon Buckley, began coming around as well. Jon was a man of peace and a very deep soul, as well as a talented songwriter who went on to record for Fillmore Records—Bill Graham's stab at owning a record label.

When I returned home from driving the school bus one day, a note from my neighbor Ron was taped to my apartment door, telling me to come over right away. I made a U-turn and dashed across the street. On his table was the poster for the Fillmore show. It was magnificent. I stood still, staring at it. Of course, my eyes rolled straight down to the script that read "LIGHTS BY CRIMSON MADNESS."

There were a handful of select artists who created the posters for Graham. This one was by the only team artists for the Fillmore, Satty and Singer, a German and an American who created turn-of-the-century French collage art. Satty died soon after this, but David Singer went on to become a stand-alone Fillmore artist. They had created a masterpiece for this show. Ron had made my day, my week, and really my life, since this poster would become part of the lore for my children and grandchildren. Many years later, I saw an identical poster hanging behind the bar at the Hard Rock Café in Jakarta, Indonesia, enclosed in an elaborate hand-carved frame. It blew my mind! I was fifty at the time, but it took me straight back to the moment that Ron gave me my copy.

On the afternoon of May 22, 1970, we headed to the Fillmore on a mission. Herb and I were Belushi and Aykroyd as we drove up Highway 101 in the bus with the crazy guy logo on the side, a ton of equipment in the back, and a dream to become the best at this art form.

The rest of the team came in cars, the unlucky ones in Rollie's new VW station wagon, which his grandfather had bought for him. Rollie drove like the guy on the side of my bus—smoking, talking, passing a joint, and, from time to time, unexpectedly turning the FM radio up to full blast when he liked a song. We all brought our shorts and sneakers so we could play basketball, as invited.

Several close friends were coming to see our first Fillmore show, including Tom McCarthy, who was now out of the Marines.

As we set up and tested the lights in the auditorium, several of the employees stopped by the tower, greeting us warmly and saying how much they enjoyed our show at the audition.

Before dinner, we played basketball and got our asses whipped. Our team of roadies, light artists, and a few musicians got killed by the Fillmore crew, who played every night. Some of the musicians were good, Rollie was good, and I was tall—but not very good. Bill Graham hustled as if he were in the Olympics, playing dirty and cussing everybody out, including his own team mates. After the game, we were all friends and sat down to enjoy a fine dinner provided by the in-house restaurant staff.

After dinner, I changed from my basketball outfit into "evening attire": a rainbow-patterned western shirt with pearl snap buttons, a turquoise bracelet, and low-slung brown wide-wale-cord pants, topped off with a gold-plated western belt buckle, which had a large but tasteful agate in the center. My long curly hair was in a ponytail, and I wore snakeskin cowboy boots, which made me six-foot-eight or -nine. Quite a vision, if I do say so!

At 6:30 sharp, the Fillmore West was ready to rock. The King bluesmen would be holding court, along with Mendelbaum. Lights by Crimson Madness, just as the poster said.

As the opening act, Mendelbaum rocked the house. Since we had played with them at the audition, I knew their rhythms and the texture of their music. We kept it light, tight, and bright for the Marin County guys. Imagine being ten feet above the crowd on a long catwalk twenty-five feet across the back of the room. At our disposal were more than fifty pieces of equipment, sending out a psychedelic light experience to thousands of young stoned compadres. It was heaven for the boys from Palo Alto.

Bill Graham himself introduced Albert, King of the Blues Guitar, and his band, who opened with "Kansas City." The small horn section and a raw guitar sound stabbed right through me. No pretence. His style of the blues was nasty—stinging nasty. Albert had never played before an audience like *this* before. Smelling and seeing the pot smoke in our lights, he seemed like he didn't know quite what to make of it at first, so he just flashed a giant grin and played like hell for those longhaired white youngsters, who loved everything he did. He played for over an hour and a half. Being around all the lights, we were sweating profusely and were exhausted, but still had to make the changes for B.B.'s show. We took turns going downstairs to cool off, but it was obvious that we needed more bodies to help.

Bill did a wonderful introduction for B.B., who came out dressed to the nines in a beautifully tailored suit and tie, the consummate gentleman. The crowd blew him away—I later heard him speak about his first night at the Fillmore in several interviews over the years. He opened with "The Thrill Is Gone," one the crowd would know. The audience sang along with the chorus while smiling their silly stoned grins. When he looked left, he saw the light show; when he looked right, he saw the light show; and when he turned around, he saw the light show. Both Albert and B.B. got a contact high, inhaling pot all night, and had rainbows in their eyes by the end of their sets.

The first of our four nights ended, as most Fillmore shows did, when Bill decided it was over. That night taught us that performing at the Fillmore for more than four hours behind a mountain of superhot projectors and overheads was hard, sweaty work, even for a bunch of guys in their early twenties. Herb and I shut everything down and were the last to leave. We received a smile and a nod from Bill as we headed to the bus. For Herb and me, who usually did all the heavy lifting and sorting, it was an acknowledgment by the Man himself. We had passed the first night's test.

Shows two and three with B.B. and Albert were pretty much the same, except Bill rotated who followed Mendelbaum each night. It had to do with something in the contracts. But the final show was the special one. B.B. and Albert dropped the pretences and ego and played together to close out the evening. I'm sure Bill had his finger in the mix somewhere, but baby they rocked!

I wanted to keep going for another four shows, particularly after that last set, but all great things have to end. To begin our Fillmore experience with such a great line-up was setting the bar very high for us. We knew how lucky we were to pop our Fillmore cherry with the grace and dignity of the blues, the real deal. It prepared us for everything that followed.

With the first Fillmore appearance now under our belts, we approached the summer of 1969 with a head of steam. Besides Crimson Madness, Vortex was continuing to produce concerts at local—and some not so local—venues. Rollie was making contacts at all the colleges in the area to expand our reach. Of course, each concert we promoted allowed us to try new gimmicks with the light show, and bring that added dimension to the audience.

The bands we had started working with, Together and Blue Mountain, were now joined by Kidd Afrika, a tight R&B outfit from Palo Alto, featuring the extremely talented Politzer Brothers, as well as Snail, a Santa Cruz–based rock band, great guys and a hoot to work with. Venues like The Château Liberté in the Santa Cruz Mountains, which we booked exclusively for a few months, allowed us to spread our sparrow-sized production wings.

Prior to Woodstock, which truly launched Santana to world acclaim, Vortex had an opportunity to participate in one of the band's first public performances. It was staged at the Frost Amphitheatre, on the Stanford campus, a perfect outdoor setting for a concert of that magnitude. Just weeks later, they would release their first album. Rollie had worked some angle that put us in a favorable position to collaborate with Bill Graham on this show. As Santana's keyboardist and lead singer, Gregg Rolie was looking every bit the soon-to-be rock star king of the hill.

As Gregg and I exchanged handshakes and smiles, I thought, *God, weight-training class seems so many years ago.*

Who will ever forget the evening news coverage of Woodstock, featuring a mesmerizing teenager named Michael Shrieve, Santana's young drummer, performing that amazing solo? That moment defined the powerful role that music played worldwide in the youth movement that was taking hold.

The very next morning, Rollie and I were about to sit down to breakfast at Bennington's Café in Palo Alto, when who should walk in behind us but Michael Shrieve and Gregg Rolie, fresh off the plane from New York. We asked them to join us and ended up laughing all the way through breakfast, listening to their stories about Woodstock.

My scrambled eggs shot out of my nose when Michael said, "Playing with Carlos was like playing with a guy who had just eaten three dozen mushrooms!"

"I wasn't altogether innocent, either," Gregg howled.

We just about got kicked out of that damned restaurant for disturbing the other patrons.

Copyright © Barry Z. Levine, 1969
Gregg Rolie at Woodstock

Robert Altman Archives
Michael Shrieve at Altamount

Eating My Own Face

Jake's One and Only Fillmore Poster

When the phone rang in July, inviting us to return to the Fillmore for a second four-night run, we were thrilled. The shows were scheduled for August 20 to 23. That was a birthday present for me, since I would turn twenty-three on August 21. We were to provide the light show for Albert King again, along with Cold Blood and Mason Proffit (another band from the audition). Cold Blood, a local band featuring lead singer Lydia Pence, had a hot album and a single or two on national charts. Their blues-infused rock would be a perfect foil for Albert.

By this time, almost all the major light show companies in the Bay Area had formed a collective, the Light Artist Guild. This was about money. The Fillmore would not do a concert without a light show, and they wanted the best, which drove us to compete for the business. On the other hand, the pay was minimal for the hours and dollars invested, so we wanted a raise. When the Guild told Bill Graham that things had to change, he just laughed. Then he railed against us in the media, saying that we were a bunch of stoned numbnuts, which really hurt, since Bill had been a theatrical labor organizer in New York.

With a line drawn in the sand, a strike loomed.

In the basement of Waverley House, we had been producing our own 16mm version of outer space movies, featuring plastic rockets we put together from model kits we bought from a hobby shop. By projecting light from behind a large black velvet backdrop with various sized pinholes cut into it, we created the illusion of a starry night sky. We dangled the spaceships in front of the backdrop on thin black wire and moved them slowly across the universe. The damned thing would look great on the screen behind the stage at the Fillmore.

But all this work would come to nothing if we didn't find a way to compromise with Bill Graham. After Bill and the Guild had several knockdown dragout sessions in his office, and a strike that went on for two weeks, Bill agreed to give us a whopping $250 more per night. A lot of money in 1969.

Back in Bill's good graces, we plowed ahead preparing for the upcoming opening show on August 20th. Jake Pierre was now experimenting with complete fantasy suites, featuring all new characters. We matched his dragons and wizards to the spinning color wheels, experimenting with different cellophane colors to enhance each movement. It was homemade animation, Crimson Madness style! How far could we go and still keep it from being too much was always the question at hand.

On the afternoon of August 20th, Herb and I managed to fit the ever-expanding load of equipment into the bus and haul it to the Fillmore. We were up for a basketball game, but Bill no longer wanted the light artist guys to be a part of it, just the musicians and their crew. No doubt, spillover from the strike.

Mason Proffit opened the show. It was great to be back rocking with them. Most bands never acknowledged the light artists, but Mason Proffit was different. They told us they had never seen anything like our show before. Every one of their sets of that four-night run was interrupted by their asking for a hand for Crimson Madness. Each night the crowd stood up, turned around to face us, and screamed and clapped for more than a minute. Many rock aficionados and critics alike felt these guys were the best rock band that never made it. I certainly share that opinion. It was a great pleasure and joyful experience to work with them at the Fillmore West.

On the second night, Herb told the in-house restaurant staff that it was my twenty-third birthday, so, after dinner, they brought out a big cake with my likeness on it in icing. Everybody from the bands and crew sang "Happy Birthday," and so did Bill. This was fucking way cool, especially when I got to eat my own face!

After the birthday show that night, Bill came up to Rollie and me to ask about the artist who had drawn the fantasy sequences in our show. We told him it was our in-house illustrator par excellence, Jake Pierre. Bill wanted to meet him.

Rollie called Jake as soon as we got home, and the next night, before the show, Bill and Jake had a talk. When Jake came out of Bill's office and climbed up to our catwalk, he was beaming.

"Bill wants me to do a big poster," he said. "And he told me to go for it…, total fantasy with all my flaming everythings. And Crimson Madness will be on the poster for the first of three weekend shows. But Bill swore me to secrecy. None of you guys can see the work until it's printed."

Jake was about to join the exclusive club of artists whose names would become part of the long history of the Fillmore/Winterland poster legacy.

At the end of the third night, Bill asked if we would work three more nights to cover for Little Princess 109, the scheduled light show. He mentioned something about an accident or medical situation. We had never done seven nights straight, but—hell, yes!—we would be more than happy to do it. The bad news was that the show was headlined by Iron Butterfly. That meant the long version, the concert version, of "In-A-Gadda-Da-Vida," three nights in a row. Fuck me dead! We were doing Bill a favor, but God almighty, there's a limit. I was starting to understand Little Princess's sudden absence.

Black Oak Arkansas (audition mates again) were also on the bill, so it was bone-wrenchingly loud for four hours every night. But we did it and lived to tell the tale. It was fun working with the guys from Black Oak Arkansas again. By this time, they were recorded and getting a lot of regional playtime in the South. Jim Dandy was quite the showman, a fucking madman who loved to drop acid and hang out on the light platform with us. He considered us brothers from our audition night. Talk about a fish out of water, San Francisco was a hell of a long way from Black Oak. I've often wondered what became of Jimmy.

A. Bernstein Archives

Iron Butterfly

For the poster, Jake came up with a castle motif, featuring all of his characters: dragons, lizard kings, firestorms from castle walls, and on and on. It was classic Jake, and then some. Seeing the poster was a thrill for all of us as we walked past store windows *everywhere* in the Bay Area. On the left side of the poster was the show we would be lighting: Fleetwood Mac, Tom Rush, and Clover (Huey Lewis's first band out of Marin County).

A. Bernstein Archives

Fleetwood Mac with Peter Green (ca. 1970)

One week before the show, I was driving the VW bus down El Camino on the way home from the bus yard, when I noticed a young woman standing on the side of the road with her thumb stuck out for a ride. I thought she looked a bit young to be hitchhiking, but I pulled over anyway. She ran up to the bus, looked in, and saw one of the Furry Freak Brothers—me. But that didn't put her off.

I smiled from behind my granny shades.

"Hop in," I said. "Where ya goin'?"

"To Los Altos High School," she said as she climbed into the passenger seat.

"School's almost over. Why bother?"

"I've gotta pay my ex-boyfriend for some hash I just sold. He's waiting for me there."

"Oh. Ya have any more? I'll buy some."

She reached in her purse and pulled out three or four small bundles of hash wrapped in aluminum foil. "It's Afghan blond…, very mellow."

"Why don't we go over to my cottage and sample some?"

"Ohhh…, okay."

She was very beautiful, with long brown hair, big brown eyes, pale skin, and the cutest little mole on her left cheek. She was wearing a long, colorful Moroccan skirt with little mirrors on it and a peasant blouse, off the shoulders.

Trouble!

"So, you go to Los Altos High, huh?"

"Yeah, I'm a senior."

At least, she's not a freshman. Probably under eighteen, though.

I was twenty-three and didn't give a thought to what had happened the last time I got involved with a seventeen-year old—and her knife-wielding papa.

"What's your name?" I asked.

"Lisa. What's yours?"

"Andy."

As I pulled off University Avenue to head down the dirt road to my cottage, she got wide-eyed.

"You live in the redwood grove?!" she said. "I can't believe it. This is where me and my friends all come to get high, down by the creek."

"I'm not surprised. I see kids come and go all the time."

As we pulled up to my creekside cottage under an old oak tree, I could see that she was impressed.

"Welcome to my little hippie hobbit house!"

Inside, we sat down on my sofa, she took out the hash and a small pipe, and put them down on my coffee table, which had once been the front door of a restaurant in Mendocino. It was redwood with dozens of names and initials carved into it.

As she lit her pipe, she said, "So what do *you* do?"

"I'm a member of a light show called Crimson Madness. We're performing at the Fillmore for Fleetwood Mac this weekend. Would you like to come?"

"Are you kidding? But I have to be home by one, or my parents will kill me."

"No problem. Have you seen the poster for the show? I've got a copy right over here."

When I unrolled Jake's poster, she said, "Oh, my god! I've seen it all over town. I *love* it! And there's Crimson Madness." She pointed to our name on the lower left side under the bill. "My friends won't believe this!"

This is too good to be true!

"I'm sorry, Andy," she said as she wrote down her phone number, "but David's waiting for me at the school. I gotta go."

After I dropped her off, and headed back home, I realized, as I stared at the piece of paper with her phone number on it, that I was feeling a very strong attraction to this young lady.

I won't be breaking any laws just by taking her to the show.

For the next few days, all I could think of was 5:00 P.M. on Saturday, when Lisa said she would have a friend drop her off at my cottage.

Sure enough, at 4:45 on Saturday, I heard a car pull up in front. There she was, with an attractive blond at the wheel.

"So, here's the plan," Lisa said, after introducing me to her girlfriend— who had already lit up a joint. "I'll be sleeping over at Sharon's tonight…, unless we get home too late. In which case, I'll sleep on your sofa."

"Sounds good to me."

No laws will be broken.

We entered the Fillmore through the secured back door and floated through the backstage area on our way to the light platform. When the guys got a look at Lisa, they were knocked out.

But Rollie the Realist couldn't resist whispering in my ear, "I'll be visiting you at San Quentin, pal."

For this show, David O'Neil put his best foot forward with his new and better mousetrap, the Infinity Light Machine—a kaleidoscope on a grand scale, with prisms and shards of glass fused together in an aluminum tube that rotated in several directions at once. A powerful light source ran the length of it, which allowed for focus. This special gift came out of his frantic Brooklyn brain.

Our experiments with lighter mineral oil viscosities and new colors were also on display at this show. We became frontline pioneers of video looping, after we met some Berkeley people who headed up an outfit named Video Free America. Their technology was expensive, but after seeing what they could do, we managed to come up with the money. The results were video feedback loops that we recorded on 16mm black-and-white film and had colorized by a photo lab in Palo Alto. Nobody else doing lights had that effect, and we used it for the first time that evening. We had four 16mm projectors aimed at each wall, two behind the stage. David fired up his new contraption and aimed it at the screen right behind the band. With all the work we had done to get Crimson Madness up to this point, standing tall over a Fillmore audience that was blown away was a crowning jewel.

Lisa was clearly in heaven, but it was hot as hell on that platform from all the lights, so she went back and forth to the floor below, where I could see her dancing whenever I got a chance to look down.

I love watching her body sway to the music!

Glow Fades at Fillmore West

Jake Pierre Archives

Vortex was now firing on all six cylinders. We were a Rambler, not a Lincoln Continental, and the junior college campuses were our proving grounds.

Stoneground was a band formed by Big Tom Donahue, a local DJ on KSAN, as part of a traveling medicine show of sorts. The band featured our good friends from Together: Cory Lerios, keyboardist, and Steve Price, drummer. Tom's plan was to take this troupe, which also included writers and painters and poets, across the U.S. in buses, then on to Europe to spread the San Francisco culture. It was a very aggressive project, to say the least.

Tom talked Cory into disbanding Together and starting Stoneground with some other first-rate Bay Area talent.

The road show didn't succeed, but Stoneground did. Vortex ended up booking the shit out of them locally, once they returned from the failed medicine show tour. The band ended up with a charted album that Tom Donahue had produced. It was the only positive outcome from the whole mess. One of the other members was guitarist David Jenkins. Annie Sampson, a wonderfully talented vocalist from the East Bay, was the lead singer. The band turned out to be a springboard for Cory and company down the road.

Vortex also produced a few shows for a former member of Steve Miller's Blues Band, Boz Skaggs. Although not yet a household name, he had already recorded his first solo album, *Boz Skaggs*, which featured "Somebody Loan Me a Dime," a hit on alternative radio stations nationwide. He was about to break through in a big way.

In April 1971, Bill Graham announced that he would close the Fillmore West in July for good, with a weeklong closing concert series, featuring his favorite San Francisco bands and light shows. Of the five nights for light shows, Crimson Madness was to do two. Love Bill or hate him—and most people did one or the other—we sure loved him when he gave us the nod. (It was a lot better than getting his famous finger.)

Robert Altman Archives
Boz Skaggs

Bill selected Crimson Madness to do the opening show on a Tuesday night, which featured Boz Skaggs, Tower of Power, and our old friends Mason Proffit. We also did the Saturday night show with It's a Beautiful Day, Elvin Bishop, and Cold Blood. These were great line-ups, and we were excited. As the big week approached, I listened to Boz's old material and brand new album as often as possible, formulating lighting ideas for each of the songs. I had become a big Boz fan. His new album, *Moments*, didn't only knock *me* out, but the rest of the country as well.

On opening night, I insisted to Herb that we arrive early to set up. Since I had the bus that transported the equipment, I really didn't care if the rest of the group showed up early or not. I wanted to hear the songs live when Boz soundchecked, so I could synchronize the slides and loops. Herb and I set off at noon, hauling in all the gear ourselves and lugging it up the stairs to the platform. I was in my hometown with my close buddy, about to be serenaded by my newest favorite band. All the stars were aligned.

When Boz lit into the first song for the soundcheck, "We Were Always Sweethearts," the vocals were like raindrops from a summer storm. My eyes teared up as I soaked them in. From the catwalk, I felt like the only one in the auditorium—Boz was playing for me alone. I didn't touch a knob or a projector, but just sat and listened. When everyone showed up later to prep for the show, emotions were running high as we ran through the routines, discussed set changes, and made notes for the slides. We had moved from getting high and doing our art, to performing the art and getting high from doing it. Many of my ideas trumped that night.

A. Bernstein Archives
Mason Proffit

With Mason Proffit opening the show, we needed to make a good first impression on the crowd, since the guys would undoubtedly do what they had always done in the past—namely, ask for a hand for the light show. We wanted it to be deserved. For the first set, we used film footage of horses running through fire on a beach, with Jake's towers burning along the top and down the sides, building in intensity with the music. When the music suddenly stopped, we froze the scene cold and quick. Right on cue, the band asked for a hand for Crimson Madness, and the crowd went nuts. What a way to start the night!

Tower of Power set up next. We had worked with them before, so we knew their style and to a certain degree their music: a big sound, with horns and swing and vocal harmonies woven through the instrumentals—a style that later came to be called East Bay Grease.

A. Bernstein Archives
Tower of Power

During the long set change between Tower and Boz, the Fillmore hummed with anticipation—and pot smoke. Boz performed his set at a high level—like a human jukebox, spilling out one new hit after another.

Although we had one more show to go, this was the best night ever for me at the Fillmore West. On the way out, Herb and I stopped to say goodbye to the guys in Mason Proffit and smoked a joint or two. We all felt a part of history, Fillmore veterans who had brought so much entertainment to the fans.

For our final show at the Fillmore West, I took it on myself to put together the piece that we would use for It's a Beautiful Day's signature song, "White Bird"—a long piece of music with many changes in tempo. I had Jake design a series of white doves trimmed in blue, which appeared to move from side to side with the use of blue and red color wheels, alternating with 16mm colored loops of moving clouds and sky. The centerpiece was two film loops of hundreds of actual doves being released, which we used as the song built to a crescendo. During this song, the other guys in Crimson Madness stood in awe at this sequence that Jake and I had put together. At one point, all the screens in the auditorium were alive with flying white doves changing colors. It was a fabulous sight.

Exhausted after this long day and night, Herb and I packed up the gear one last time and hauled it to the bus. We knew this was the end of an era, as well as the end of Crimson Madness.

Homer's Warehouse

By the time the Fillmore closed, Lisa and I had been living together about a year. I was getting tired of the school bus routine, so we decided to move to Hawaii. My plan was to do carpentry, and Lisa figured she would make custom-fitted dresses at home. Instead, I wound up cleaning toilets, and Lisa made tourist jewelry in a sweatshop owned by a Chinese slave driver. The bonus of her job was that she got to steal tiny diamonds and rubies that fell on the floor. My job had no bonuses. When we got back to Palo Alto after six months, those gems paid our first month's rent *and* deposit. I went back to driving the bus, and Lisa got a sales job at Sears.

Rollie was still booking shows around the area, but it was a struggle because the same old local bands were not drawing the kind of crowds needed to keep his production company going. Both of us missed the action and great music of the Fillmore days. We wondered how we might break into the music scene someplace besides endless community college gigs. Rollie suggested we open a nightclub, but I pointed out that Stanford was a powerful influence on the morals of the community, ensuring that Palo Alto maintained very strict red light district laws. In Your Ear (formerly The Poppycock) had closed down while I was in Hawaii. Aside from that, there was a dingy biker bar on Homer Lane off El Camino Real, called Homer's. It was on an unlit alleyway behind a hardware store in a cluster of old steel warehouses. I had been there once or twice, but it was too rugged for me.

A. Bernstein Archives
High Street and University Avenue Today, Former Home of the Poppycock

Rollie and I stopped by one night to check it out. The parking area out front was full of motorcycles. The music was rock 'n' roll played loud. We paid the fifty-cent door charge and stepped in. A cheap

8x10 poster on the front door announced the name of the band playing that night, the Doobie Brothers. I recognized the name. Their manager had called me, trying to get us to book them at one of our church gigs the year before. When I had asked Rollie if he wanted to book a band from San Jose named the Doobie Brothers, he laughed, so I blew the guy off. Now here they were at Homer's, playing for a bunch of drunk bikers, mostly Hells Angels.

The room was big enough, but smelled really bad and was in need of a lot of work. Rollie asked me if he should get the manager's phone number.

"Can't hurt, man," I said. "But this fucking place needs more than a few coats of paint and a can of Lysol."

I didn't dare to check out the men's room—toxic was my first thought.

After this initial exploration of Homer's, Rollie and I let it go, never calling the manager, but we kept his number just for shits and grins. Then, in November, a game changer came along out of the dark. On the front deck of Homer's, a man was stabbed with an ice pick. According to the *Palo Alto Times*, he wasn't seriously injured, but the story made for bad press, and the police shut the place down as a public nuisance. Since we still had the manager's name and number, we gave a call.

During the day, Bill Gussi (pronounced "Juicy") was an insurance salesman. He was a nondescript guy with a family in San Jose—not what we had expected. While looking for a place to open a small bar, he said, he had discovered the old warehouse, which was owned by an elderly woman named Katherine Urban. Homer's was the largest of eight warehouses. Altogether, the old steel buildings housed twenty businesses, mostly small auto shops, furniture makers, and welders. Everyone who leased from Katherine loved and respected her—but they all agreed that she was a tough cookie. Bill admitted that he hadn't been totally honest with her, since she had approved a hamburger joint for the local blue-collar workers, not a nightclub with a pool table, pinball machines, and loud bands. Katherine hadn't contacted Bill about the stabbing incident, but he was highly motivated to talk to us. For one thing, his wife had not been favorably impressed by the front-page newspaper story.

When we went to look at the place again, it had been locked up for a while and was even funkier than before. A shitload of work would need to be done to get this dump into shape. Bill agreed to sublet to us cheap, only $1,450 a month, and not say a word about it to Katherine. The lease would have to be renegotiated in a year. If anybody asked, we were managing the club for Bill. We created a handwritten contract on the spot, and Rollie and I finally had ourselves a nightclub. We dubbed it Homer's Warehouse.

We set a target date forty-five days out for the grand opening, and got busy. Somehow a silk purse had to spring forth from this sow's ear. We each chose our jobs and gathered up "friends of Homer's"—people willing to help, who believed Rollie and I were on to something. The whole place had to be painted, 220-watt power brought in, an entire new stage built, the ceiling reinforced to hang a lighting rig, the miniscule office enlarged into a combined dressing room and office, and on and on.

While Rollie went fishing on the phone for musical talent, spreading the word far and wide to the booking agent community and reaching out to the record label representatives, I did most of the heavy lifting with the help of a master carpenter named George. He was from the east coast, intelligent, burly, and loud. At our very first meeting, he told me that he lived with an exotic woman in downtown Palo Alto. Then he told me he was gay.

I was open about such things, but I had never before worked alongside a gay man, day after day. George was not necessarily interested in me, but he talked nonstop about sex with men. While working on 15-foot ladders, putting up 25-foot ceiling rafters, I would tell him to shut the fuck up, and he would explode in laughter. He loved to get to me. But, God bless him, he knew his shit, and I would have been lost without him. I didn't pull a single permit except for upgrading the power to 220. That was expensive and required an electrical contractor.

The new office/dressing room, designed by George, was a masterpiece. Since Rollie had been sitting on his ass with his feet up most of the time, calling booking agents all over the country, I asked him and Gail to paint the room, one of the few major jobs left. I was relieved when they agreed to do it over a long weekend, because Lisa and I planned to go camping on the Feather River. Driving the school bus and renovating the club had exhausted me. After our trip, I headed over to the club to see what Rollie and Gail had done to the room. As soon as I walked in the front door of the club, I smelled fumes.

Christ, he must have used oil-based paint!

When I turned on the light in the dressing room, I found myself in the middle of a funhouse. Our green room was neon purple!

Although I hated it, and was really pissed at Rollie, I didn't have the energy to do it over.

We need to get this fucker open!

The final big piece of work was to deaden the sound at the back of the stage with a soundproofing drape to hang along the wall, which was 45 feet wide by 15 feet high. It was time to call my Uncle Sid, who owned a company that made stage curtains and drapes for schools. When he saw the place, he generously offered to make the acoustic drape for free.

Two weeks before opening, a police Captain showed up unannounced with another officer to ask a few questions.

"So, boys," said the Captain, "what kinda music you guys gonna be puttin' on here?"

"Oh, sir," Rollie said, "just local talent. We're gonna promote Palo Alto bands."

What a fucking liar!

"How many people you fixin' to have in here?"

"Oh, about a hundred," Rollie said without missing a beat.

Try four hundred…, twice a night.

"We had a little problem with motorcycle gangs here. Are you aware of that?"

"No, officer, we didn't hear about that. What kind of problem?"

" Hells Angels kinda problem…, including an ice pick."

"Thanks for the information, officer."

We'll cross that bridge when we come to it.

After a while, the Captain got around to telling us what he wanted: the entry ramp rebuilt with handrails on both sides; floodlights mounted over the door and in three locations in the parking lot; and no motorcycle gangs with colors on their jackets.

"We won't hassle you, boys, but we got the right to stop in unannounced anytime we want, to be sure no one under twenty-one is admitted. Your place looks great. Good luck."

We also got a visit from the Palo Alto Fire Marshal—once again, a very nice guy, who wanted to make sure we were up to code for the number of people we expected to put in the place. For him, Rollie upped the number to two hundred. The Marshall took notes and went around the place, measuring stuff, and said he would get back to us the next day with a short list of things we would need to do.

In fact, his list did turn out to be short: electric exit lights over the doors, battery-powered emergency floodlights that would come on if the electricity failed, and panic bar exit devices for the doors.

Before he left, he said, "You fellas gonna present any blues acts? I'm a fanatic for blues. If any of my favorites come in here, you'll be seeing me."

Wow! Within a week, we've got the cops and the fire department in our pocket. It's full steam ahead!

In our minds, every classy joint needs a picture of a tastefully disrobed woman behind the bar, so we brought Jake in for a consultation. He wanted to do a 20-foot-long mural, 4 feet high, but we were in a hurry, so we talked him down to 12 feet. Off he went.

A week before opening, to produce our radio advertising, Rollie hired a media manager named Cliff Feldman, who was tight with the two major Santa Clara Valley FM stations, KSJO and KOME. Cliff knew all the jocks at both stations, so we just dropped in one evening and recorded our spots for opening night. The whole time there, we smoked joints and fucked around with the studio guys and gals while they were on the air. It was terrific fun.

Also for opening night, Jake had worked up a wonderful poster with Blue Mountain as the opener and Stoneground as the headliner. In the left bottom corner of the piece, he had drawn caricatures of me behind the bar and Lisa sitting on a stool in front of me. Rollie and Gail were chatting away in the bottom right corner. Between these two adoring couples, there was a sketch of Homer's exterior with my old Castro Valley firetruck out front. Under that, there was a simple line map, showing how to get to the place.

Four days before opening, Jake showed up with his mural for behind the bar. He was carrying a piece of plywood, about seven feet long and four feet high. Laying it down face up on one of the tables, he said, "I went fourteen feet. This is the left side."

"What the fuck did you do, Jake?" I said.

"I felt compelled by artistic freedom."

"Well, I'm only payin' ya for twelve feet, you asshole!" I said in mock anger. "That's what we agreed on, and that's what you'll get."

A. Bernstein Archives
Lisa, ca. 1973

"Then, I'll take two feet home with me…, the middle two."

"Fuck off, Mister Pierre," I said. "Let's get this thing hung. I can't wait to see it from the bar!"

Jake and I hung it ourselves while Rollie sat in the office yakking on the phone and smoking up a storm. When we finally got the two parts of the mural lined up, I stood back to see what we had.

Jake had created a three-dimensional masterpiece. In the background of the mural, a blue-eyed blond woman was lying on her side, her body forming a fourteen-foot-wide mountain range with rainbows overhead. In the middle distance, there was a country scene coming off the slopes of the foothills below the woman's snowcapped breasts and hips, with little communities of elves and dragons running and playing. Up front were four of Jake's favorite alligator and snake characters, all with human-sized heads and pierced ears. They were sitting at a bar, looking at us as they passed a joint around and drank beer.

Homer's first customers!

"You fucking nailed it, Jake!" I yelled. "Get your fat ass out here, Grogan. This thing is the real deal!"

When Rollie got a look at the piece, he started laughing so hard, I thought he was going to pee in his pants.

What would we have done without Jake?

There was a crappy old sign outside over the front door, which said, "Hamburgers and Beer." Jake painted over that a scene of alligators with top hats dancing under an enormous rainbow.

The last major decision was which beer to offer—Bud or Coors. We only had four days to decide and make a commitment.

We were using the beer license that Bill had procured, which remained in his name, with us tagged as managers. I needed to work with a distributor who would provide the hardware to pour draft beer from at least two stations with multiple spouts. Since we only had an unrefrigerated cold box that could hold about ten kegs for a short time, we had a big challenge. We did have refrigerated cabinets that held ten cases of bottles, but what to do with the kegs?

The rep from Budweiser (the brand we favored) offered to put in ten thousand dollars for new refrigerated cold boxes at a low interest rate, but that was exactly the kind of investment we didn't want to make up-front. We chose Coors after the rep told us his beer was pasteurized and therefore could keep without refrigeration for up to forty-eight hours. Coors set us up with a couple of four-pour stations, including lines and air tanks, all for free.

The keg driver would be our primary contact, a middle-aged teamster named Lou. The first time he made a delivery, the afternoon before opening, he seemed okay out in the parking lot, but was disgruntled when he saw that he had to push kegs up the ramp with his hand truck. Since the drivers got a percentage of the gross on kegs, I had little sympathy for him. Our account could mean good dollars in Lou's wallet.

"I'll be stopping by twice a week," he said. "Tuesdays and Fridays at nine-thirty sharp. If nobody's here, I split."

"I'll be the guy, Lou. My bus yard is only two blocks away."

We started out with ten kegs for the opening weekend plus twenty cases of bottles.

To tend the bar, we had hired four girls who lived across the street from Rollie. I also brought in Tom McCarthy, who loved to tend bar with all the beauties. Gail managed the bar and kept an eye on things, Lisa sold the tickets, and Rollie and I traded off as doorman. Because we were selling beer, IDs were required. One of our major concerns for the first night was that the Hells Angels would show up and demand to be let in with colors on.

Opening Night

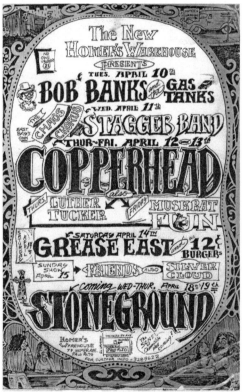

Jake Pierre Archives

At 5:00 P.M. on opening night, which was a Friday, the Fire Marshal showed up to go over his checklist. The exit lights above the doors had gone out, so we needed Fiore, our electrician back out on overtime, since the Marshal said he wouldn't leave until those lights were working perfectly. Fiore was happy to make a quick hundred and fifty bucks, so less than an hour later, we said goodnight to the Fireman and invited him to come as our guest anytime he wanted.

"I've got your card," I said. "I'll call you just as soon as we start booking blues acts."

Everything was in place as we locked the door for our first soundcheck. The plan was to open for business at 6:30 sharp. Both bands had their own sound technicians, who were concerned that their female lead singers' voices would be lost in the vastness of Homer's. But they resolved that in no time, and by 6:25 the bands were cooling off in the Purple Room.

Minutes before Rollie opened the doors, I stood behind the bar, taking in the whole scene. The only person at the bar was Jake, admiring his work.

"Hey, barkeep," he called. "How about a cold glass of beer?"

I poured him a draft, took his dollar, and put it in the register.

"Hey, asshole!" he shouted, "what about my change?"

I spun around and looked for the quarter that should have been sitting in front of him. In my excitement, I had forgotten to make change for my first customer. We both erupted in laughter, and then I opened the till and gave him his two bits.

"I'm opening the doors!" Rollie yelled.

As the first patrons came in for the 7:30 show, Rollie checked their IDs, and then Lisa took their money and stamped their hands. Many curious folks were standing out in front, apparently having heard the radio spots, but still uncertain about coming into this warehouse at the end of a pothole-riddled cul-de-sac. Nevertheless, by 7:00, we had close to a hundred people inside. By 7:30, we were ready to rock.

Blue Mountain got the evening started with a rhythm-and-blues infused rock 'n' roll set, complete with Motown standards and some original material. Although this band never recorded an album, they had a strong local following who received them warmly.

When Stoneground hit the stage, they knocked the nails out of the floor. Annie Sampson stood front and center, with Cory, David, Steve, and the other musicians backing her up. It was such a delight to finally have music bouncing off the walls. Although our club sat right next to the railroad tracks, the rumble of the trains only added to its authenticity. We'd all come a long way to get here—the shows at the junior colleges, the church, Addison Elementary School, the Fillmore West, and now here we were at last. The Palo Alto boys finally had their own place to rock, and it was heaven!

Dan Roach, the entertainment editor for the *Palo Alto Times*, dropped in that night and gave the club and Stoneground a very positive review, but didn't mention Blue Mountain at all. He noted that the old Homer's had been cleaned up, but still had enough funk to make it an adventurous night of music with the occasional train rumbling by. Fortunately for us, this was not his last visit.

Raising Hell on a Mountaintop

Saturday night was basically a repeat of Friday, except better. All of us were more relaxed, this time around, and word on the street filled the house.

We sacrificed Sunday night at the club to get Rollie and Gail married. They were both from Italian families, so all the parents, siblings, aunts, uncles, and cousins were there in force. (Rollie had taken the name Grogan from his mother's second husband.) We all convened at noon at the new volunteer firehouse on Skyline Boulevard in the middle of the redwoods above Woodside.

Rollie's clan came from Stockton, where they had emigrated from Italy early in the century. They were all farmers, so the San Joaquin Valley was well represented that afternoon. The members of Gail's family were all from the Bay Area, many of them teamsters. Besides the two Italian families, the other wedding guests were the extended family members of the Crimson Madness gang and assorted "friends of Homer's."

Throughout the entire day, the gods unleashed a horrific Pacific storm that dumped buckets of rain on Skyline Boulevard. The new roof on the firehouse leaked like a sieve, so the Palo Alto contingent rounded up a bunch of plastic buckets that had been left over from the construction and placed them strategically around the room.

The guests were all wearing their wedding best: the Italians in dark suits and shiny shoes; the Palo Alto boys in ponchos, moccasins, and trench coats. One of the guys, René Comeaux, was in a full-blown Cajun outfit topped by a Mississippi gambler's hat with a big white feather on top. I wore a three-quarter-length Moroccan leather coat with camel's hair trim, embroidered all over with pot leaves.

Just before the ceremony, during a break in the rain, Rollie and I sneaked out to my firetruck to smoke a joint. When we returned, all the Italians were seated in foldup chairs, looking as if the Pope would be arriving soon to officiate at the union. Instead, our friend Jon Buckley, a mail order minister of the Universal Life Church, made his entrance with hair down to his waist, dressed in a long, white, flowing shirt with his guitar over his shoulder. I thought the Italians were all going to walk out in single file when Jon asked Gail and Rollie to join him for the ceremony, which started with a song. But he won them over with a beautifully sung ballad he had written just for their special day.

Rollie and Gail had written their vows in advance, and Jon delivered them with much tenderness and grace. I noticed a few of the old ladies dabbing their eyes. It was the visuals that most upset the old folks, but the nuptials were sincere and tender. They were also short, thank God, as the buckets were overflowing onto the floor.

Somehow and some way, the caterers showed up during the middle of the ceremony and were able to get the tables set up at a dry corner of the firehouse. Champaign corks were soon popping, and we finished off the food, cut a cake, and celebrated the happy couple with a toast.

Meanwhile, the firetruck remained open for business for the rest of the day. Out of respect for Rollie's grandfather, Papa, a well-respected patriarch of the Italian community in Stockton, we waited until he and his clan left to start the rock 'n' roll. The next challenge was getting Blue Mountain plugged in without short-circuiting the entire place, thereby killing the musicians and burning the new firehouse down to the ground. But by the grace of God, we somehow pulled it off. I remember manic Herb frantically dropping nonflammable drop cloths over everything that could spark.

For the remainder of the evening, the forty-plus non-Italian freaks who were still left danced around the sometimes overflowing buckets of water until the wee hours, without killing anyone or doing permanent damage to the firehouse.

We did, however, deflower that place wonderfully. To this day, every time I drive by it, I remember the night of the rollicking zombies, dancing at times by flashlight when the circuits blew, raising hell on a mountaintop in the redwoods.

Dan

Lisa and I had found an affordable home in a nice Palo Alto neighborhood, on Forrest Street north of Middlefield Avenue. Our little mutt, Trinity, loved it because there were tons of squirrels to chase up trees. Lisa and I were very much in love. She had other interests outside of the club, always the spiritual traveler, horse lover, and home designer. I felt very lucky. When there was no one in line at the club, I smiled at her from behind the bar, and she would step out of the ticket booth and shake it to the music.

By our second week, Homer's had become the place to be seen and heard. The radio spots worked like a charm. Rollie managed to book several weekends ahead with headlining bands, and we filled in as best we could with local talent for the midweek dates. The idea was to keep the doors open seven nights a week. Sunday afternoons and evenings were for auditions. Monday nights were for football. Hell, whatever it took to make a buck. Because of the media exposure for our grand opening, the phone was ringing off the hook with bands looking for a chance to play, and even audition for free. Rollie booked the auditions, but we shared most talent decisions.

By the third weekend, we were pulling in near-capacity crowds. On that Saturday night, I was working the door when the unmistakable sound of several Harleys danced around my eardrums, getting louder and louder until they appeared in the parking lot. We were being paid a visit by the Daly City chapter of the Hells Angels. And they were in colors.

Rollie and I strolled down the ramp to greet our new friends, about ten of them. Obviously, Homer's had changed. They no sooner got off their bikes than a Palo Alto police patrol car rolled in after them. The cop stayed in his cruiser and observed.

As we approached the Angels, Rollie extended his hand. Two guys got off their bikes and greeted him. Rollie told them very politely that we had reopened the club and would be featuring excellent music on a nightly basis. They were welcome to attend as paying customers, but the Palo Alto Police Department had informed us that no motorcycle club colors could be worn anywhere within five hundred feet of the entrance. Otherwise, the cops would immediately shut us down for good.

"So," Rollie concluded, "we would definitely appreciate you and your brothers supporting the new rules."

I got nervous as I saw skeptical looks cross their faces, but with all the new floodlights in the parking lot—and the patrol car sitting right there—they decided not to push the issue, fired up their bikes, and were gone as fast as they had come.

"We dodged a bullet that time, Andy," Rollie said.

"I know. We're gonna need a Plan B for when they come back."

The officer got out of his car and walked toward us.

"Do you boys understand that no motorcycle colors will be allowed in your club?"

"Yes, Lieutenant," Rollie said, "We spoke to your Captain, and we know the rules. In fact, we just told those Angels the same thing."

"I think I'll have a look around, all the same, boys."

"Make yourself at home, sir."

He came into the club, looked around for a few minutes, and left.

Rollie and I immediately retired to the dressing room for a quick toke. We had rigged a warning bell in there that could be triggered by Lisa at the door if there were ever any problems.

We didn't have to wait long. About 4:00 P.M. the very next day, a Sunday audition afternoon, we heard the familiar rumble of Harley Davidsons approaching.

Oh, shit! Here we go again!

In walked two couples in full leather. The guys had "1%" patches on the front of their vests, so I assumed they were Angels. One of the men was extremely broad in the shoulders, with a black beard and medium-length dark hair in a pompadour. The other was a tall skinny guy with a pockmarked face and several missing teeth.

"Welcome to the new Homer's," I said as they walked up to the bar. "What can I do for you?"

"Where's the ladies' room?" asked one of women, a tough-looking redhead.

"Right over there, ladies," I said, pointing toward a corner near where Rollie was playing a pinball machine.

She and the other woman, an even tougher-looking blond, marched off.

Turning back to the men, I said, "And what would *you* like, gentlemen?"

"A pitcher of beer and four glasses, please," said the broad-shouldered one.

Please?!

"Hey!" said the other man, with a lot less manners. "What the hell's the name of this band? They sound pretty good."

"Bob Banks and the Gas Tanks. They're auditioning today."

"What the fuck kinda name is *that?!*"

I just smiled. It was true that the band looked like twelve-year-olds with cowboy hats on, but they were actually a lot of fun and pretty good musicians.

Wanting to see what the bikers had on their backs, I said, pointing toward one of our industrial spool tables, "Have a seat, and I'll bring the beer over to you."

When they turned around, I saw the words *UNFORGIVEN SINNERS* on their vests.

Shit!

Fortunately, because it was a Sunday afternoon, the cops were not likely to stop by, so I left the bikers and their women alone to enjoy an afternoon of music and beer.

After a while, the Sinner with the black beard came up to the bar to get another round. I could see right away that he was very articulate and quite charming.

"The club looks great," he said. "You've done a fine job. I remember this place from the old days. It was a first-class shit hole."

I laughed. "Thanks," I said. "It took a lot of elbow grease."

"Used to be a bit rough here, brother. The Angels used to have after-initiation parties in this place."

How could a Sinner be at an Angels party?

Not being up on biker politics, I knew I would be treading in deep water if I asked that question, so I kept my thoughts to myself. Instead, I simply said, "I'm Andy."

"Pleased to meet you, man, thank you. I'm Dan."

We shook hands.

At this point, Rollie came over to the bar to size things up.

"Dan, this is my partner, Rollie," I said.

Rollie gave me a curious look.

"Would you gentlemen like to join us at our table?" Dan asked.

"This pitcher's on the house," I said.

Rollie gave me an even more curious look.

As Dan walked back to the table, and I began to pour another pitcher, Rollie whispered, "What the fuck are you doing?"

"It's alright, man," I whispered back. "Just play it out. I got a good feeling about this guy."

Handing Rollie two glasses, I headed around the bar with the pitcher. When I got to the spool, I filled all the empty glasses and set the pitcher down on the varnished table top.

"Here's to new friends!" I toasted.

"*L'chai-im!*" said Dan.

Wow, a Jewish Sinner! How cool is that?

I never did find out if Dan were Jewish, but I did learn a lot of other things about him that afternoon. To begin with, he had a B.A. degree from the University of Oregon in philosophy with a minor in comparative religions, was a high-ranking member of the San Jose chapter of the Unforgiven Sinners, and had a day job as a manager of an electrical supply company in San Jose. The more we talked, the more I was impressed. It was immediately clear that he loved music. When I told him some of the groups we planned to have at Homer's, his face lit up.

"Are you guys hiring?" he asked.

Rollie, in one of his more surprising moments, said, "Yes, we're looking for a doorman…. Are you interested?"

What the fuck, Grogan! Are you crazy? He's a nice guy, but how the hell are we gonna have an Unforgiven Sinner as a doorman?!

"When can I start?" Dan asked.

I glanced nervously at Rollie, but he winked back the famous Rollie fisheye. A plan was clearly hatching in his insidious brain.

As he explained the ice pick incident on the ramp, and what the cops had said about colors, I could see that Dan was taking it all in. When Rollie finished, Dan began to tell us some things that would become very important for the future of Homer's.

"The Sinners and the Angels," he said, "have an alliance and coexist without any hostility. In fact, we party and occasionally even ride together.

I feel confident that I can communicate to my brothers in the Angels that the guys running Homer's can be trusted and really want it to be a good place to hear music. I understand that the Angels are welcome, but the colors have to stay off."

"Dan," I said, "you're a godsend! We'd love to have you work the door."

As our new doorman and his friends roared off on their Harleys, I turned to Rollie and said, "There's our Plan B."

The Wheel Goes Round and Round

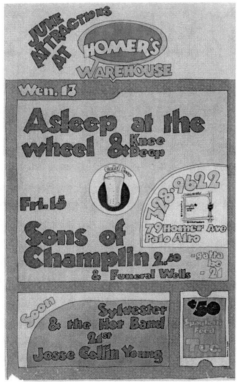

A. Bernstein Archives

Going into our second month, two things were clear: we could continue to draw big houses on weekends—with the right acts, of course—but we needed a midweek boost. Rollie's homemade Stroganoff for Monday night football, plus his fifty-cent spaghetti on Wednesday nights featuring unknown talent, was not paying the bills.

By now, we had become friends with Freddy Herrera, who owned and managed The Keystone, a club in Berkeley that was highly successful at the time. When we discussed our mutual problem of poor midweek attendance, Freddy mentioned a new band making a name for themselves on the East Bay club circuit: Asleep at the Wheel. They were a country swing band from Pennsylvania, via Paw Paw, West Virginia, led by a guy named Ray Benson.

"We already have a country band," Rollie said. "Some kids from Stanford…, Bob Banks and the Gas Tanks. They pull students in from the campus."

"These guys are different, I'm tellin' ya," Freddy insisted. "They're slick as shit…, country pros. You've gotta come over and check 'em out. They'll blow you away."

And they did. Somehow, they miraculously channeled the sound of Bob Wills and His Texas Playboys from the late '40s. Ray Benson was a tall baritone guitarist with a huge Stetson on top of a ponytailed melon. Like us, he was a stoner dude, but a fucking one-of-a-kind wunderkind. I took to him immediately, and we became fast friends. Rollie, on the other hand, thought he was weird.

I made arrangements for the band to play Homer's the following Wednesday. They had a brand new publicity photo of themselves standing on an old Kenworth truck in a junkyard in Emeryville, a brilliant backdrop. Benson was no slouch when it came to self-promotion. I gave the picture to Jake and asked him to do his best for handbills and a poster advertising fifty-cent spaghetti with our new friends, Asleep at the Wheel.

That Wednesday, after the noon bus runs, I bought twenty giant loaves of French garlic bread, ten pounds of onions, twenty-five pounds of ground beef, five huge cans of tomato sauce, ten pounds of pasta, and a ton of herbs, and threw it all in the back of my firetruck. Then I went over to a restaurant supply house in Menlo Park and bought two twenty-gallon aluminum pots, an aluminum ladle with a long neck, and a long wooden spoon. Back at the Warehouse, I fired up the Wolf industrial stove behind the bar (a leftover from the old Homer's) and started chopping onions until I was nearly blind. Then I threw all the ingredients for the sauce into one of the pots and let it simmer slowly. (The other pot would take care of the pasta later.) By the time I had to leave for afternoon bus runs, Rollie came in and looked after the sauce. The whole club smelled delightful when I returned.

The band arrived about 5:00, with all their gear packed into an old delivery truck. The plan was for them to start playing as soon as we had twenty-five people in the house. The handbills we had plastered on the thousand windshields in the parking lot at Stanford Medical School did the trick: by 5:30, there were a hundred butts in the chairs, all eating spaghetti and drinking pitchers of beer. We didn't want the audience to stop eating and drinking, so we held off the band till 6:15, but the jukebox was going at full blast.

The Wheel began with "Take Me Back to Tulsa" and didn't take a break for an hour and a half, by which time there were two hundred customers in the house—and no spaghetti. The band played all the old hits from earlier decades, which were nevertheless familiar to our generation through our parents and early country music shows on TV. Lucky Oceans was on steel pedal, Floyd Domino was on piano, the lovely Chris O'Connell was on vocals and rhythm guitar, and Ray was on lead guitar and lead vocals, with a big presence on stage.

Presenting this country swing music to our grateful audience was a godsend for us. The second set was even better than the first, with songs like "I've Been Everywhere" and several boogie-woogie tunes driven by Floyd Domino on piano. He was red hot. By the end of the evening, the crowd was clamoring for more, but the band had run out of songs and were exhausted.

After the show, I said to Ray, "I wanna book you for every Wednesday you have open for the next year…, and maybe some weekends."

He got a big smile on his face. "Andy," he said, "we love your place, we love this crowd, and we'll come back as often as we can."

"On that promise, Ray, let's burn a fatty."

After that, we had calls coming in for days, asking when the band would be back.

Thank you, Benson, we rocked it, buddy!

The first blues act we presented at Homer's was Nick Gravenities, a Chicago bluesman who came out west with Michael Bloomfield, Elvin Bishop, and Mark Naftalin. They all made contributions to those first Paul Butterfield albums in '66 and '67. That music transformed boomers' college dorm rooms into institutes of *higher* learning and schooled us all in the Chicago blues. The music had come from West Africa with the slaves, been pollinated in the South, and become electrified after World War II. But these white boys who loved it so much, and been exposed to it as young men, took it to another level.

Smoking pot and listening to the *East/West* album was a religious experience for me and many of my contemporaries. Although other blues artists we later featured at Homer's drew bigger crowds, the idea of having two or three parts of the Paul Butterfield Blues Band perform was enough for us to get very excited.

Nick arrived late in the afternoon of the performance date and was quite friendly, even complimentary of the club. When a train came rumbling by, he said, "Oh, man! Just like home! It reminds me of all the places we've played in Chicago, with the EL trains screeching overhead."

As we sat at the bar chatting, the rest of the musicians came in one by one, and Nick introduced them to me. Mark Naftalin was on keyboards, along with a bass player and drummer, who worked regularly with him. The drummer looked familiar. Nick said he used to be the drummer for Clover.

THAT'S *where I remember him from..., the Fillmore shows..., Marcus David.*

Nick mentioned his deep admiration for John Cipollina. "He's a fine musician and a great guy," he said. "I love working with him."

I had forgotten that Nick produced the first Quicksilver album and had written a few of the songs with John and the band. He also collaborated with Janis Joplin, and produced several hits for her.

This show was on a Tuesday night, with only about a hundred and fifty people in the house. Rollie showed up between sets with a smirk on his face, as if to say, "You and your fuckin' blues bands!" But once the musicians got back to playing, he came out from the Purple Room and paid attention.

After the show, once the gear was out the door and gone, Nick and I shot the breeze for a while. I was drawn to his experiences, and wanted to hear just a tad more before saying goodnight. But I was tired, and he had a long drive back to Marin, so we finally called it a night.

Right after he left, I poked my head out the dressing room door and saw his guitar case leaned up against the wall next to the front door. He had forgotten his precious Les Paul, a real beauty and a classic!

I flew over the bar and sprinted through the front door. His brake lights were blinking at the end of the alley, a hundred feet away, as he waited for traffic to clear on El Camino before making a right turn. I reached him just in time to pound on the trunk of his car.

Jon Sievert Archives
Nick's Musical Brother, John Cipollina

"You scared the shit out of me!" he said when I came around to his window. "What the fuck is wrong?"

"Where's your guitar, Nick?"

He looked around. "Oh, shit! I did it again." He burst out laughing. "I thought that thumping on my trunk meant I had run over some poor soul."

The Sons

Jake Pierre Archives

The next weekend show at Homer's featured The Sons of Champlin, one of Lisa's favorites, and mine, too. Cutting the radio spots for The Sons with Cliff was a great joy. I got to choose my very favorite Sons songs to use as background for the ads.

We had set up outlets with a couple of local record shops, so tickets for The Sons' Friday night performance sold out by Wednesday. We scheduled a second show for that night, and that sold out as well. We recruited Lisa's older brother, Kim, as our parking lot attendant, a somewhat thankless job, but the cops were putting some heat on us about the traffic on weekend nights.

On Friday, The Sons' equipment truck arrived at 2:00 P.M. Being a logistics guy, I was impressed by the vehicle, a customized straight truck with a very cool sleeper built in behind the cab. The cargo box, which had a rail gate on the tail, was set up for quick loads and unloads. This was a $70,000 rig. I asked The Sons' manager, Wally, about the cost of this operation. He really believed in the group (as did I) and was doing everything he could to help them. At some point, he told me his last name, Haas—Walter Haas, Jr. Without asking, I knew that he was an heir to the Levi Strauss fortune.

With the equipment set up, and Dan on the door, we opened early to handle the crowd for the first show, which was lined up in the parking lot. We had stocked up on beer, fifteen kegs and forty cases of bottles. There was plenty in reserve if we needed it for the second show, which we did.

Before The Sons came on for their opening performance of the night, a fan approached Rollie and me about our five Pong tables, which we had just gotten from the cigarette machine vendor a week before.

"How are my machines doing for you guys?" he asked.

In his vaguely sarcastic way, Rollie said, "Whaddaya mean, *your* machines?"

"I invented the damned things…. I'm Nolan Bushnell, the CEO and co-founder of Syzigie/Atari in Sunnyvale."

Being the science fiction fan he was, Rollie had an immediate attitudinal adjustment: "Oh, man! Your machines are doin' great! Nice to meet ya, Nolan."

"I've been looking for a place to sponsor some Pong tournaments and test prototypes of new games. Your place looks like it might be perfect. You interested?"

"Nolan," I said, "we'll give you fifty square feet in the back and all the radio advertising you want. How many tables were you thinking about bringing over?"

"How about ten?"

"Perfect."

"By the way, I'll also drop off two kiosks with my latest game…, Space Race."

"Great," Rollie said. "Enjoy the show tonight."

Shit, this is our second month, the paint's barely dry on the walls, we've got two sold-out houses tonight, and the inventor of Pong is coming to us!

From the opening song of the first show, The Sons shook the walls of that old steel-sided warehouse. We sold beer at a brisk pace, two and three deep at the bar. Lisa had held back fifty tickets to the second show, which would put us over our legal limit of 350, but we sold them anyway. She was in heaven: her favorite band was playing, and she was dancing and swaying as if she were in our own living room. I was dancing, too—when I

CALIFORNIA SLIM | 111

wasn't clearing the cash registers of twenties and hooking up new kegs. The audience was having a great time.

This is what it's all about…, people having a ball to the unmistakable groove of The Sons of Champlin.

We turned the first house on time, the band took a well-deserved break, and we did a clean sweep of all glasses, bottles, and ashtrays. Then I went back to the dressing room to congratulate The Sons and thank them all, including Wally, for their major contribution to putting Homer's on the map.

Before we opened the doors for the second show, I brought Lisa back to meet her favorite musicians. She was shy at first, but after a while made fast friends with the guys. Bill Champlin was a genuine no-bullshit human being, and put everyone around him at ease. Not one pretense about that man. Lisa was over the moon.

By the end of the night, we learned how much beer we could sell for two shows: fifteen kegs and forty cases, give or take a few bottles. Once everyone cleared out, Rollie and I locked the front door, went into the Purple Room, and emptied the money bags onto the table.

Shit, there must be five thousand dollars there!

It turned out, I wasn't far off.

Rollie took the locked bag of cash to the bank for a night deposit. A larger bank deposit bag would soon be needed

In Monday's *Palo Alto Times*, Dan Roach wrote that he was thrilled by the show's production, the enthusiasm of the audience, and, most of all, The Sons' great music.

Pickin' and Grinnin' with Jerry

Jake Pierre Archives

A few days later, Rollie rushed out of the office with some important news.

"I just got a call from Sam Cutler."

"The guy from Altamont?"

"Yep. He's now booking side gigs for Jerry, who's got a new acoustic bluegrass band called Old and in the Way. Sam wanted to bring him down for one night, so I gave him March fourth."

"God*damn* that's good news, Rollie! Well done. With that bill, we'll be able to turn two houses and sell a helluva lotta beer. Time to roll a big one!"

A little later, I called Jake to get his butt over to the club to plan the poster. We had just over ten days to prepare.

1973 is shaping up to be a mighty fine year for Homer's!

Sam Cutler and a couple of his Dead lackeys made a trip down to the club to check out the site. Sam was decked out in a fringed leather jacket and snakeskin boots, and was dripping with turquoise jewelry. With his

British accent, he had a way of coming across as a real scene maker, but to my mind he wasn't representative of the Dead mentality. Jerry had felt sorry for him because Sam was still wearing the Altamont disaster around his neck, so he gave him a job after the Stones stranded the poor bastard. The Dead were complicit in the nightmare as well, so it was only right to pick Sam up. Since he was only booking Jerry's side gigs at this point, how much trouble could he cause?

Sam did have a taste for Peruvian marching powder, however. It's no secret that the taste went further into the Dead organization than just Sam, and we were expected to pony up on show night. Sam drove that point home more than once that afternoon. I thought it was a little sleazy, but, okay, we could go along with it. When Sam asked for a sample, I wondered if that was the reason for his trip to Palo Alto that day. But the guy was hard not to love, he'd been so shat on by Mick and the boys.

Although PMP was around, we tried to minimize its appearance at the club. Unless specifically requested as a must for the artist to agree to play, we had a zero tolerance rule in effect. Our audience base was a cross-section of the community that wanted a relatively clean, well-managed, and safe place to hear music. Local community leaders came to our shows, along with Stanford students who were old enough to get in—or at least get past Dan. (There was one underage co-ed with pierced nipples who got in every time. Quick sweater pull, and bingo, Dan stamped her hand.)

This would be a homecoming of sorts for Jerry. He'd not been around Palo Alto for a while, and we wanted him to feel comfortable. Perhaps he would return for more appearances if it felt right to him. We knew this was a great opportunity to make a splash. All fingers and toes were crossed.

Treat them right the first time, and they'll come back to play again.

The players in the band this time were Jerry, John Kahn on standup bass, Peter Rowan on guitar and vocals, and the great David Grisman on mandolin (playing under the name David Diadem). With a minimum of radio spots, both shows sold out in days.

On the afternoon of the performance, around 1:00 P.M., while I was sweeping the front ramp, a brand new gold P-1800 Volvo sport wagon rolled up, looking oh so good—and out stepped Jerry.

"Well, well! My old banjo teacher! How the hell are ya?"

"You gotta be kiddin' me, man. I was your teacher?"

"Yeah, but I got tired of dragging you out of Saint Mike's Alley, you fucker!"

He laughed. "You got a cup of coffee, man?"

"I'll brew one for ya. C'mon in."

As he approached the bar, he smiled at Jake's mural.

"It's cool to be playin' back in Palo Alto," he said.

"Hey, Jerry," I called from the coffeemaker, "do you remember the time you and Pigpen came to the Foster's Freeze without any money, and I gave you double cheeseburgers, fries, and strawberry shakes out the back door?"

"That was *you*?"

We both cracked up at that one.

While I was still brewing the coffee, he wandered over to check out the video games, which were beeping and flashing from across the room. He walked right past the Pong tables to one of the two Space Race kiosks that Nolan had recently put in.

"Hey, man," Jerry yelled, "what the fuck is *this*?"

"Hold on, let me get this coffee and grab some quarters, and I'll show ya. Pull over a couple of bar stools."

A minute later, the two of us were seated in front of the kiosks.

"Alright, Jerry, the goal of this game is to shoot down alien rockets. The more you shoot down, the faster they come, and the steeper the angle."

"Fuckin' cool, man! Let's get started."

We played that dammed game for the next two hours. Jerry was addicted. *We're bonding over Space Race and black coffee! Thank you, Nolan!*

Jerry was sold on Homer's before he ever opened his banjo case.

"This fuckin' game's the future, Andrew," he said. "Right here in this steel warehouse."

Later that afternoon, the Dead's sound crew arrived, led by a manic Owsley. Once the musicians were present and accounted for, they took the stage for a soundcheck, which went perfectly, with the instruments and Jerry's vocals coming through crisp and clear.

For the early show, the musicians hit the stage right on time. Unlike a Dead show, this one was relatively well structured. As the harmonies soared through the warehouse, the subtle fuse was lit. After an hour and a half, the band finished the third encore to thunderous applause. We had to be ready to go in thirty minutes for the second show.

PMP was making its way around the Purple Room—not copious amounts, just enough to keep things lively. The band all wanted coffee, no beer or anything stronger. Of course, there was always a joint going around. At the bar, we had sold more beer than anticipated and thought we'd run out of kegs because Lou, the driver, had not completely filled our order. I called the president of the Coors franchise, a nice Italian guy, and told him the driver cut me short on kegs. He apologized. He couldn't take a truck out of the yard, but he would leave his home, pick up six kegs with his Lincoln, and bring them over to us. Midway through the dynamite second show, he arrived with his son and brought all six kegs through the back door. He said the keg driver was cutting everyone short, just to make trouble in anticipation of a teamsters' strike in the Bay Area.

The audience went wild over the second show. Afterwards, as the sound guys were loading the truck, Jerry hung around for an hour to play Space Race. Peter Rowan had to hang around for the hour as well, since he had decided to go home with Jerry. He spent the time chatting with me.

"Blue grass music's in my blood, Andrew," he said. "When I was eighteen, I was playing with Bill Munroe and the Blue Grass Boys. Fuck, I was just a kid. Can you imagine?"

"Score a lotta chicks back then, Peter?"

"Oh, man, I was usually too tired! I think I was still a virgin anyway."

We both laughed.

Old and in the Way
(set list, March 4, 1973, early show)

Homer's Warehouse

"The Willow Garden"
"Going to the Race"
"Wild Horses"
"Soldier's Joy"
"Land of the Navajo"
"Lonesome L.A. Cowboy"
"Blue Mule"
"Panama Red"
"Till the End of the World Rolls 'Round"
"White Dove"

Old and in the Way
(set list, March 4, 1973, late show)

Homer's Warehouse

"Going to the Races"
"Katie Hill"
"Till the End of the World Rolls 'Round"
"Panama Red"
"White Dove"
"Knockin' on Your Door"
"Fanny Hill"
"Land of the Navajo"
"Wild Horses"
"Blue Mule"
"Lost"
"Hard Hearted"

"Fooled Around"

Jake Pierre Archives

Rollie hit another home run after the first Jerry show. Elvin Bishop, one of the original Butterfield Band guitarists, would be making a one-night, two-show appearance at Homer's, but we couldn't advertise it as such.

We were told that, in our ads, we could use the name "Crabshaw's Outlaws" with Elvin Bishop and two band members' names, but nothing about the "surprise." There was to be a special guest: Mickey Thomas, lead singer for the Starship at that time. But we couldn't use his name in the advertising. It was all very mysterious, something about record contracts and the like. But whatever the issue, we jumped at the chance.

I called Jake and told him to come over to my house for a special project. Together, he and I came up with a likeness of Elvin, with his straw cowboy hat on and a bandana over his face, holding up a stagecoach with his band mates. It was straight out of Jake's imagination and was cool as hell.

Trying to get the radio spots right for this show was tricky, since the promotion could make no direct use of Mickey's name or music. So we went with Elvin's music, and that of his former band as well, The Paul Butterfield Blues Band. He had played on Butterfield's *East/West* album, so we used the guitar parts from the "East/West" single as the background music for the radio spot. Anyone who knew that album, and that song in particular, remembered the guitar exchanges between Michael Bloomfield and Elvin Bishop. The songs on that album were (and are) ageless classics, with Butter's harp either playing over or under them, but always there.

Cliff and I chose a different riff from the *East/West* album for each station.

Friday afternoon before the first show was spent getting Homer's into shape technically for a noisy night of electrified blues. We brought in an expensive PA system from Wally Heider Sound in San Francisco. We also had Morpheus Lighting out of San Jose bring in a couple of towers to enhance our in-house overhead light rig. Everybody was working their asses off to whip the production into shape. Between the speaker towers and the lighting towers, the usable stage area was shrunk by fifty percent, but looked bad-ass as hell.

Now we're talkin'!

When Elvin arrived with his band around 4:30, the club was ready for launch. I had a crew of high school kids do a vigorous scrubdown to defunkify the old place. Even the johns got a once-over. Our little showboat was sparkling, and the cockroaches had to see a therapist.

During the soundcheck before the show, the walls rattled. Shit, you couldn't even hear the trains! Elvin was grinning from ear to ear, clearly loving the acoustics. Mickey Thomas arrived just in time for the final number of the soundcheck.

The fact that Elvin was willing to do Homer's, with or without Mickey Thomas, was really a big accomplishment for Rollie.

Once again, the show required some creative customer parking to accommodate the 350-plus cars that showed up for the two shows. Chaos Chorus, a great young band out of Santa Rosa that we had auditioned, opened with a short set that was very well received. A young Norton Buffalo, the leader of that outfit, was cutting his teeth on Homer's patrons, and doing a great job. He knew how to work the audience with humor, dancing, and unbelievable brilliance on the harmonica. These eighteen-year-olds from Santa Rosa were the most unlikely great band we ever featured at the club.

Joe Hester Archives

Norton Buffalo's First Band: Chaos Chorus and Stagger Band

Mickey Thomas was already a celebrity from his years with the Starship. Although I didn't know him personally, I'd heard through other musicians that he was a good guy. There was a period when his voice was on the radio every time you turned it on. His personality was totally different from Elvin's, but when they were onstage together, there was great electricity and unfiltered exuberance. They had played and practiced long enough to work out a bunch of great tunes, most of them blues-oriented, which was a departure for Mickey, but he could handle it. Before Steve Perry hit the local scene with Journey, Mickey was the "voice" of the City with the Starship. Replacing Marty Balin was no small feat, but Mickey had pulled it off, with the new Starship charting hit after hit for several years.

In any event, it was the Mickey and Elvin show that night. They both loved playing clubs, and it showed. Some top Bay Area musicians were in Elvin's band, including Rich Kellogg.

Elvin and Mickey chose songs to suit everyone's tastes, sticking the future hit "Fooled Around and Fell in Love" in the middle of their first show, then again at the end of their second show. Many fans bought tickets for both. The second show went pretty late, as Elvin was feeling the groove, and they needed the practice before hitting the road. This would not be Elvin's or Chaos Chorus's last appearance at our place.

After the success with Elvin, I was able to persuade Rollie that booking blues bands was a good idea, so we proceeded at full throttle. The next blues show featured Luther Tucker, another Chicago-style blues guitar player and vocalist, with roots in the Mississippi Delta. Luther was stunning with his sharp, brilliant blues runs and moaning vocals that reflected his hard-earned chops. Once again, we filled the place with enthusiasts of the genre, including the jubilant Fire Marshall from the City of Palo Alto. I wanted the blues and folk shows to be something I could be proud of. Some of these senior players were not going to be around forever, so this was a wonderful opportunity to bring them to a city that really appreciated them. Over the next few months, we featured some excellent blues artists, and our loyal customers loved us for bringing them.

In-between our featured blues artists, The Wheel and The Sons of Champlin continued to dazzle Homer's audiences with periodic appearances.

By the end of June, the club was well established. We were still struggling to draw audiences from Monday through Thursday (with the exception of The Wheel on most Wednesdays), but the weekend shows continually sold out. In early July, we booked Jesse Colin Young, better known as the leader of The Youngbloods, who had had a national hit six years before, in 1966, "Get Together." When he played Homer's, I had a hard time believing we were presenting yet another of my favorite singer/songwriters.

The first time Jesse set foot in the club, he wasn't impressed by the potholes out front. From the way he greeted us, I could tell he felt the place was "another shit hole." We assured him we expected close to a full house. Chaos Chorus was opening for him, and they had developed a big local draw. Once Jesse settled down and the soundcheck was complete, he proved to be a very pleasant guy. He told me that having a national hit on his first go of it had been a blessing and a curse at the same time. He was able to get airplay for other songs from his catalogue, some of which were far more original and brilliant, but he was associated with one "catchy" song that people simply couldn't get out of their heads.

A Weekend with Merl and Jerry

Jake Pierre Archives

Rollie's biggest triumph to date came on the afternoon he booked Jerry Garcia and Merl Saunders for a weekend show. Joining them on May 4th and 5th, 1973, would be John Kahn on electric bass and Ron Tutt, Elvis's old drummer and famed Nashville studio percussionist. Jerry was spreading his musical wings when the Dead were off the road. This was an early incarnation of what would later become the Jerry Garcia Band.

There was yet another surprise waiting in the wings. Lobster, one of our regulars, was part of the FM radio scene in the Bay Area at the time. He was big, loud, and both a DJ at KSJO in San Jose and the musical director of KZSU, the Stanford radio station. One afternoon, he approached Rollie and me about broadcasting the Merl and Jerry shows live from Homer's on KZSU. Rollie and I both thought it was a great idea, so Lobster connected us with Mike Lopez, the student manager of the station. Lobster had told us that we would reach the whole Northern California market, but Mike had even bigger plans than that. It seems that Stanford had access to a transatlantic phone cable that had been dormant for many years, so Mike decided that what several Iron Curtain countries needed was a heavy dose of Jerry—via pirate radio from Homer's!

Mike's plan called for Hungary, Belarus, and parts of East Germany to receive the feed. However, we first needed to get permission from Jerry, which meant going through Sam Cutler. (More blow, please!) When Sam gave us the green light, it was full speed ahead. Of course, the university would know nothing of this little international broadcasting caper.

For the poster, Jake did a drawing of Jerry and Merl off their newly released record album. Decades later, ten years after Jerry's death, a songbook from Jerry's various bands, *The Jerry Garcia Songbook*, was published by Warner Bros. The inside covers of the book feature two posters of shows Rollie and I produced: one of them was Jake's poster for this special weekend at Homer's.

Around 10:00 A.M. on the day of the show, our Purple Room started to take on the look of a command center, overrun by cables and wires with crazy-looking guys from Stanford hooking up 20,000 watts. Both shows would be taped on a gigantic Memorex reel-to-reel. It was a fuck-all, balls-to-the-wall extravaganza.

Jerry arrived unceremoniously around 2:30 P.M., and walked straight to the Space Race kiosk.

"Hey, Andrew," he called as he pulled up two bar stools to the machine. "Great to be back! Can you bring me a cup of black coffee and a few stacks of quarters, please?"

A couple of minutes later, I set the coffee down next to him, along with *two* stacks of quarters, and we shot down alien spaceships for the next hour.

Around 3:00 P.M., the sound truck arrived with the road crew, and out stepped the lead technician for the night—Owsley Stanley.

Because of his eccentric and unpredictable character, Owsley didn't know how to finish a project on time, so he was banned from any involvement with sound when the Dead were on tour. However, for the Jerry shows, he was "the man." His first task, when he got to Homer's, was to make sure the broadcasting guys from Stanford knew who was running the show. General Patton had arrived. Sound mix, PA levels, acoustics, tape speed, the whole shebang was under his direct control. The packed Purple Room was known that night as The Command Center.

Sam Cutler showed up around 5:00, decked out once again in space hippie togs, with a couple of slackers who seemed to have no role other than to make sure that Rollie or I got them enough blow.

By this time, Owsley was like an obsessed woodpecker. He was a pain in the ass, but a perfectionist, and eventually, with only fifteen minutes before the doors were scheduled to open for the Friday night show, we got the sound up and working to his desired metrics.

The music for the show started at 7:30 P.M. sharp. Lobster was the live DJ, operating the radio control board for the broadcast out of the Purple Room. He was hyped, as we all were. I did the stage intros.

This is history in the making! I thought as I introduced the band.

Then I ran out to Rollie's car and turned on the radio. (Castro Valley didn't have one.) There we were, coming through loud and clear! I tried to imagine some Hungarian family puzzled by what in the hell they were listening to. I hope they enjoyed it!

A. Bernstein Archives

Merl and Jerry at Homer's Warehouse, May 5, 1973

Merl and Jerry made amazing music, ranging from rhythm and blues to Dylan and everything in between, with a couple of Dead songs tossed in for good measure. Although the musicians came from different musical roots, their love of open jamming and the tunes they chose for the shows fused together. Jerry was having fun, making music he loved with people he respected and enjoyed playing with.

It was something of a miracle we didn't blow that old tin can sky high, with 20,000 watts hitting a much overloaded line back to the Stanford transmitter.

When I arrived at the club the next morning around 11:00, the scene was surreal. To begin with, the place needed a top-to-bottom bath. The Friday night show had been so much work that the thought of doing it all over again, complete with Owsley and the Stanford radio crazies, wasn't very appealing.

Rollie showed up when I was already scrubbing away, and went straight to the office, as if I were hired help. My immediate reaction was to toss the mop over the bar, which broke a couple of beer glasses, and scream at him to get the fuck out of there and help me.

"This club is a goddamn mess," I said, "and we have an early start tonight. Once the techs get here, nothing'll get done, so start washing glasses and dump the trash. I'll do the bathrooms and swab the floor."

He got busy.

By the time the Stanford crew arrived at 3:00, we had the place spic and span. As usual, Jerry showed up at 4:00 and began filling the Space Race kiosk with quarters and downing cups of black coffee that I refilled every once in a while—right after I emptied his ashtray. I was too busy to join in the fun, so he just sat there alone and shot those damned aliens all by himself.

Once Owsley, Sam Cutler, and their wild-eyed sound crew arrived, the madness set in once again. Unlike the day before, however, all the gear was already set up, so all they had to do was push some buttons and turn some knobs. I could tell by the soundcheck that the musicians were in a groove for the evening's performance.

In fact, it was a show that was not to be missed. The crowd went nuts, which gave the band energy to take the music to another level. I still have a picture from that night's performance. To think that show was also enjoyed by millions around the world is mind-bending.

Dan Roach came that night and reached the same stellar conclusion I did. There must have been something in the air. Maybe it was the disinfectant, who knows? People still talk about that weekend, and bootlegs of the music are traded over the internet forty years later.

Jerry stuck around after the show, waiting till everyone left, to play more Space Race. He and I played for a good hour, while the crew loaded everything into their truck, and the radio guys cleared their gear out.

Before Jerry left, he said, "Andrew, we'll be back. I've got some more dates planned. Sam will be in touch."

"Nothing would make me and the community happier, Jerry," I said. "By the way, the Space Race guy told me he's working on some new gadgets, so come prepared."

"Cool, man. Thanks again. We love this great little place. See ya soon."

Merl Saunders and Jerry Garcia
(set list, May 4, 1973)

Homer's Warehouse

Set One
"That's the Touch I Love"
"Expressway"
"Instrumental"
"After Midnight"
"It's No Use"
"That's All Right Mama"

Set Two
"It Takes a Lot to Laugh, It Takes a Train to Cry"
"Honey Chile"
"Lonely Avenue"
"Soul Roach"
"Georgia on My Mind"
"The Night They Drove Old Dixie Down"
"How Sweet It Is"

Merl Saunders and Jerry Garcia
(set list, May 5, 1973)

Homer's Warehouse

Set One
"Hi-Heel Sneakers"
"Honey Chile"
"Here There and Everywhere"
"Jam"
"Are You Lonely for Me Tonight"
"After Midnight"
"I Second That Emotion"

Set Two
"It Takes a Lot to Laugh, It Takes a Train to Cry"
"Expressway"
"Instrumental"
"The Night They Drove Old Dixie Down"
"How Sweet It Is"

Wheels, Commanders, Copperheads, and Jewboys

A. Bernstein Archives

One afternoon, I got a call from Benson, who had been out on the road for a month or so with The Wheel. Now back, they were ready for some gigs at the warehouse. On the following Wednesday, they showed up in their old van, which was overflowing with equipment. Benson and I sat down after the soundcheck, lit up a joint, and shot the shit about his plans for the band. Moving to Austin and touring forever, with albums in-between produced in his own studio, was Benson's dream. But at the moment, he needed a bus and a driver. He already had plans to go back to Knoxville to buy an old double-decker Scenic Cruiser from Greyhound. Knowing that I had been a bus driver, he asked if I were interested in the job. It immediately hit me between the eyes that if I didn't want to do it, I knew who would.

Fuck, he'd be perfect!

"I'm pretty sure I got a driver for you, Ray."

"Well, give 'em a call, Andrew. See if he's interested."

I went back to the Purple Room and called Maynard Lutts to explain what was up. In his unflappable way, he said it sounded interesting, but he wanted to think it over. The next day, he called back to say he'd like to talk to Benson, and before I knew it, they cut a deal.

At the Wheel show that Wednesday, we had a lively crowd and sold all the spaghetti. Afterward, I told Benson that Rollie and I had been thinking about doing a big Fourth of July celebration.

"I like the idea, Andy," he said, "but who did you have in mind to open?"

"I'll find out who's available, Ray, and I'll call you for approval if I get lucky."

"Better do it quick, Andy. The Fourth is only two weeks off."

We put some feelers out, and, lo and behold, a booking agent in San Francisco had the perfect band to compliment The Wheel: Commander Cody and His Lost Planet Airmen. It was a done deal—one show, two long sets, one by each band, both headliners, and we would rock the joint for the Fourth.

I immediately called Benson, and he was onboard.

George Frayne Archives

I knew that show was bound to draw a lot of bikers and be a wild ride. The question was, could we pull it off while keeping the cops at bay? We would have a full house, with very little ventilation, on a hot summer night. I beefed up security, telling Dan that I was bringing in a few ex-Marine friends to be available if he needed help. The Hells Angels had been coming to every show the Wheel played. They were always respectful, but the Fourth could present problems. For one, I expected firecrackers. The cops and the Fire Marshal would not tolerate any of that inside the club.

The show sold out a week in advance. Meanwhile, Benson took off for Knoxville, bought the bus, and drove it back to California in time for the big night. Once again, we called on Morpheus to light up the old warehouse for Cody and The Wheel. Wally Heider came back again for the sound. The speaker stacks had an almighty aura, plus a crisp and clear sound—more what you'd expect from Winterland, not our little tin-walled shack.

By 7:30, we had seventy-five Harleys parked in front of Homer's, many with the Angels' death head painted on the gas tanks. Fortunately, no one wore colors. I can't thank Dan enough for the tightrope he walked that night. The Wheel stormed the stage, and Benson was feeling it. Before they completed two songs, firecrackers were going off inside the club. Then a beer bottle flew by my head.

Oh, shit! This is getting out of hand.

Dan and I had a quick powwow. He suggested that we meet in the Purple Room with a few reps from the Angels chapters that were there that night.

"Maybe we can get them to help out," he said, "so the cops don't shut us down for the night."

A few minutes later, he brought three brothers into the Purple Room.

"Andrew," he announced, "this is Nazi Dave, from the Daly City chapter…, this is Larry, from the San Jose chapter…, and Denny, also from the San Jose chapter. Denny's a close friend of Benson's."

"Guys," I said, "this ain't the old Homer's. We have to tone it down."

"We sure love seeing The Wheel here, Andrew," Denny said. "Just tell us what we gotta do."

"Well, take the fireworks outside, and don't throw beer bottles. That's about it. When the cops see all those bikes out there, they're bound to come in. One firecracker or one flying bottle would be all it takes for them to pull the plug on the music."

Nazi Dave looked agitated. "Oh, great!" he said. "First, no colors. And now we gotta behave like schoolboys."

But Denny and Larry looked at each other, and then nodded to me.

"Don't worry," Larry said. "We wanna continue to hear The Wheel, so we'll spread the word."

"Thank you, boys," Dan said. "We can use all the help we can get."

We had over three hundred people in the club that night, all there to have a good time and listen to lively music. George Frayne, the Commander, was a boogie-woogie player with a vocal range from deep growl to happy-go-lucky traveling man. The Airmen featured Bill Kirchen, one of the most versatile guitarists of the era, who kept up with George's piano riffs. With his long black hair flying around, Cody covered all his hits with a cigar on the piano and a bottle of whiskey on his amp.

I had the club cleared by 2:30 A.M., with everyone gone but Rollie, who was in the Purple Room, entertaining some Angel, who I later learned was the president of the Daly City chapter. His guys were waiting outside, bored. As I was sweeping the floor, out of nowhere five Angels rode their bikes up the ramp into the club and started weaving between and around the tables. I was caught in the middle with no place to go. They finally left when their president came out and told them to wait outside.

Dan Roach ran a glowing review of the show in Monday's *Palo Alto Times*. He had as good a time as everyone else with the great bands and "colorful" audience. No place else within forty miles, he wrote, was presenting the kind of music and good times we were.

Benson was very proud of his new bus. He had been dreaming for years of being just exactly who he had become, and doing what he had set out to do: bring his county swing to the masses.

Maynard was now onboard as caretaker of the old Grey dog, a job that suited him just fine.

Around this same time, we got a call from an agent in L.A., who wanted to book Kinky Friedman and The Texas Jewboys into the club. They were a comedic country band out of Austin, touring behind their first album. We agreed to have Kinky open for The Wheel, but his agent insisted that the Jewboys had to be the headliners, since a couple of their songs were getting radio play—"They Don't Make Jews Like Jesus Anymore" and "Kick Me,

Jesus, Through the Goal Posts of Life." Benson was coolly receptive to being the opening act, but knew the audience would really be coming for The Wheel.

A. Bernstein Archives

A 1951 Super Scenic Cruiser

Four days before the show, I got a call from the agent, saying that he had shipped ten thousand pictures of Kinky and the band to Homer's, and asking me to please give them to the band when they arrived. The pictures came the morning of the show, freight collect! I was the proud guardian of all the promo pictures for the tour, and then some.

Kinky rolled in with his boys about 4:00 P.M. in an old van pulling a trailer. He walked up to the bar in boots and a wide cowboy hat, smoking a big cigar and wearing dark aviators.

"Who owns this shit hole?" he said, looking like he was about to spit on the floor.

"My partner and I do," I said casually. "Welcome to Palo Alto."

All hat and no cattle!

Just then, a southbound train roared by, shaking the floor. Kinky's lips were moving, but I couldn't hear what he said. When the train was gone, he made his meaning clear: "I said, have ya got a fuckin' bottle o' whiskey?"

"Only beer, sorry."

He looked like he wanted to slug me.

Jake happened to be there, dropping off some poster artwork, so I pulled a twenty dollar bill out of the till and said, "Hey, Jake, mind running over to Ernie's Liquors and getting a bottle of Wild Turkey?"

"Fuck the turkey!" Kinky said. "Get me some Old Overholt."

I took another twenty out of the till and handed it to Jake. Later I learned that Old Overholt was cheap crap, and Jake made a killing on the change.

"While we're waiting, Kinky, let's you and I go in the back room. I've got something special for ya."

Back in the Purple Room, over a big fat joint, we soon became pals—Bernstein & Friedman. We could have opened a law firm in San Francisco. All was good in the ghetto.

"So what about this band, Asleep at the Wheel?" Kinky asked.

"They're a fuckin' great swing band, Kinky…, pull huge crowds from Stanford. Their first album is about to come out on United Artists."

I wanted to scare this Jewish cowboy a little. For a second, he looked shocked. Then he got it, and flipped me off. The two of us roared.

The Wheel opened to a full house of old and new fans. As usual, they pleased their loyal following, who asked for more at the end of their set, which of course the band gave—with a little extra just to throw the fear of God into The Jewboys.

Kinky was clearly impressed. "Jesus Christ, Andrew! These fuckers are good!"

"Go up there and knock 'em dead, Kinky. Your fans are waitin'."

He took a big swig of the Old Overholt and hit the stage with the Jewboys in tow, opening with "Put Your Biscuits in the Oven and Your Buns in the Bed." The crowd loved him, for he sure knew how to work the room with his patter and gags in-between the songs.

After the show, I got to spend a little more time with Kinky. He was one of the funniest SOBs I'd ever met. The more he drank, the funnier he got. After he and his boys finally pulled out for Portland that night, I went back to the Purple Room to clean up and spotted something in the corner.

Oh, shit!

There were the ten thousand pictures of the Jewboys, still in the boxes.

Kinky never even saw them. I eventually got them to him, but he still owes me a bundle.

We could now feature just about anyone we wanted at Homer's. Promo albums were arriving daily from the labels, and the phone was ringing off the hook with agents wanting to book their talent.

The day Copperhead's agent called was a grand day indeed. This Marin County–based band featured the lead guitar player and co-founder of Quicksilver Messenger Service, John Cipollina. Quicksilver was an early outstanding San Francisco band, thanks to John's stunning mastery of the electric guitar. He had retired Quicksilver several years earlier, but continued to write and record with an exceptional evolving group of local musicians.

I was beside myself that John was coming to our club. So were three hundred other people, who began hanging around at 3:00 P.M. for the early show. The poster was on yellow paper, the text in black, with the only color being the head of a snake in copper ink. In cutting the radio spot, Cliff and I, both big-time fans of John's, once again had a ball deciding which song to use, "Pride of Man" or "Silver and Gold." We compromised by cutting two spots.

At 6:00, we were ready to roll. We had ample beer, an outstanding touring sound system, and an amped up crowd. More than half the house bought tickets for both shows, and they got their money's worth. The band played old songs as well as new. The older tunes got the audience into a lather—including yours truly. The second show went late, since the band was feeding off the exuberance of the crowd. Maynard, a big Quicksilver fan, attended both shows, and was totally lit up.

A. Bernstein Archives

After the performance, John came into the dressing room, exhausted. I made sure he had cold water to hydrate himself, and was delighted when he told me how much he had enjoyed the intimacy and funky nature of our place. He actually loved the trains rumbling by.

"Could I have a copy of that poster with the copperhead on it, Andrew?" pointing to one on the wall. "I really like it."

"No problem. You can have that very one."

As I walked over to take it down, he said, "I'll always remember your club and all the fun I had in Palo Alto tonight. I'll tell all my friends about you and urge them to play here."

That version of the Copperhead band was not around long, so we were fortunate to book them when we did. John died in 1989 from a respiratory illness he had had his entire life.

Me and Sonny

A. Bernstein Archives

We got a real blessing with the next blues act Rollie booked, at my insistence: Sonny Terry and Brownie McGhee. I suggested that a great opener would be Jon Buckley, our old friend from Foothill, who now had an album out on Fillmore Records. Jon was at our doorstep the same afternoon that Rollie called him. His music was a deep and powerful personal statement. Appearing on this bill would be a wonderful mentoring opportunity for him.

The booking arrangements for Sonny and Brownie were more complicated than most, since their agent told us we would be responsible for transporting Sonny and booking his hotel. Rollie thought that was a pain in the ass, but I was happy to help an elderly blind man, who I felt was one of the greatest artists who would pass through our club.

A. Bernstein Archives

Sonny and Brownie were scheduled to play Homer's on Friday night and the Paul Masson Mountain Winery in Saratoga on Sunday afternoon. Then Sonny would fly out of SFO on Monday morning for a show in Portland. Rollie thought this was way too much work, and he was determined to make this a "you and your blues shit" deal, but I told him to fuck off and not worry about it.

Sonny arrived at the Holiday Inn in Palo Alto on Thursday afternoon, in a cab provided by his airline. I called him about 7:30 that evening from the club to introduce myself. He sounded just the way I imagined he might—a well-spoken, raw-voiced gentleman.

"Would you mind joining me for dinner, Andrew?"

"It would be an honor."

When I hung up, I told Rollie I was taking Sonny to dinner and might be back late, if at all. Then, out of respect for Sonny, not wanting to look like the Wild Man of Borneo, at least for that night, I pulled my hair back in a tight ponytail and dressed appropriately.

To make picking Sonny up something special, I had Lisa borrow her father's gold four-door Oldsmobile sedan with leather seats. I couldn't bear the thought of driving Sonny around in my firetruck or the Volkswagen.

When I pulled up in front of the Palo Alto Holiday Inn, I saw a black man standing just inside the door. I immediately recognized Sonny from his pictures. He was definitely a dapper dresser, with shades on and a white cane. As I walked up to him, I estimated that he was about seventy, which turned out to be close.

"Mister Terry," I said, "I'm Andrew. A pleasure to meet you, sir."

Mom taught me right.

He put out his extraordinarily large hand, which totally engulfed mine.

As we shook hands, he said, "Please call me Sonny…, and the pleasure is all mine, sir."

He was a tall man, at least six-foot-two, but he said to me, "My goodness! How tall are you, sir?"

"Six-foot-seven, Sonny."

"Wow!"

When I helped him into the car, I heard him sniffing the aroma of the leather interior.

"This is a roomy, comfortable car, Andrew," he said, settling into his seat.

"You up for barbequed ribs, Sonny?" I asked, as I started the engine.

"That would be just fine."

Getting to know Sonny over dinner was totally natural. We spoke in general terms about life, music, and a little religion. When he got around to talking about his relationship with Brownie, he said, "Andrew, a man can lose his patience over the years, and I'm afraid that's what's happened with Brownie and me."

I was all ears. At twenty-five, I never felt younger in my life. But Sonny did his best to put me at ease. He was very upbeat.

"Andrew, as long as I have the energy to make the next gig, I'll be working. I'm just so grateful to each club owner who makes the effort to escort me around."

I'm the grateful one.

We enjoyed the rib dinner and talked and talked. The more comfortable he became, the more he opened up to my questions. By the time we were driving back to his hotel, he was telling me whatever came to his mind.

I wanted to hear specifics about the Chicago scene in the Thirties, a city he and Brownie knew well, since they had taken up many social causes and marched arm-in-arm with Woody Guthrie when the government was railing against Communists and liberals. As young men, they used music to further their nonviolent ideals. I also wanted to know about various artists, and I hit a winner when I asked about Lead Belly.

"You wanna know how he got his name, don't ya?"

"I sure would."

"Lead Belly liked the ladies, but he really pissed one of 'em off. She walked into the bar, drunk, and pumped two low-caliber slugs into his belly."

"Did you take him to the hospital?"

"No, that sumbitch said it would be too expensive…, and he never *did* take 'em out."

He told me this and other tales in his slow and deliberate tone, laughing at some of the highpoints. He knew all the greats, but was obviously a humble man. Sonny was a soulful historian, a teacher, and a genuinely cool guy to be around. But he also had a stubborn streak, especially when he talked about Brownie.

When I dropped him off at the Holiday Inn, we agreed that I would I pick him up for the show the next night at 5:00 sharp. With no one from the hotel around to escort Sonny to his room, I happily volunteered to do it. He put his arm through mine, and we strolled down the hall together. At his room, I took the key from him and opened the door. The vibe I felt was "new friendship," not musician and lackey.

When Sonny called me the next afternoon, we agreed to meet in the lobby and have dinner together at his hotel before the show. Once again, he looked like a million bucks, with a black felt feathered porkpie hat, perfectly creased.

How does he do it as a blind man?

This was just another aspect of Sonny Terry that fascinated me.

At dinner, Sonny asked about the club and the opening act.

"Jon Buckley, Sonny. A local musician, who just cut his first album. He's a friend of mine, and a fine folk singer."

"Splendid, Andrew. I'll look forward to hearing him. Does he have a band?"

"No, he's solo."

Sonny looked relieved. I could tell he didn't want to follow a big noisy act.

He wanted to know about my family, my education, and my plans for the future. I gave him some quick answers, doing my best to direct the conversation back to him. When he mentioned that he hadn't heard from Mountain Winery about his ride to the show on Sunday, I told him not to worry. If they didn't call, I would take him. Sonny perked up at that.

When we got to the club, I escorted him to the Purple Room. Brownie and his crew were already there. To my surprise, no one got up to give Sonny a seat, so I said, "I need half the people in this room to leave."

At that point, Brownie and the whole rest of his entourage walked out—with attitude.

I led Sonny to the sofa, and said, "Jon Buckley would like to meet you before he goes onstage. Would that be okay?"

"Invite him in, Andrew. I'm always happy to meet another musician."

I gave Sonny a cup of coffee, made sure he was comfortable, and asked Jon to come in.

When Jon saw Sonny sitting there, dapper in his fine clothes, shiny black shoes, and stingy brim, he lit up with a wide smile. Jon had confided in me that Sonny was one of his folk heroes. I sat back, pleased that this night at Homer's had made this exchange possible. When it was time for Jon to go on, Sonny asked me to open the door so he could listen to the music. After the set, Sonny took the time to let Jon know how important his music was. As Jon left the dressing room, he was beaming.

When it was time for Sonny to go on, I brought him out to the stage, where Brownie was already set up. After I helped Sonny into his chair and adjusted his mike, I made a brief heartfelt introduction to the audience. Then Sonny and Brownie ripped into their music with abandon, particularly Sonny. His wild harp playing, with whooping and yawing, was mesmerizing. Their deep-throated vocals, Brownie's masterful guitar, and Sonny's amazing virtuosity on the harmonica were what this music was all about. Even Rollie was struck by it. He had that crooked smile on his face, with his head bobbing, which meant that we were dialed in. As I looked over the audience, I realized that this was the most diverse crowd we had ever had. The people included folk and blues fans, whites and blacks, young and old.

It crossed my mind that I hadn't seen Sonny and Brownie interact offstage for as much as ten seconds. I was amazed that two people who hardly spoke to each other could make such beautiful music. Because Rollie handled the business transactions, I didn't have anything to do with Brownie myself. Later, I learned from Rollie that Brownie lived in Oakland, so he and Sonny, who lived in Long Island, had a continent between them in more ways than one.

Between the first and second show, I made sure that Sonny had me at his disposal for a bathroom visit, a full cup of coffee, and no grief from the Brownie Posse.

After the second show, Sonny looked tired.

"Andrew," he said, "could you take me back to the hotel right now? I wanna check about my ride to Sunday's gig."

I could tell he was still worried.

It turned out that the hotel hadn't received a message from the Mountain Winery.

"In that case, Sonny," I said, "it's a done deal. I'll be taking you."

"Well, that's just splendid, Andrew. By the way, tomorrow's my rest day, so you don't have to fuss with me. I'll be just fine here by myself."

"Well, take my home phone number just in case you need me for anything. If not, I'll see you Sunday morning at nine."

When I got home that night, I said to Lisa, "Being with Sonny is like a dream, except I'm wide awake. He's the first true gentleman I've ever met."

On Sunday morning, I met Sonny for breakfast at his hotel. As usual, he was looking terrific. By now, we were so comfortable together that I knew what he needed before he had to ask for it, and I let him do what he could without my help.

Over bacon and eggs, he said, "I told my wife last night that with you I'm in good hands."

I could tell from the way he talked about his wife how much he loved her.

"Andrew, I'd like to have your address so my wife can add you to her Christmas list, and we can keep in touch."

I wrote the information on a napkin, folded it over, and handed it to him."

"What would you like me to do today when we get to the winery?" I asked.

"Just do everything you've been doing for the last few days. I don't wanna be handed off."

"Don't worry. I'm your assistant till you're on the plane tomorrow morning for Oregon. Since you're spending the night at the winery, I'll come back and take you to the airport."

We loaded up my father-in-law's golden Olds with Sonny's suitcases and headed to Saratoga. It was a beautiful morning as we rode through the green and yellow foothills and then climbed up toward the ridgeline. The view was spectacular when we reached the top of the winding driveway to the winery. Sonny kept asking me what I saw, so I did my best to share it with him. He wanted to know about colors, which I found interesting, since he had told me he "felt" colors.

When we arrived at the mansion on top of the hill, we were greeted by the three producers of the show, two men and a woman, who were ecstatic to be meeting Sonny. At some point, the woman asked a young man standing nearby to take Sonny and me to Sonny's cottage. As we were driven there in a golf cart, I described the layout of the winery to Sonny as best I could. He wanted to hear every detail.

As the driver unloaded Sonny's bags from the cart, a man came out of the next-door cottage, whom I immediately recognized as Jon Hendricks, the jazz performer, who would be opening the show. When he came over to introduce himself, it was obvious that he was pleased to be on the same bill as Sonny and Brownie.

"You know, Sonny," he said, "the Masson family, who own this place, are hosting a special dinner tonight after the show."

I was thrilled, figuring it would be a meal to be remembered.

Sonny wanted a little nap before the show, so I went back to the reception area, where the producers introduced me as Sonny's assistant to some important-looking people. I asked a few questions about the setup, especially where Sonny could sit out of the sun as he waited to go on.

For one day, I've got the best job in the world!

When I drove a golf cart back to Sonny's cottage to pick him up, he was waiting for me. He looked splendid in a lightweight summer suit and a feathered fedora. When we got back to the reception area, I introduced him to a few of the big shots, some of whom turned out to be members of the Masson family.

Sonny and Brownie had been picked to help "move along the blues" for what would become one of the premiere concert venues on the west coast in the years ahead. At that performance, three hundred people sat on wooden folding chairs on the lawn behind the mansion.

Jon Hendricks was a great one-man act, with a fabulous scat singing style, which set him apart from most other jazz singers. After his set, I walked over to Sonny, who was sitting backstage at a table under an umbrella.

"Showtime, Sonny! Take my arm."

I felt as if I had been groomed to do this my whole life.

I led him over to the performing platform, got him seated comfortably, and set a glass of water on the table next to his chair.

Brownie winked at me and nodded his approval.

One of the Masson family sons got up in front of the audience to give a warm welcome to these two old pros. As they started to play, it was a beautiful experience to see them performing with the entire Santa Clara Valley spread out a thousand feet below. I was impressed that they could entertain a group of elite wine-sippers one day, after they had been tearing it up in front of the beer-guzzlers at Homer's the night before.

It was hot in the sun, so Sonny and Brownie took a brief break after forty-five minutes, and then did another short set. Afterwards, I brought Sonny from the stage over to a shaded area, where guests came by to meet him and Brownie and take a few pictures. Sonny was hot and tired, and wanted to get back to his air-conditioned cottage before dinner, so we soon excused ourselves.

While I roamed around the vineyard, Sonny napped for an hour. About five o'clock, I picked him up in the golf cart and took him over to the mansion for a pre-dinner winetasting party, which was held in the living room, with a spectacular view of the valley below.

Sonny and I were the first ones to arrive. As always, he asked me to describe the house and the view in great detail, so he could tell his wife about it later. Soon there were twenty people in the room, talking and drinking and laughing. Sonny and I worked the room together as if we had been doing this forever.

At dinner, we all sat at one large dining-room table covered with large plates and bowls of food. As I filled Sonny's plate, I quietly told him what was for dinner. He and Brownie played off each other without a trace of bitterness, with Jon Hendricks acting as a go-between, using his knowledge of folk music to keep the conversation rolling along. Everyone was cordial, and the wine and food were out of this world.

After dinner, Sonny and I went straight back to his cottage so he could call his wife and go to bed. After I made sure he knew where everything was, we arranged for me to pick him up the next morning after breakfast and take him to the San Francisco Airport.

As I drove home that night, I imagined leaving my bus-driving job and Homer's to go on the road with Sonny and take care of him for as long as he performed. In the course of four days, I had grown to love this man. I certainly wasn't looking forward to saying goodbye to him.

When I arrived to take him to the airport on Monday morning, he was waiting for me in the reception area by the mansion. As soon as he recognized the sound of the Olds pulling up, I saw a big smile cross his face.

When I got out to open the trunk, he greeted me with a hardy "Good morning, Andrew! How are we this glorious morning, sir?"

Yeah, right! Calling me "sir" like I'm any measure of a man compared to you.

"I'm just fine, Sonny," I said.

Some of the hosts were on hand to see Sonny off.

We headed back down that curvy road in the gilded tank, barely making the tight turns all the way down. Once back on I-280, heading north, we talked freely about anything that came to mind, finishing each other's sentences and laughing.

As we neared the point where the highway crossed through the foothills of Palo Alto, there was a quiet moment. Sonny put his hand on my shoulder and spoke directly to me: "Andrew, I want you to know that you are a man…, an honest and a good man…, and that's just what I told my wife this morning. She said you and your wife will always be in her prayers and mine."

Then he was silent.

My eyes opened up like floodgates, but I couldn't speak. I made a mental note of exactly where we were at that moment, glad that we had just crossed into Palo Alto, my hometown. Sonny knew that he had touched me, and didn't expect me to respond. I was twenty-five and didn't yet have a clear idea of what it meant to be a man. But at that moment, I felt I had the answer for the rest of my life.

After I finally settled down, I said, "Thank you, Sonny. That means a lot to me."

He had taught me about being a man just by being himself. He couldn't know how that one statement had changed my life, and I didn't want to be overly dramatic, but I knew I would never question my own manhood again. It had been defined by an expert.

When we reached the airport, I pulled up to the curb, got his bags out of the trunk, and asked a redcap to stay with him while I parked the car.

As the redcap lifted Sonny's bags to take them to his stand, he said, "My! These bags are heavy!"

There are seven wardrobe changes in there.

I parked the car and rushed back to Sonny's side. With him holding my arm, we headed for the gate. The agent there assured me that they were ready to look after Sonny's needs.

"Will someone be meeting Mister Terry at the gate in Portland?" I asked.

"Yes, sir, arrangements have been made to get his bags and escort him to a taxi for the ride to his hotel."

With all my heart, I wanted to go with him to Portland, to take care of him, and spend the rest of his touring years doing just what I was doing at this moment. As we sat together and talked, he invited me and Lisa to visit him and his wife on Long Island.

Soon it was time to board. Sonny gave me a firm handshake and a promise to stay in touch. We exchanged Christmas cards for years, right up till he died, but that day in 1973 was the last time I ever saw him.

Jerry Garcia and Vassar Clements

A. Bernstein Archives

S am Cutler called Rollie two weeks later to bring Old and in the Way back to Homer's once again, on July 24th. Ray Benson had great respect for Jerry Garcia and wanted to play on a show with him before The Wheel left the Bay Area for good. Jerry's blue grass fans and the Wheel fans would love that, so we dropped the idea on Sam Cutler, who said he would get back to us.

Sam also told us there would be a new musician with Old and in the Way. Vassar Clements, the most respected blue grass fiddler alive, had joined the band. In a few weeks, he would be making sawdust on our stage.

The next morning, we got a call back from Sam that Jerry was okay with The Wheel opening the show.

"Jerry's only request of them," he said, "is please don't blow the audience into center field with volume."

When I called Benson to tell him the deal was on, he flipped.

In many respects, we had managed to choreograph a pretty sophisticated little production, bringing together a diverse group of people who spanned Tennessee (Vassar), West Virginia (Benson), and planets as yet undiscovered (the Dead family).

Lobster, Mike Lopez, and his guys needed a few days to once again turn the Purple Room into a broadcasting and recording studio. By Friday afternoon, the dressing room was toast, with cables once again running in and out of the warehouse walls.

Owsley, the Dead crew, and the truck driver arrived at 2:30 in the afternoon. Owsley was engineering the sound for the live audience, the overseas radio audience, and the recording he was making.

When the Wheel showed up around 4:00, I was scurrying around as usual—checking on the parking and storing extra kegs of beer. At some point, I saw Jerry sitting at the bar, having a cup of coffee and a cigarette. I walked over to chat.

"Who owns that old red panel out front?" he asked. "Sure is fuckin' cool!"

"You mean 'Castro Valley'? That's my rig."

"What was it? An old plumbing truck?"

"No, man. It's a 1942 Chevy rescue wagon…, custom-built for the Castro Valley Fire Department during the war."

"It's looks like a Furry Freak Brothers truck, straight out of R. Crumb's imagination."

"You got that right!"

"Anyway, Nolan Bushnell arranged for his guys to drop a Space Race kiosk in my living room at home. I think he got my number from Rollie, which is cool. By god, he made good on his promise, and I don't have to put quarters in it!"

After that, Jerry never even looked over at our gaming area.

"By the way," he said, turning more serious, "did you have a chance to spend any time with Sonny Terry last month?" He saw the look of surprise cross my face. "I heard the spots on the radio, but unfortunately wasn't able to make it to the show. Sonny was Pigpen's idol, ya know. More like his god."

Although I had a lot on my plate, I pulled up a stool next to Jerry and told him some Sonny stories. I was selective, since I didn't want to betray Sonny's trust, especially about his rift with Brownie. I spent the better part of an hour talking about Sonny's music and what a gentleman he was, delighted to share my stories with someone who "got" them.

As I was talking with Jerry, I noticed a guy sitting by himself at the other end of the bar. Since I knew all the musicians from both bands, I figured he must be the truck driver for Owsley. He was older than the rest of us, with short hair, Levis, and a well-ironed shirt.

"Do you need anything?" I asked, walking up to him.

He replied in a deep southern accent, "A cup of coffee, sir."

"No problem."

I went around the bar and poured him a cup.

"Any trouble finding the place or getting the semi in?" I asked.

He looked at me quizzically.

"I don't know, sir. I came here with Peter Rowan and didn't notice how we got here. I wasn't around when they brought the semi in."

Oh, shit! This is Vassar Clements! The best fiddle player in the world! And I just asked him if he's the driver! That's like asking Einstein if he's the waiter!"

I put out my hand.

"I'm Andrew…, I own this place. You must be Vassar."

"Yes, sir, I am. And it's a pleasure to be here, playing with Jerry Garcia. I'm an old friend of Peter Rowan's, and he kindly invited me to come out and play with this group. I'm very honored."

"Welcome to Homer's Warehouse. We're proud to have ya."

A nicer, more humble country man I had never met.

By 7:00 P.M., Homer's was once again transformed into a spaceship ready to launch. The audience included a good sprinkling of Hells Angels, who never missed one of Benson's shows.

The Wheel opened with "Take Me Back to Tulsa," hitting the high notes to counter Benson's smooth baritone. They sounded wonderful. Many purist blue grass fans in the crowd got a schooling on Bob Wills's swinging style. The Wheel left the stage to a grateful, robust round of applause.

But Jerry whispered in my ear, "I thought you told me they were gonna keep the fuckin' volume down."

"For them, that *was* down, Jerry. The walls are still standing, aren't they?"

He smiled.

When he and the other musicians hit the stage, Vassar brought the magic dust that turned the night into a tight, exciting musical experience. The band's rendition of "Lonesome L.A. Cowboy" reached a new high, with Peter and Jerry singing harmonies that were the Dead meets "Panama Red" on a Kentucky afternoon. In fact, we were in Homer's Warehouse, in Palo Alto, California, being transported to another time and place. The radio guys blasted the music to the ends of the planet. Owsley recorded it for posterity (and maybe an album), and bootlegs were recorded by hardcore fans.

Old and in the Way
(set list, July 24, 1973)

Homer's Warehouse

Set One
"Billy in the Lowground"
"Going to the Races"
"Catfish John"
"Good Woman's Love"
"Lonesome Fiddle Blues"
"Eating Out of Your Hand"

Set Two
"Lonesome L.A. Cowboy"
"Hobo Song"
"Pig in a Pen"
"Panama Red"
"Workin' on a Building"
"Hard Hearted"

Mr. and Mrs. Doeskin

Rollie was burning up the phone lines with booking agents. Our main source was the San Francisco Booking Agency, run out of the second floor of a mostly abandoned South of Market factory by a guy named Michael Oster, a rotund hippie with long curly hair, thick glasses, and a mouth that never shut. I liked Michael, and got to know him well, but for now Rollie was the main contact. I left him alone to book, and he left me alone to run the place. It was always exciting when Rollie walked out of the Purple Room with a half-smile on his face, puffing on a Camel. I knew from his look that we would soon be presenting another great act.

Although the club was clicking along, I was still driving the school bus, and Lisa was working as a textbook editor for a small publisher in Portola Valley. We talked about getting married, since we wanted to have kids.

Lisa was fascinated by Native Americans, and often dreamed about being one in a past life. In one of those dreams, she was marrying a brave who was wearing white knee-high doeskin moccasins decorated with silver conchos up the side. What made this dream amazing was that she didn't know I had white doeskin at my mother's house. It was nearly impossible to find, since doe hunting was illegal. However, my father (God rest his stylish soul) had fashioned himself a garment out of white doeskin. I don't know the whole story of how Dad and Mickey came home with a doe from a deer hunt one day, but within a few weeks, my dad had a God-awful ugly bleached doeskin cardigan. Mom just about died laughing. Dad wore it out in public a few times and then hung it up for good after being laughed off the golf course by his friends. But I retrieved the blasted thing from mom's closet, and Lisa made moccasins out of it—the very ones she had seen in her dream. Once she sewed the silver conchos on, we decided it was time to get married.

We wanted a small wedding, so I called the pastor at the local Unitarian

Church in Palo Alto and arranged for a quickie two days later. After work, I picked Lisa up with the moccasins, met Bob and Carla, our neighbors, at the church, and fifteen minutes later we were Mr. and Mrs. Doeskin. Afterward, we had Chinese dinner with my mom, but we didn't tell Lisa's family for a while.

The lifeblood of our burgeoning enterprise at Homer's was beer. No wine or hard liquor, no choices in beer—it was all about cold Coors. But then the teamsters' strike that we had been warned about hit on a Monday night, and things got ugly quickly: front-page news, with shootings and threats in most Bay Area counties. The union drivers took potshots at the scab-driven trucks and sabotaged the distributors' yards. We had The Wheel coming on Wednesday night and Copperhead booked again for Friday night. This time, I asked the franchise president if I could come over and fill up my old truck with beer and pick up some air tanks for the lines. He said yes on the beer and told me where I could get tanks of air. He also warned me that it was very dangerous outside his property, and they had to have security inside.

"Expect to be harassed by the teamsters," he said.

"Fuck them!" I said. "I have a club in need of beer, and I'll be over this afternoon."

My big red fire wagon could hold lots of kegs and cases.

The drivers who serviced Homer's, mostly Lou, knew the firetruck, since it was always parked in front of the club. As I rolled the old rig up to the entrance of the distributor's yard in Redwood City, the yelling and threats began. I was surprised at the level of antagonism. These guys looked like dock workers from pictures of the 1930s labor unrest in San Francisco. Lou, the guy whose pockets I had lined with money from all the beer he brought us, stood just outside the big gate with hatred in his eyes. As security opened the gate to let me into the yard, Lou called me names. I quickly looked away.

The president met me at the warehouse door.

"Thank you, Andy, for coming over to pick up product. But, you know, it's pretty dangerous out there. You might be followed."

"Hell, I'm six-feet-seven, look mean, and will put it right back in their faces!"

"That's a bad idea. Get the beer, don't look at them, drive back to your club, and leave the face-putting alone. These guys are animals."

As I drove the packed truck back through the gate, Lou came up to the window and barked, "Your club will be torched!"

"Good luck," I told him.

It's an all-steel building, you dumb fuck!

I had enough beer now for a week. After that, I had to make two more trips, which went pretty much the same way.

With the beer strike into its third week, and big acts on weekends, we were getting a little frantic. Rollie and I had a full schedule keeping up with the demand for food and drink and staying sane. Then, just as quickly as it started, the damned strike ended. We got a call from the distributor that beer deliveries would resume on our usual Wednesdays.

I had put up with a good bit of abuse from Lou—this from the asshole I had made into a hero for his record sales at Homer's. Sure enough, right on time on Wednesday morning, the Coors truck pulled up, and out hopped Lou with a big shit-eating grin on his face.

"Hi, Andy, good to see ya!"

Full of resentment, I said, "Get back in your fucking truck and leave before I call the cops!"

"It was just about the strike, Andy. I was never serious about hurting you or torching the club."

"I'll give you thirty seconds to get the hell outta here!"

He climbed into his rig and backed out. I went inside and immediately called the distributor. It seemed I was not alone. According to the president, other customers on Lou's route had also gotten the same treatment during the strike, and, like me, had requested another driver. I never set eyes on Lou again.

The Wheel was in the midst of recording their first album, but United Artists didn't spend a lot on the band's production costs, and even less on their tour promotion. In fact, nothing. I suggested to Benson that we do one of the album release events at Homer's before they left for Austin. The first two thousand copies of the album were to be completed on a specific date and shipped out on a tight schedule.

Benson took the band down to L.A. to do the formal release, and we made plans for a release party at the club as well. A few days later, Benson called me with bad news. The trailer with the two thousand copies in it had gotten lost. He was pissed, and wasn't getting any answers from UA about what the fuck had happened. I told him we would still do the date even if the albums didn't make it. He had one copy, so we had it hanging on the front door as people came in.

Later that month, Benson told me the album was now in the stores and on the radio. Sure enough, "Cherokee Boogie" by The Wheel would be topping alternative country charts.

One midweek afternoon, I blew into the club, and there was Rollie, feet up on the desk in the Purple Room, with one of those grins I had come to know so well. He had just booked Elvin Bishop for Saturday night for a follow-up show. Mickey Thomas would not be with him this time, just his band for two nights.

We hugely respected Elvin and knew he liked playing Homer's. His new manager preceded him, to be sure we were still a bunch of crazies. When he saw we were, he was relieved. Elvin loved chaos. When he arrived, it was like seeing an old friend again. He was easygoing, more interested in how we were doing than in his own interests, asking about the club and what it was like working with Jerry. He had heard about the radio show and was blown away by it. He and Rollie got on from the moment he walked in for this second set of shows.

Because the band was playing for two nights, we would be able to hang out with Elvin and his guys after the Friday night performance. Once we locked up, we got together in the Purple Room for tea and crackers until at least 3:00 A.M. Nobody remembered too much about it the next afternoon when we opened up.

Sunset at Homer's

A. Bernstein Archives

Maynard Lutts was now in charge of The Wheel's bus and called to say he needed a place to park it. It was okay with us to park the old dog at Homer's for three weeks until the band split, but I had to promise our neighbors it would be gone no later than that.

Maynard asked me to wait for him out on El Camino Real at 10:00 A.M. the next morning so I could help to guide the 40-foot double-decker bus in. As I was standing out there, five minutes early, I saw it a quarter-mile away, making the right turn off Embarcadero. It was a monster, hissing air from the compressors and rumbling from the Detroit Diesel engine. When he pulled up, we set about calculating how to get the beast into Homer's front lot. All the neighbors came out and couldn't believe their eyes. Maynard backed that sucker all the way down the road, then the alley, and tucked it nicely into the space I had envisioned for it. I really wanted to drive it, but I didn't bring that up. However, as I looked at the bus every day, I could see myself wheeling around town in that big old grey dog.

One day, Maynard called to tell me he was going to take the bus over to the East Bay for some paint work. When it had been gone for a few days, I was driving east on the Embarcadero in the firetruck one morning when I saw it coming toward me. Maynard immediately recognized the truck, and blasted his air horns, scaring the shit out of me. Emblazoned across the driver's side of the bus in big orange letters were the words *ASLEEP AT THE WHEEL*, with a big steering wheel in the middle. As he whizzed past me, I could see that Maynard was laughing. But not for long.

When I arrived at the club the next morning, Maynard was waiting for me, looking upset.

"I found this under the windshield wiper this morning," he said, handing me an envelope.

Inside there was a typed message signed by Katherine Urban, the property owner, stating that she had not given us permission to park a Greyhound bus on her property.

"I gotta leave it here one more night, Andy," Maynard said. "I've got no place else to keep it. Tomorrow, we're hitting the road for Austin."

Just then, Rollie pulled up. When I showed him the letter, he said, "No problem. I'll call Katherine and tell her it'll be gone by tomorrow."

Early the next morning, the phone rang, waking me up.

"Andy, get the fuck over here!"

"What's happening, Maynard?"

"Just get over to the club. You won't believe your eyes."

When I arrived, ten minutes later, he was standing next to a trench that had been dug around the bus. It was three feet deep and three feet wide. Maynard was as pissed as I had ever seen him.

I rushed into the Purple Room to call Katherine, who was fit to be tied.

"I want that bus out of there right now! Why is it still there, when I told you yesterday to move it?"

Oh, my god! I'm dealing with an eighty-two-year-old woman who's lost it.

"Didn't you get a call from Rollie?"

"I most certainly did not!"

"He said he would tell you that the bus would be gone by today.... The driver's here, and now we can't move it."

"Alright," Katherine said, "I'll send a crew right over to fill in the ditch."

Thank you, mom, for teaching me diplomacy with little old ladies!

"But," Katherine added, "I wanna meet with you and Rollie tomorrow morning at nine sharp."

"Yes, ma'am."

That afternoon, a backhoe arrived, filled in the ditch, and Maynard was on his way.

The next morning at 9:00, a tall, thin, distinguished-looking white-haired lady showed up at the club, threw a disapproving glance at Jake's nude mural, and said, looking me straight in the eye, "I have some things I wish to discuss with you."

"Won't you sit down, Mrs. Urban," I said, pointing to one of the cleaner spool tables. "I'm Andy, and this is Rollie."

As soon as we sat down, she got right to the point.

"Bill told me that you young men are subletting from him.... Much to my displeasure, I might add."

Rollie and I looked at each other, but decided to keep our mouths shut.

"This place," she said, gesturing toward the stage and the overhead lights, "has obviously grown way beyond burgers for the neighborhood workers."

"Yes, ma'am," Rollie said, "we present music from time to time...with homemade spaghetti."

"I told Bill, no music!"

"Yes, ma'am."

"But I do have to admit, my husband would be very proud of what you've done with his old storage warehouse. In fact, he wouldn't believe it. But I have to tell you, the lease is coming up in a couple of months, and I'm not sure I want a nightclub here any longer."

"I assure you, Mrs. Urban," Rollie said with his smoothest snake oil salesman charm, "no more rock and roll, just blues and jazz."

"Thank you, boys, I'll be in touch."

Despite Rollie's promise to Mrs. Urban, we had already booked two rock bands for the very next night: Cat Mother and the All Night News Boys, a great outfit from the city, with Elvis Duck, a band from Marin, opening. After getting the musicians set up, Rollie and I took off to hear a new band in town, Tom Petty and the Heartbreakers, who were playing at The Bodega in San Jose. Ken Rominger, the owner of the club, had told us we might want to book them. We had chosen this night to go because Wednesdays were slow, now that The Wheel had left town. Since it would be an early night, with the last set scheduled to finish at 10:30, we felt comfortable leaving Lisa behind to sell tickets at the booth, Dan to guard the door, and Gail and another girl to work the bar.

However, around 10:00, Ken came over and told me that Lisa had called, and wanted to talk to me right away.

As I headed to Ken's office, I tried to imagine what was wrong.

I hope it isn't the cops.

"Get up here right away!" Lisa said, sounding upset.

"Why?"

"Just get up here!"

"Alright, but it's gonna take us half an hour."

Rollie and I hopped into his VW station wagon, and drove 80 miles an hour to the club, with him chain-smoking Camels and tailgating every car in front of us the whole way.

When we walked into Homer's, the place was empty, Dan was nowhere in sight, and Cat Mother was packing up early. Lisa and Gail rushed up to us.

"Where's the hell's Dan?" I asked.

"Slow down," Lisa said, "lemme tell ya what happened.... About an hour ago, two bikers showed up and started giving Dan a hard time about paying the lousy dollar cover charge. Dan told 'em to pay the fuckin' dollar or get the hell out. They paid the money, but Dan said to me, 'I better not have any trouble with those pricks..., or this'll be my last night.'"

"Okay, so where's Dan now?" Rollie asked.

Gail piped up, "Well, lemme tell ya what happened when they came up to the bar to buy beer.... First, they called me Sweetie. I said, 'My name's Gail. How can I help ya?' And one of 'em said, 'Give us some free beers. We already paid a couple o' bucks to get into this dump.'"

"Dan was watching this whole scene," Lisa said, "and getting more and more pissed."

"So when I waved for Dan to come over," Gail said, "one of 'em turned around, looked at Dan across the room, and spit on the floor. Bad move."

"Dan looked at me," Lisa said, "and asked me to hand him his vest..., the one with 'Unforgiven Sinners' on the back. 'I'm now officially no longer working for Homer's,' he said. 'Tell Andy and Rollie, thanks for the great time, and I'll be in touch.'"

"Dan walked over to those punks," Gail said, "and told 'em they had one choice..., leave now. They made the wrong decision and got sassy with him."

"It happened so fast, I couldn't believe my eyes," Lisa said. "He laid 'em both out in thirty seconds. One of 'em was out cold, and the other was crawling towards the door, begging Dan not to hurt him and crying. Dan picked him off the floor and literally tossed him out on the ramp. I think he ended up with a busted nose, 'cause he was bleeding all over the place."

"Yeah, I saw that out there," I said.

Rollie started laughing. "Shit, I'm sorry I missed it."

"The other guy was still out cold on the floor when I called ya," Lisa said.

"Dan was gonna toss him, too," Gail said, "but the stupid motherfucker managed to stagger out on his own, so Dan saved his energy."

Lisa laughed. "When the pricks rode off, Dan said, 'Goodnight, ladies, it's been a pleasure workin' with ya,' and he roared off on his Harley. I don't think we'll ever see 'em again, Andy."

Dan did stop by a few days later to get his money, but I wasn't there at the time. I never saw him again. I hope he's well.

With The Wheel no longer around as our mainstay, with Dan gone, and with Katherine insisting that there be no more rock 'n' roll—when she wasn't threatening to double or triple the rent—it seemed like a good time to find a new location. Before we could do that, there were two more weekends of shows that we had already booked, including Copperhead, which was sold out.

When we locked the doors for the last time, I said, "How many fuckin' bands you think we put through this place, Rollie?"

"The list is long, my friend."

A New Journey

Not long after we closed down Homer's, Rollie and I began looking for another venue in Palo Alto. Our experience with the college shows, Crimson Madness, and Homer's had given us reputations in the local music scene. We knew other Bay Area club owners and felt like part of an extended family. One day, Ken Rominger told us that the Zinzinnati Umpapa, a polka club on California Avenue in Palo Alto, had folded.

"It's already got a stage and a bar in it," he said, "and a small restaurant. It could be perfect for you guys."

As soon as we drove up, I recognized the place as the old Purity Market, a grocery store where I had often shopped with my mom as a kid. Since then, it had changed hands a few times. When we got inside, it was a mess, with dirty dishes on the tables and a foul odor coming from the kitchen.

"There's either a dead junkie in there," I said, "or a whole lot of Polish sausage has gone bad."

"Kinda makes Homer's look a palace, don't it?" Rollie said.

"It's gonna cost a shitload o' money and time to clean this place up."

"Not so bad," Rollie said. "This place'll hold seven or eight hundred people. One good night, and we're in the chips."

"Somebody's gonna take this club, Rollie. And it may as well be us. It's on a main street with plenty of parking. Homer's proved there's a loyal and supportive base of rockers in this area."

I saw a sparkle in his eyes as we mulled things over.

Carlos Santana was experiencing the first of many personal changes in his band since it had burst on the music scene, three years before. Gregg

Rolie, the Palo Altan whose voice and keyboards had been key in the first group of megahits for Carlos, had decided to move on.

After his phenomenal success with Santana, Gregg had the wind at his back. He was twenty-five, rich as hell, and had a Midas touch if he played his cards right. He could attract great talent and a lucrative record deal, and those of us who knew him were paying close attention to his new project with Neal Schon, which had evolved into a band, rumored to be named Journey.

Gregg and Neal felt that if forming a new band was worth doing, it was worth taking the time to find the right players—who turned out to be Ross Valary on bass, George Tickner on guitar, and Prairie Prince on drums. Gregg told Rollie that he was going to be very careful not to overexpose his new band until the training wheels came off. We signed a one-night, one-show contract with the polka club, figuring it would be a great coup if we could get Journey to play Palo Alto, a real homecoming.

Since Rollie knew Gregg a lot better than I did, he was obviously the one to try to persuade him to come home to showcase his new group. Lots of friends and fans would turn out to see what their native son was up to, Rollie suggested. Gregg liked the idea and agreed to do it.

This would be one of Journey's first public appearances.

I set about getting the polka club into shape for a rock show. The stage was too small for all the equipment Gregg would be bringing in to create his thunder and lightning, so I rented several risers for the PA speakers. The stage lighting was inadequate, too, so I called John at Morpheus Lights. When he stopped by to measure the room for the lighting towers, he suggested also bringing in one big spotlight and one small one.

"You want us to provide the operators, Andy, or are you gonna do it?"

"Package deal, John. Send 'em along."

The club owner had a beer license, and since all the beer tap lines worked, and the bar was in good shape, I called my friends at Coors and ordered a shitload of kegs and bottles.

Gregg left it up to Rollie and me to do the advertising, but he didn't want any radio spots or any use of Santana's music—or, for that matter, any mention of Santana. Jake did his poster thing, and with that and word of mouth, we sold the show out in less than a week.

On the afternoon of the performance night, which was on a Tuesday, I went over to the club around 9:00 A.M., right after my last morning bus run. By 10:00 our beer order had arrived. Just as I expected, the first of two semi-trucks floor-loaded with gear arrived at the back door early in the afternoon. It took several hours for all the lights, PA system, mixing boards, speakers, monitors, keyboards, including Gregg's custom Hammond B3, and other miscellaneous sound gear to be loaded onto the stage.

This place could hold over five hundred legally, not including the "Friends of Gregg" list—mostly females.

Jake's wife, Bee, had hooked up with Journey's management and was on the ground floor with the band as a technician and roadie. They weren't touring yet, but Bee would soon be traveling the country with them. She had been bitten hard by the bug and would eventually take this rock 'n' roll deal to the stratosphere, touring with the Stones, McCartney, Bowie, you name it. Bee earned her keep as a rigger and scrim cloth seamstress. But this night in old Buttholeville, we all got a chance to make a big splash in the old pond. A little more Palo Alto musical history: Journey was busting out.

By 5:00 P.M., the club was set up. The PA guys were playing taped music at top volume, trying to get the sound mix right. Apparently, no one had seen Gregg all day. I wasn't worried, because soundcheck was not until 6:00. At precisely 5:45, a big white Silver Cloud, with tinted windows and six-inch-wide white walls, pulled up to the front door. I watched through the window as Gregg got out, all hair, full-length ermine coat, snakeskin boots, and mirrored shades—a cross between Elvis and Liberace. He had a small posse with him in the Rolls, some of the Palo Alto music mafia from the south side of town, where he grew up. I unlocked the door and welcomed them all. Bee whispered in my ear that, while I was out picking up supplies, Gregg had stopped by the club and told her that he and Neal were ready to set Palo Alto ablaze.

Soundcheck was loud and uplifting with the interplay of Neal's guitar and Gregg's keyboards that so marked the early Journey sound. I flashed on "William Penn and His Pals" at the dance hall in Sunnyvale from years past. The crowd was anxious to get in, so once the soundcheck was completed, we opened the doors and started selling beer.

During the first set, the band ran through several new tunes, and then cranked it up for a few Santana gems. Even though Gregg and Neal had played these songs thousands of times all over the globe, this night was not about Carlos Santana, it was about Journey.

The second set was absolutely on fire. Gregg sang with every ounce of energy and passion he could muster, an awesome display of the Journeyman chops that had been honed over four years of constant touring, playing arenas in front of millions of fans. It was a great evening for me and Rollie, and one hell of a party for everyone there that night. Homer's had been my entry-level drug; after this evening, I wanted the hard stuff. I ached to see it from the top of the mountain.

Rollie had told a few San Francisco agents that we were once again planning to present talent in Palo Alto. The fact that we had scored this coup with Journey prompted a phone call from an old friend of ours, Cory Larios from Together and Stoneground, who asked if it were true that we were going to be opening a new club. Rollie gave him the scoop, and soon found out that he'd put a new band together, featuring David Jenkins and Steve Price, two of the guys from Stoneground, and old friends of ours. They were also joined by a new bass player named Bud Cockrill, a regular on the city music scene. Cory invited us to come up to their rehearsal studio the next day.

It was great to see the guys again and tell war stories while we shared a joint before they played. Bud sat transfixed as we all howled at Homer's tales and earlier escapades of Tahoe and the old Church shows. David knew I picked a little and asked if I wanted to join in on rhythm guitar.

"Thanks, Dave, do you really think I'm up for it?"

"C'mon, Andy, just strum along in the right key."

"Maybe later, man. You're so kind to invite me, but let's see what you guys are up to first."

And with that, they played a slew of new material that was catchy, soulful, and had Hitsville woven into almost every song. They didn't have a name that day, but I was certain that whatever they ended up calling themselves, the rest of the country, maybe even the world, would soon be asking radio jocks to play their music. After an hour, they took a break, and Cory turned to me.

"So, whaddaya think, Andy?"

"Well, Rollie smoked seven Camels, butt to butt…, a sure sign he liked you."

Everyone laughed.

Then I said to Steve, "You're the best fuckin' drummer in San Francisco. Finally, you guys are destined for the attention you deserve."

He came over and gave me a big hug.

"Brother Andy, we been through some shit, man. I hope you're right."

This unknown band soon signed a record contract under the name Pablo Cruise. But the album was a year out; they had to record it first. Like Journey, they were still in the rumor stage.

A Decade of Dust

When Lisa and I got a chance to move into the Santa Cruz Mountains, we jumped at it. My high school friend Jon gave me first option on the log cabin he'd been living in off Skyline Boulevard, deep in the Redwoods. The commute up and down Highway 84 to Palo Alto each day would be a challenge. It would also require a vehicle other than the firetruck for the drive.

The cabin was perched on the side of a steep canyon, dense with second-growth redwood trees. A stone staircase led down from the dirt road to the front door, perhaps a vertical drop of twenty feet. Jon's brother had seriously injured his back while moving Jon's piano up these stairs. A true log cabin, the house was made from redwood railroad ties harvested from northern California in the 1930s. The mighty ties had hard mortar between them. Inside was an open beam A-frame ceiling with a beautiful handcrafted stone fireplace and hearth. A tiny staircase (more a ladder, actually) went down to the kitchen, bathroom, and a small guest bedroom.

The California coastal redwoods exist in a microclimate that combines salt air, fog, and sun. The house sat high on a ridge, which had been carved out of the mountain with the foundation posts driven right into the earth. The fog would occasionally surround that little house, and then blow away an instant later.

Our very first night in that house, I learned that we were sharing it with another family, the Ariolimaxes—otherwise known as banana slugs. They formally introduced themselves to me that night when I was walking barefoot to the bathroom, and suddenly slipped on my ass. When I turned on the light, I saw giant yellow banana slugs slithering around the floor, leaving God-awful slimy trails behind them. I immediately realized that that was the last time I would ever walk in the dark in that cabin without a flashlight.

A. Bernstein Archives

Our Log Cabin in the Redwoods

A few days later, Lisa and I went down to Carlson VW in Palo Alto to shop for a used car. The one that caught our eye was a VW station wagon that was banana slug yellow. We immediately fell for it, and nicknamed it the "Slug."

Meanwhile, as I discovered a few years later when I moved out, the real slugs had set about eating my entire high school yearbook, including half of the cover, and were working on the one from ninth grade, both of which were stored in the shed next to the house.

After the Journey show, Rollie and I decided that the overhead on the polka club was way beyond us. Also, we both needed a break from each other. Most of all, I was ready for more time to enjoy the new home in the woods. Lisa and I had been talking for a while about having a baby. So she and I went off for a long weekend of backpacking at Yosemite, along with her brother Kim (who was living in our guest bedroom at the time) and a couple of his friends. In the privacy of our own tent, Lisa and I practiced Babymaking 101 at 10,000 feet, every chance we got.

Shortly after we returned to our cabin paradise, I became curious about one of our neighbors down the road. Jazz, blues, big band sounds, musicals, a whole spectrum of music (and laughter) drifted over on the breeze to my property from a little house up on a hill. One morning when I was taking a walk, I met the neighbor in front of his house.

"The name's Glen," he said. "Glen Battle. Care to come in for a beer or a coffee?"

Although Glen was fifteen years older than me, I recognized one of those ageless souls who drifted through my life from time to time. While we listened to John Coltrane, he offered me a few hits on some good weed, and we were instant friends.

A. Bernstein Archives

Slim in the Log Cabin, 1975

During the day, he ran the hematology lab at Stanford Hospital. At night, he had another life altogether. He also knew Maynard's mother from the hospital, which completely tripped me out!

"I'm a stage guy," he said, and told me that Woody Allen had seen him in an off-Broadway play in New York and cast him in his first big studio-backed movie, *Take the Money and Run*. I tried to place his character. Knowing what I was thinking, he smiled and said, "Andrew, how many black men were in that movie? C'mon!"

"Just one, I guess."

"That's right. I was one of the prisoners who escaped from jail with Woody."

"I remember you perfectly now," I said. And I did.

Glen told me that Woody had asked him to become one of his regulars, but he had passed up the opportunity so he could try to make his Broadway dream come true. Obviously, that hadn't worked out, so now he was acting at night and on weekends in the Whiskey Gulch area of Palo Alto at an independent playhouse, a progressive theatre that interwove dance and drama.

Although the school bus job paid the bills, I was finally getting bored with it. As I drove down the hill to Palo Alto every morning, I felt the tug of getting back into the music business.

"Why don't you produce shows by yourself?" Glen asked me one day. "Why do you need Rollie?"

"I've always worked with a partner," I said.

"You don't need a partner," he insisted.

He got me thinking about that.

Where will I produce the shows? Do I really want to put up with the bullshit? What will I call my venture?

Half Gaffed Productions was the name I came up with. I guess because I wanted to see what I could do without Rollie. Jake drew me a logo of a fish smiling through the hole of a life raft with a gaff in the fish's hand and a top hat on his head, celebrating the half gaff that allowed him to stay free.

The next challenge was finding a venue. The Stanford Theatre in Palo Alto had sat empty for years. Originally an old vaudeville house, the building was converted into a movie theatre in the early '50s. I had gone to watch movies there for most of my young life. Recently, I had noticed a little activity around the old place: the marquee lights were on at night, but without advertising anything.

I drove over one lunch hour to snoop around the entrance. Much to my surprise, one of the front doors was open. I walked in and looked around. The candy counter, stairs to the balcony, and beautiful carpets and chandeliers hadn't changed a bit.

"Can I help you?" a man asked, walking toward me. I guessed he was in his late forties.

"Yeah, what's going on with this old place? I used to come here to kiss girls and watch movies."

He laughed. "My name's Dennis," he said, putting out his hand.

"Andrew," I said. "I'm a concert promoter. I just closed down Homer's Warehouse, and I'm looking for a place to put on live music."

"I've heard about that place. Jerry Garcia used to play there, right?"

I nodded.

"Is there any money in that business?" he asked.

"Well, Dennis, if you do it right, you can make a few bucks…. So, what are your plans for this place?"

"I've got a year lease on this old house, and I want to put on stage plays."

"Would you consider letting me put on some rock 'n' roll shows here, to generate some cash?"

"Let's go up to my office and talk," he said, "if you've got the time."

"I got nothin' *but* time."

His office smelled musty—as if the door hadn't been opened in ten years. He sat down behind an ancient oak desk, and I sat across from him on a steel folding chair. He opened a drawer and took out two pads of paper, tossing one to me.

"So, tell me about your idea," he said.

"Well, I've got a lot of connections to name bands out of San Francisco, and I think we could book the shit out of this place."

He wrote down *shit* on his pad and underlined it.

I laughed.

"You realize," he said, "this old lady needs a lot of makeup. I've only scratched the surface in bringing her back to life…. Wanna take a walk around?"

"I'd *love* to take a look under the skirts of this old girl."

She was dusty, but had a backstage worthy of a grand burlesque theatre from the '20s. The stage had all the scrims, ropes, pulleys, and lighting rigs, none of which had been used in years. The floor itself was sound. As I looked around, I saw that although the stage wasn't as big as I would have liked, to accommodate all the equipment to produce a modern rock show, I could work around that.

Dennis turned up the house lights, and I saw that the auditorium looked spectacular, with red carpets, chandeliers, and all the baroque trimmings.

Awesome!

"Eighteen hundred seats," Dennis said. "But we can't use the balcony, since it's not earthquake-proofed, and kids jumping and dancing around up there might bring the thing down. So that subtracts about three hundred."

"Where are the dressing rooms?" I asked.

"Come with me."

I followed him down a staircase behind the stage to the basement. There was a small lounge with a bar in it, a few couches, and some cocktail tables scattered around. Everything was covered with a decade of dust, but I could easily imagine the vaudeville performers of the '20s and '30s scurrying around here, grabbing a shot of moonshine gin between acts.

In front of me, there were five doors, all of them closed.

"What's in those rooms?" I asked.

"Take a look for yourself."

I opened the middle door, and found myself inside a dressing room, perhaps ten by fifteen feet, with tall mirrors on facing walls and a sprinkling of old furniture.

This will be party central!

I took a quick peek behind the other four doors, and found those rooms were all the same as the first one.

Dennis could see from the look on my face that I was hooked.

Back in his office, he said, "So, Andy, are you still interested in putting on a show here?"

"I am, but I've gotta talk to some people, run some numbers. I think I can get back to you in about a week. So, how do *you* feel? Is this something you wanna get involved in?"

"I can really use some cash flow."

Whoa! How my life has changed in the last hour!

That evening, I told Lisa I wanted to try to get a bank loan to begin promoting shows again.

"Is Rollie involved?"

"No."

"Go for it!"

Lisa never trusted Rollie.

The next morning, after the early bus runs, I walked into the downtown Palo Alto branch of Wells Fargo and asked to speak to a loan officer. A young man in a suit and tie came over.

"Can I help you? My name's Rob. Let's go over to my desk."

As I began to explain my plan, he stopped me in mid-sentence.

"Did you use to present shows at Homer's?" he asked.

"Yeah. Did you come?"

His face lit up, and I got an earful about a couple of his favorite shows.

Once we finished talking about Homer's, he finally got around to my business with him. When I explained my idea to present name bands at the Stanford Theatre, he immediately got excited.

"I want to open a business checking account," I said, "and get a credit line for ten thousand dollars."

"No problem. Will that be enough?"

"Fifteen thousand would be better."

"No problem…. What's the name of your company?"

"Half Gaffed Productions."

He didn't flinch. "How do you spell *gaft?*"

This guy's willing to put it on the line with the old fat bankers for the sake of rock 'n' roll!

Within thirty-six hours, I had fifteen thousand dollars in my new account, and Jake working on a scaled-down logo for the checks.

Let's Rock This Joint

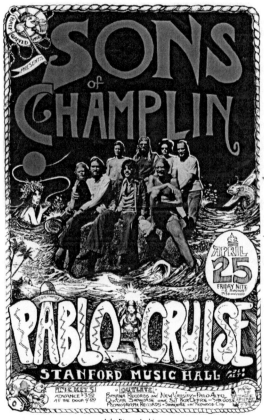

Jake Pierre Archives

I was excited to see how Dennis was feeling about my idea of setting University Avenue on fire with rock 'n' roll. I'd taken the time to run some realistic numbers, examine the margins, and speak to Michael Oster at San Francisco Bookings about bands.

Dennis was in the lobby as I walked in after a week of planning.

"Great to see you, Andy," he said. "I've been thinking about you all week, and how we can make this thing happen. I'm sure glad you waltzed in here that day."

"Well, damn, Dennis, so am I. Let's go over some numbers I put together."

As we walked up the plush carpeted stairs to his office, he said, "I have a surprise for you."

He led me to a room across from his office and opened the door.

"It's your new office, my friend. Hope you like it. My son and I hauled this desk from my house in his pickup."

I was blown away. He had old movie posters on the walls and an overstuffed chair from the dressing rooms, along with a working telephone and an old Tiffany-style lamp on the desk.

When we went over the numbers, he liked what he saw.

"But I've gotta warn you, Dennis," I said, "these figures are based on turning two houses for each show. That's a helluva lotta work, but I did it at Homer's."

"I've got good news for you, Andy," he said. "You run your business, and I'll run mine. All I want out of this deal is the concessions and the publicity that the place is open for business."

"What are you saying, Dennis? Are you sure?"

"Hell, I don't know a thing about rock 'n' roll, but I can sell a ton of candy, drinks, hot dogs, deli, the works. Even posters, if you have enough made up. Besides, I don't need the money, I just wanna be able to turn this old lady into a playhouse someday."

So the deal was done on a handshake, with no contract. When he left my office, I went to work on the first show. I knew who I wanted: the Sons of Champlin and Pablo Cruise.

The first step was to call Michael Oster to see if they were available on the same date, and then arrange for contracts. Within a week, we had the dates, and the paperwork was in the mail to me. Michael was a magician at this shit.

I set up studio time with Cliff Feldman to cut musical radio spots, just as in the old days, and got the ball rolling for me to be interviewed on the local college radio stations. I relied on Jake to use his imagination to make the poster. He was fired up, but what really pleased him was that our old friends Cory, Steve, and Dave were on the bill. That inspired him to pull from deep within his devious mind.

Since the Stanford Music Hall was much larger than Homer's, I realized that it was going to be a much bigger challenge to make these productions professional. This place had been designed in the 1920s for live acts of every kind, so we just needed to grease the old wheels up for rock 'n' roll. I hired Wally Heider from San Francisco to do the sound, and brought in John again from Morpheus for lights. Although we couldn't use the balcony for the audience, we could place spotlights and operators up there. A perfect perch.

A. Bernstein Archives
Stanford Music Hall (aka Stanford Theatre)

In exchange for free tickets, Dennis got his teenage kids and some of their friends to clean up the old hall, top to bottom. Soon they had put a big grin on her wrinkled art nouveau face. It was like rummaging through an old estate sale, finding remnants from another time. In some old milk crates, I came across all the plastic letters for the marquee and soon had them up for the show. Dennis was thrilled because he had been looking for them for months. Lower University Avenue was soon lit up with my sign:

SONS OF CHAMPLIN, PABLO CRUISE
PRESENTED BY HALF GAFFED PRODUCTIONS
FRIDAY, APRIL 25th, 7:30 & 11:00

With two houses to turn, I had a lot of seats to sell. It was important to me that this first production be an absolute winner, so I advertised in the Sunday pink section of the *San Francisco Examiner*, as well as on the South Bay radio stations. Jake created a two-color separation poster, the first for one of my own productions. My brother Mickey, who owned a print shop at the time, did the posters, a beautiful piece of period artwork. I placed handbills under the windshield wipers at the Stanford parking lots at night. Both shows sold out well in advance.

On the day of the show, I had things well under control. The sound and light teams had set up the day before. Lisa ran the door with help from a few of her friends. Chris, one of her brothers, ran the spotlights. I went all-out in the dressing rooms with flowers, a bartender, and plenty of food.

The head of security was my Cajun friend René Comeaux, but he drank all day and had to be replaced ten minutes into the show. We had a house to turn in two hours, and I had my hands full with other responsibilities, so I called Rollie. He was happy to come over and save my ass, no bad vibes, just a helping hand.

This was the first time I introduced bands at my own production. Cory, David, Steve, and Bud plugged in and tuned up behind the curtain as I walked to the front of the stage. When I heard Cory say, "Okay, Andy," I introduced "Palo Alto's own, Pablo Cruise!"

The curtain went up, and the guys stormed into one of their originals. They sounded so good, so tight. The audience loved them from the opening chords.

It's funny, I was listening to my good old buds playing, but was so busy keeping up with all the production bits and pieces that I never got to tune into their music. However, it was clear from the audience reaction that these guys were killing them.

When the band completed its set, we dropped the curtain to move The Sons' equipment center stage. Bill Champlin, ever the genuine charmer and consummate professional, and his band mates helped out to get the stage reset on time.

A. Bernstein Archives

Bill Champlin, a Man of Great Soul

Once again, I got to introduce my favorite band at my production, and it felt great. Their big band sound resonated throughout the hall and kept everyone rocking their asses off for this first set. The horn section, Bill's booming voice, and the boogie beat were exactly why I had booked them.

After their performance, we cleared the house and changed the set back again for the second show. And we were ready on time, even though half the security team was drunk. I learned a valuable lesson for the next shows: hire professional security.

After everyone left that night, Dennis gave me a thumbs up. He had made a small fortune from selling everything from popcorn to posters.

As Lisa and I headed to the car to drive up the mountain, she said, "I missed my period again. I think I'm pregnant."

Tuna and the Commander Come to Town

A. Bernstein Archives

The little office in the Stanford Music Hall was a perfect place to conduct my business. No more burning up the school district phone. Dan Roach not only gave the first show a glowing review, but he stopped by the office to ask me about the future of the venue, and the importance of what I was trying to do. His comments were both supportive and encouraging.

"I'm looking forward to reviewing all your shows, Andy…, putting this place on the map, and giving local fans an alternative to traveling to one of Bill Graham's shows in San Francisco. This is an important artistic investment in our community. Keep it up!"

"Thanks, Dan, I appreciate your support. This is a great old place, and I sure as hell hope we can keep it rolling."

All this started with Homer's, and it was that experience that I counted on to keep Half Gaffed moving forward.

By now, my old buddy Maynard Lutts had been driving the bus for Asleep at the Wheel for a year. He called me from time to time with an update on his adventures touring around the country. In a recent call, I had told him that there might be a baby coming. Of course, I also told him everything about Half Gaffed.

A. Bernstein Archives

Dolly, Porter, and the Tube

One day out of the blue, Maynard called to tell me how he was sick and tired of being broke in Austin.

"I'm thinking about changing jobs," he said. "I need your opinion on an opportunity that came up last week."

It seems he had met a harmonica player named Mickey Raphael at a gig The Wheel was doing with a hippie cowboy band called Willie Nelson and Family, which had recently gotten national radio time with its concept album, *The Redheaded Stranger*. Nelson had just bought an old GM bus that had been owned by Porter Wagner and Dolly Parton, and he needed an experienced driver. Mickey had confided to Maynard that the guys currently driving the vehicle didn't know shit about driving a bus. Since the family were about to hit the road in a serious way, Mickey wanted a driver who wouldn't get him killed, and Maynard fit the bill.

"Shit, Maynard, seems like a no-brainer. I've heard of that guy. He's got a couple singles with Waylon Jennings that are just starting to chart."

A week later, I saw a blurb in a Bay Area music rag about a local bus driver, Maynard Lutts, driving for Willie Nelson out of Austin, Texas.

I was looking forward to the next time I crossed paths with Maynard.

A week later, when I arrived at my office at the theatre, Dennis said that Michael Oster wanted me to call him right away.

"Andy, I've got a great idea for the Music Hall," Michael said.

"I'm all ears, buddy."

"Hot Tuna and Commander Cody and the Lost Planet Airmen are doing a short West Coast tour of mid-sized venues."

"Sounds great. Tell me more."

"Well, the problem is, they want a *lot* of money. At least seven thousand, with half up front, and fifteen percent of the door."

"Hell, Michael, that means I'll have to double my ticket price to five bucks, plus turn two full houses."

"Well, do your math and get back to me. But you better get back quick, 'cause the dates are filling up fast. You'll have the only South Bay appearance if you book by the end of the day."

At 4:00 o'clock, I called him back.

"Michael," I said, "I've taken a look at the numbers. I can give them their guarantee of seven thousand, but no percentage of the door."

"I'll get back to you on that."

Two days later he did, and the deal was sealed.

Commander Cody was George Frayne, a very bright guy from Michigan, who drifted into music in college through the graphic arts. George fit into the Bay Area as if he had been born here. Members of his band, the Lost Planet Airmen, were among the best musicians around, attracted to his loose but true-to-the-original approach to boogie woogie/rockabilly. I knew that George and the boys loved a good party as they wandered around the country in Ozone 1, their double-decker Greyhound cruiser. They were Homer's alumni from the night the beer bottles were flying. George also illustrated his own album covers, drawing and coloring them by hand, often featuring Peterbilts and other modern and antique rigs. He was a remarkable man with an equally talented group of fun guys, who could play their asses off.

The contract for the show specified how much sound equipment would be coming. It was a load and a half, but I figured, somehow or other, I'd find a way to fit it all onstage. The scary part was that the rider specified that if the road crew couldn't get everything onstage, they would leave with my deposit of $3,500.00. This was a serious contract, the kind that had attorneys' names at the bottom. I also had to provide a grand piano for Commander Cody at my own cost, tuned prior to the show and ready to go. According to the contract, I also had to agree to feed them like potentates.

On the Monday before the Wednesday night show, I still had a few things to do to meet the terms of the agreement. The most important one was renting the piano. I had no idea how much it was going to cost, but I was willing to go the distance. There was a Yamaha piano dealer on El Camino that I had driven past hundreds of times, so in I strolled, my arrogance leading the way—Mr. Promoter. I wandered through the store, looking at pianos, until a representative saw me. I don't remember what kind of bizarre outfit I was wearing, but the five-foot-two Japanese salesman in a black suit and horned rim glasses looked a little concerned. Leaning on a brand new ebony grand, I told him I was promoting a concert in Palo Alto and needed to rent a fine piano. In a pronounced Japanese accent, he asked a few questions about the show. Before he could ask any more, I told him it was a jazz concert.

Robert Altman Archives
Commander Cody and Crew, ca. 1975

"No wok an' woll," was his only comment.

"No, sir," I replied, lying through my teeth.

The salesman said I could rent the very piano I was leaning on. I was almost afraid to ask how much, but it was reasonable at $500 for the night, including tuning before the show, delivery, and pickup. The security deposit was $2,000. Brand new, the piano went for $15,000. I wrote the checks and arranged to have the piano delivered on the morning of the show. It was a beauty.

With that off the list, only catering was left. The food requirements on the catering rider to the contract were over the top, but I obliged, right down to the ten packs of Beeman's chewing gum. There was to be no pizza and plenty of tequila.

The poster turned out to be a little more complicated, because I couldn't reach Jake. I found out later that he was out of town. So Lisa and I sat down in our bedroom at the cabin and created a spacey poster for a couple of spacey bands. It was the only poster I ever did, but fortunately George and I both loved trucks, so the theme was easy.

On the morning of the show, I called in sick to the bus yard and got to the Stanford Music Hall by 9:00 A.M. The piano arrived at 10:00. When the tuner showed up at 11:00, he commented on what a beautiful instrument it was. Then he said, "I know Commander Cody is pretty rough on pianos, so be careful."

He knew who was playing, because it was right on the marquee.

I pretended to be distracted.

The light towers were going up about the time I heard the air brakes from the first equipment truck. At the back door, a burly man introduced himself as the road manager for the tour. As we approached the stage, he spotted the piano and immediately made it clear that this was Tuna's tour, and he was going to move that "big fucker" out of the way for the soundcheck. Then, looking at the stage itself, he began spitting out a string of expletives in my direction. The gist of it was that the stage size didn't meet the contract requirements, and he had no intention of unloading anything.

"Did you read the contract, idiot?"

"I did, asshole!"

"Tuna only plays with a full sound rig," he said, "and this piece o' shit tiny stage won't hold half of it. I'm gonna turn my two trucks around and leave."

"Give me fifteen minutes to make a few calls, man," I barked.

Fuck this guy!

"Go make 'em," he said. "I'll wait."

My first call, which turned out to be my last, was to Michael, who in turn called Bob Brown, Tuna's manager. I don't know what they said to each other, but within half an hour, Bob was there, and equipment started rolling off the trucks. The roadies pushed the piano out of the way, stacked speakers on top of speakers, and filled the entire stage with amps and equipment.

I still don't know how we did it, but by 4:30 a huge truckload of gear was sitting on that stage. The soundcheck went well, and the sound engineers loved the acoustics.

One important lesson I had learned from the previous show was that to turn two houses, I needed competent, professional security, so I had found some in the Yellow Pages. The security detail showed up at 5:00 in their sharp uniforms.

"Don't act like cops," I said. "Just keep the peace and clear the house when I tell ya…. And stay out of the basement. The bands have their own security."

That was a lie, but the last thing I needed was one of those guys walking in on snorting musicians.

Out of nowhere, Rollie showed up. He wanted to help, and God knows I needed it, so I put him to work keeping the backstage in hand.

By 6:00 P.M., the members of both bands and their managers were in the basement dressing rooms, partying and eating. When I stepped into one of the dressing rooms, I noticed that the wall mirror had been removed and was being used for some utilitarian purpose. Not the least bit shocked, I turned around and closed the door behind me. Laughter roared from those private rooms all night as people came and went from dressing room to dressing room. This was suburban San Francisco rock 'n' roll in the '70s, and they all loved it. The old lady had history, and it was dripping off her walls.

Shortly before the curtain was scheduled to rise at 7:00, I went out onstage to take a look around. I just about had a heart attack when I saw the two large pieces of the piano top leaning against the side wall. The piano itself had been moved back to center stage, with several microphones gaff-taped around the soundboard. Major surgery had been performed on that beautiful Yamaha. It was not a pretty sight. My rookie mistake had been not to watch how the piano was prepped for Cody's performance.

To make matters worse, a giant ashtray was perched just above and to the right of the keyboard. It was now ten minutes to showtime—way too late in the game to say anything. I could only imagine what the piano would look like after two shows. The sounds and smells coming up from the basement dressing rooms assured me that Cody and the Airmen would be well fueled for their flight tonight.

Every seat in the house was full. I checked with sound and lights to make sure they were ready. Thumbs up all around. I signaled Rollie to bring the act onstage. George clambered up to the piano with a big cigar, a quart of beer, and very red eyes. His band followed, all looking the same. George looked at me as he settled into the cockpit of the Yamaha and winked. He knew exactly what I was going through. Another promoter, another rental piano to trash.

He took a big gulp of beer from the bottle, lit his enormous cigar, and nodded toward me. The curtain rose. I did an intro to a screaming audience, and George slammed the first chord and left-handed a base boogie run to "Hot Rod Lincoln."

I limped to the basement to drown my $2,000 deposit woes.

"Nobody without a pass gets past you," I told a uniformed guard at the top of the stairs that led down to the dressing rooms. Then I grabbed Rollie and headed downstairs. Hot Tuna and their entourage were enjoying themselves behind closed doors. Rollie and I went straight to the bar, got a couple of beers, and sat down. The racket of piano mayhem upstairs sounded like it was coming through the ceiling. I was afraid it just might! The good news was that the crowd was roaring after each of Cody's catchy tunes.

The opening set was a little shorter than I would have liked, just over an hour. There was so much equipment crammed on the stage that we had to get a jump on it to prepare for the second set, Hot fucking Tuna. Meanwhile, Dennis was making a killing at the snack bar.

Hot Tuna used their ninety-minute set to tune their instruments and warm up for the second show. It was a good set, but not really full throttle.

Cody and the Airmen, on the hand, hammered their outrageous take on rock 'n' roll at breakneck speed for both of their boogie-infused sets. Chugging beer and flipping ash from his footlong cigar, the Commander and his hot band had a full house of high school and college kids shaking the rafters. It was probably the first concert that half of those kids had ever been to, and Cody's boys sensed virgin blood in the house. That fucking George put everything he had into both performances. Bravo, boys, the old lady shook her tush, and the crystal chandelier swayed to the roar of the crowd.

The stage change between the early and late shows took half an hour. As I walked around backstage before Cody's second opening set, I dared not peek at the piano.

Enormous amounts of tequila and beer were consumed in the dressing rooms between sets—so much that the caterer had to make another run to the warehouse to stock up.

Just before the end of Cody's set, I walked out into the audience to hear the sound, and ran into Dan Roach.

"Very professional, Andy. What's next? Like I said, these shows are so important to this community."

"I was thinking of Neil Young for next weekend," I said with a laugh, knowing I could never afford him. "But more realistically, I'll be looking to bring in some of the side bands from the Dead."

Homer's again…, hometown boys.

"Great idea, man."

"I'm gonna give the Stanford Music Hall high marks for effort," he said. "I'll decide about the music review after the late Tuna show."

After their explosive and totally exhausting second set, George and the Airmen staggered offstage and planted themselves over the still horizontal mirror in Tuna's dressing room. They slammed the door shut, and that was the last I saw of them for a while.

The nucleus of Hot Tuna were two former members of the Jefferson Airplane: Jack Cassidy on bass and Jorma Kaukonen on guitar. Papa John Creach played electric fiddle, and Bob Steeler was on drums. Hot Tuna had morphed organically into a jam band known for long meandering jazz- and blues-infused music. Papa John added unique and fabled licks as the other guys played around his torch for hours. John must have been in his early sixties at that point, a very dapper, tall, thin black man, who could play circles around these youngsters, but he never let on and appeared to be enjoying every single minute of it. The sound was a mix of New Orleans style voodoo mystic spiced up with San Francisco light acid rock.

After a break at the seventy-minute point, the band wanted to keep playing. Bob Brown asked me if that would be okay. The tour had just gotten under way, and they wanted to go for it. I told them I had no problem with that. Once again, the old dame was extending her irresistible hospitality.

About half the house had left by 2:00 A.M.; the rest stayed until the bitter end at 3:15, when the cops came in and politely shut us down. The place smelled like—well, you know what it smelled like. I told one of the cops it was a private party after 1:00 A.M. He laughed and said, "Right. Are we invited? Shut 'er down."

Dan Roach ran his review of the show in the Friday issue of the *Palo Alto Times* special weekend entertainment section. It could not have been better had I written it myself. I was tired, proud, and pleased. The fact that Rollie had dropped by to help out was very cool.

On Thursday morning, I had to meet the piano mover to pick up the Yamaha. On Wednesday night, I had had Tuna's crew put the top and side pieces back on, but I hadn't wanted to look at it right away.

As I stared at it now, I thought, *Shit! It's a fucking mess!*

There were cigar butts on the sound board, burns on the riser where the ash tray apparently had overflowed, beer all over the place, and scratches where the top had been stacked on the floor.

Although I kissed the deposit on the piano goodbye, I made a hefty contribution to my Wells Fargo account that afternoon.

Born in the Mist

The reality that Lisa was pregnant was not confirmed for a few months, since her rabbit tests kept coming back negative. Nevertheless, her doctor's office finally called with the good news. We felt certain that the baby had been conceived at on our camping trip to Yosemite.

Lisa decided that she wanted to home birth the child, for which she had my total support. Her obstetrician was an advocate of home birthing, an attitude that was well outside the boundaries of respectable medicine in the mid-1970s. In other words, my health insurance through the school district would not pay a penny for alternative birthing.

Lisa and I joined an underground support group in San Jose, and educated ourselves on nutrition, breathing exercises, and how to work as a team. Both of us viewed birth as a natural process that had been turned into a medical procedure for the benefit of doctors and hospitals. Drugging by epidermal was state-of-the-art for healthy as well as distressed women. Get them in and get them out. To say we felt like pioneers is putting it mildly.

A member of the support group put us in touch with a midwife, who lived in La Honda, just down the road. June Whitson was a trained midwife from England, where midwifery is encouraged. She had delivered hundreds, perhaps thousands of babies in England, but was forbidden to practice her art in the States. To ensure that the baby was positioned correctly and that all vital signs were as they should be, she worked closely with our doctor. California was in the early stages of legalizing midwifery, so June was signed up for the initial "trial" certification course being offered by the University of California Medical Center in San Francisco. She could have taught the class—and eventually did.

Preparing for our baby was hugely educational. Within the home birthing community, a network of men provided counsel to male counter parts, teaching me about the events leading up to the birth and the mate's role in the process itself.

As the due date approached, Lisa continued to consult her doctor, who assured her that the baby's position was fine. She took extraordinary care of herself, following all the doctor's guidelines and recommendations, but she also continued to ride her horse regularly.

On the evening of August 10, 1975, Lisa went into labor. We were fully prepared, with oxygen available, as the doctor had instructed. Once her water broke, around 9:00 P.M., we called June, and she asked me how often the contractions were coming. I told her they were far apart—in fact, almost nonexistent at that point. She told me to call back when they were ten or fifteen minutes apart.

An hour and a half later, I called June again, and she and Arthur, her photographer husband, were at our place in thirty minutes. When June measured the dilation of Lisa's cervix, she suggested that Arthur and I get some rest.

"It's gonna be a long night," she said. "I'll wake you when it's time."

I lay down on the couch in the living room, and Arthur went down to the guest bedroom, which was empty now because Kim, Lisa's brother, had moved out in preparation for the baby coming. I didn't get much sleep, mostly just tossing and turning.

Around 4:00 A.M., Arthur and I both got up to see what was happening. Lisa was working hard. The room was peaceful, with fog drifting in and out of the redwoods outside the window.

By 10:45, we knew the baby would arrive any minute. Then two things happened. First, the sun suddenly broke through the morning fog and bathed the room in soft light.

"Get ready to catch your child!" June said.

Within sixty seconds, an arm—not a head—came shooting out!

I glanced at the clock: it was 11:11 on August 11th.

Ten seconds later, a head appeared. I cupped my hands, and the baby slid right into them.

The golden silence was shattered when I loudly broadcast, "It's a boy!"

I was immediately scolded by June, who told me to keep my voice down.

I was holding my infant son, who was still connected to the placenta. After a moment, I nudged him up to Lisa's breast, and he began nursing.

With great care, I cut the umbilical cord, following June's instructions. Ode Marin Bernstein was the most beautiful bundle of joy imaginable.

Arthur took a few pictures, then told everyone we needed to rest.

After June and Arthur helped us to change the sheets, Lisa, Ode, and I fell off into a well-deserved sleep.

As we had prearranged, June put the placenta in a big pot and placed that in the bathtub. When I got up, I carried the pot outside to a hole in the ground on a slope near the road. I had dug that hole weeks before, choosing a pleasant spot that needed a tree. Waiting for me on the porch was a redwood sapling, ready to go into the hole. I placed it directly on top of the placenta, filled in the hole with dirt, said a little prayer, and watered it. That sapling has since thrived on the fog and sun and grown into a beautiful giant redwood, which I still visit from time to time.

Kingfish and the Legend Link

Jake Pierre Archives

The next day, I walked over to Mack's Smoke Shop on Emerson, around the corner from the theatre, to buy a box of stogies with "It's a Boy!" paper rings on them. Then I strolled over to Wells Fargo to see my rock 'n'

197

roll banker. After receiving an enthusiastic reception, I passed out cigars to all the suits in the Loan Department.

With money in the bank, Lisa and I looked for a larger house—one without banana slugs and the constant dampness of a redwood forest. I found a place in La Honda, down the road, four miles closer to the coast. It was nothing fancy, but was perched on a ridge with a perfect view of mountains and valleys.

Life was good, but the drive to the Palo Alto bus yard was now twice as long as before. I was used to the steady income and benefits from the school district, and not quite ready to give them up, so I forged ahead over the mountains each morning.

A. Bernstein Archives

The long commute put a strain on Half Gaffed Productions. Having made out well from the Tuna/Cody night, Dennis was all over me to book the next show, so I committed myself to number three, putting the word out to Michael Oster. Fortunately, he had received good reports from the band managers about the first two shows.

" I've got a perfect fit for you."

"You always say that, Michael…, you hustler!"

He laughed.

"Okay, listen. You know Kingfish? Matt Kelly's band from Palo Alto?"

"Great little band. Robbie Haddinott's the guitarist. He went to Los Altos High with my wife" I said.

"Well, Bob Weir and Dave Torbert have joined the band."

"Dave Torbert from the New Riders of the Purple Sage?"

"Yup".

"Does that mean I can use Dead or New Rider songs in my ads?"

"You bet! Now let me give you the best part…. Link Wray is living in the Bay Area for a short time, and I've been given the green light to book him to open."

"Fuck, Michael! He's one of my idols. He should be the headliner."

"Settle down, Andy. He doesn't have a band. Kingfish has to back him up. So he's the opener, with Kingfish behind him."

A. Bernstein Archives

Link Wray Stole the Show

"Book it, Michael!"

"How many shows?"

"Just one. I don't think this bill would draw two full houses."

"Done. I'll send you the contracts."

Link Wray was the icing on the cake for me. His song "Rumble," from the mid '50s, was a classic. It was the first single to feature the use of fuzz tone and distortion on the electric guitar, influencing the likes of Jeff Beck, Jimmy Page, Jimi Hendrix, and Neil Young.

Cutting the radio spots with Cliff was great fun. I used a mix of Dead and New Riders material, as well as "Rumble."

I also put Jake on the poster right away.

"It was a tough call, Jake," I said, "but we're gonna feature Kingfish as the headliner on the poster, and Link as the opener. I hate to do it, but our core audience will be high school Dead fans, and they're too young to even know who Link is."

The show sold out in the first ten days. Dennis was bummed out that we were only doing one show, since that would cost him a lot of money in candy and soda sales."

"Sorry, Dennis, we can't get enough butts in all these seats to justify the expense of two houses."

A. Bernstein Archives

Kingfish at El Camino Park in Palo Alto

On the day of the show, I discovered that Owsley was doing the sound, handpicked once again by the Dead. He loved the old theatre and brought enough of the Dead's equipment to put together a wonderful sound. He also insisted that I let him design a permanent PA system for the theatre.

All I could say was, "Later, Bear, later."

The doors opened at 8:00 P.M. By 8:30, I was standing onstage behind the curtain with Bob Weir and Kingfish. It was showtime, but Link hadn't arrived yet.

"Alright, Bobby," I said. "It looks like you may be doing the whole show yourself."

"Shit! Link's one of our heroes too. We're looking forward to playing with him, give it a few more minutes."

By 8:40, we could see and hear that the audience was getting restless. I decided not to make any introduction, but just turn Kingfish loose. However, just as I was about to signal the stagehand to raise the curtain, a door burst open in the back of the auditorium, and in walked Link, carrying a guitar case, with his manager trailing behind.

Link had a fine '50s pompadour, Ray-Ban shades, a black leather jacket, and a rock 'n' roll aura. Bob and I looked at each other and simultaneously said, "Link's here!"

From the wings, I waved him over to me.

"Hey, Link, we've been waiting for you. I'm Andy..., the promoter."

"Sorry, man. We thought the Stanford Music Hall was on the Stanford campus. We've been driving around in a cab for the last forty-five minutes. The cabbie's from San Francisco, and didn't know any better."

"Well, you're here now, and we're ready to go."

After a hasty conference with Bob and the band (which had practiced his major songs), and a brief introduction by Mr. Producer, they launched into the first song.

I went out into the house to listen. Owsley had done a fine job; the sound was awesome.

All the musicians in Kingfish were fully aware that they were in the presence of a legend. It was a no-soundcheck-let's-get-to-playin' evening. Bobby and all the guys deserve a lot of credit for being able to fall right into Link's rockabilly groove and keep the focus. For Robbie Haddinott, it meant trading licks with a mentor unlike any other he would encounter in his short life. Of course, Link recognized this, and made sure he incorporated several well-known songs from his era, like "That's All Right, Mama" (an Elvis mainstay) and several Carl Perkins tunes. Kingfish rolled with his choices, and the audience was transfixed by this man of small stature with the controlled roar of a 747. Always the gentleman, Link offered generous kudos to Kingfish after his third encore.

Dan Roach tracked me down as Link was playing.

"Andy, this is a once-in-a-lifetime experience. How in the hell did you book Link Wray? This guy's the godfather of modern rock 'n' roll."

"Just got lucky."

For their headlining set, Kingfish played a mix of Chuck Berry, Grateful Dead, and rock and blues gem from years past. But this night was Robbie's, with lots of his former classmates in the audience. He laid down on a virtuoso performance on lead guitar. Toward the end of their set, Link walked out and joined Kingfish for the final two songs.

Because I didn't have to turn two houses, this show was much more low-key than the first two concerts, making it more relaxing and enjoyable for me. I didn't make a whole lot of money, but Dennis did better than he expected.

Dan's review in the *Times* mentioned me by name. But this was to be my last show at the Music Hall. I loved the old place, the audience reactions were soul lifting, but the profit margins were just too thin. I either had to find bigger venues, or hang it up for the time being. Rollie came in behind me and did a short series of shows at the music hall, so not all was lost. I ended up helping him with his productions as he did for me.

Jerry and Nicky...Old Souls Collide

Jake Pierre Archives

About a month after the Kingfish/Link show, I got a call from Rollie, who had booked the latest incarnation of the Jerry Garcia Band, which featured Nicky Hopkins. This was a real coup for him. The show would be at the Flint Center for the Performing Arts at De Anza College in Cupertino. The production needed at least two men to pull it off, so Rollie asked if I was up for it.

"Holy shit! Are you crazy? When do we start?"

"We just did."

That very day, Lisa informed me that she was pregnant once again. I'll never forget getting those two surprises the same day. Of course, the news of the baby took center stage.

Nicky's piano playing was all over *Exile on Main Street*, as well as many other Stones' classics. He was one of the most in-demand studio pianists at the time, recording with the Kinks, Jefferson Airplane, New Riders of the Purple Sage, and the Steve Miller Band, among many, many others. He was something of a studio recluse, but good old Jerry had nabbed him for a short live tour. How sweet it was. Ron Tutt and John Kahn rounded out the band.

Sam Cutler, who knew Nicky from the UK and perhaps from his studio sessions with the Stones, was once again the tour manager. At the time, Sam was working as the tour manager for the Dead, as well as for Jerry's side bands. Working with Sam again would be cool. I'd grown to enjoy his offbeat personality and smooth persona. He was also a very bright guy.

Rollie had done all the advance work for this show, something he was now quite proficient at. Jake's poster for the show was the best of the best, with lots of wizardry and magic. Cliff and Rollie's imaginative radio spots ran on three local stations, and the show was sold out a week ahead of time.

On the day of the performance, Jerry showed up early, as usual, with his partner in bad behavior, John Kahn. By 5:00, Nicky and Ron Tutt were also on hand. The dressing rooms upstairs were very comfortable, the mood was relaxed and jovial, and the catered California fusion food, which I had arranged for, was out of this world. To get from the dressing rooms to the stage, two floors below, the artists would have to negotiate several narrow walkways and a flight of stairs. It would be really easy to get lost, so I made a couple of test runs before the show, knowing that I might be the only one who could find the path to the stage.

After that, it was time to relax. When I got back to the upstairs lounge, the only available seat was on a sofa between Jerry and Nicky. They were both smoking cigarettes and drinking coffee. I grabbed a beer and sat down between them.

"Hey, man," Jerry said. "Good to see ya. Have you met Nicky?"

"No."

"This is Andrew, Nicky. He used to run our favorite little funky nightclub in Palo Alto…, Homer's Warehouse, down by the railroad tracks."

"Ah, mon," Nicky said with his cockney accent, "sounds great. Wish I coulda been there."

Nicky was a very slight man, with bushy sideburns, a scruffy haircut, and a cockeyed, warm smile. I was thrilled to be sitting next to him, and tried to keep from sounding like a fourteen-year-old girl.

He was a charming guy, very polite and very British. Sitting there casually chatting with him and Jerry made my small contribution to this evening worthwhile—and the music was still to come!

A. Bernstein Archives

Nicky Hopkins, Keyboard Genius

While I was being squeezed between two giants, Rollie suddenly showed up.

"Excuse me, gentlemen," he said, "it's showtime. Please follow Andrew."

I led the parade down to the stage. When we got there, Rollie did his introduction, and the curtain rose as the band roared into "Let It Rock." The first set was typical Jerry, with a beautiful rendition of "Mississippi Moon," featuring beautiful keyboard work by Nicky. A rousing version of "Mystery Train" ended the first set.

During the break in the small backstage changing rooms, I asked if anyone needed anything from upstairs. Jerry, of course, wanted his black, black coffee. I should have anticipated that. I had the caterers bring some down to him.

The band soon lit into the second set with "I'm a Road Runner." My favorite song of the evening was the beautiful "Lady Sleeps" halfway through the second set. The interplay between Jerry and Nicky was simply stunning, with Ron Tutt's gentle cymbal work adding color.

After the show, we all gathered upstairs for more food, a few joints, and many stories. Nicky's tales about the grit, the drugs, and the insanity when the Stones recorded *Exile on Main Street* in the south of France had us all captivated. Apparently, while acting like depraved heathens, the Stones had turned out perhaps the most brilliant rock 'n' roll album of all time.

That night on the De Anza campus was a rousing joyful experience for all—and the last time I ever spoke to Jerry Garcia.

Truck Drivin' Man

Lisa and I enjoyed living in La Honda and treasured Ode, who was now a year old. But we needed more money, and it was time for me to make a move from buses to trucks, if driving was to remain my main money stream.

Truck driving school was out. Hell, I knew how to drive, I just needed to get licensed on big rigs. Once again, John Tipton, the school bus instructor, was a big help. He arranged for me to train on the district's ten-wheel dump truck, which also pulled a twenty-foot equipment trailer, to practice backing and to master multi-gear transmission shifting. Once I was proficient in John's eyes, the district signed off on the State of California certificate of completion for mandatory hours behind the wheel. It was a crash course, outside the district's legal authority, but I was good to go, with a Class 1 license to prove it.

I found an employment agency in Palo Alto that placed tractor-trailer drivers. The guy there said he would have a job interview for me within days. I got a call the very next day from a moving and storage company in Redwood City, LDM, which was an agent for United Van Lines. The secretary said I would be interviewed by the Operations Manager, whose name was Stan.

When I showed up promptly for the interview, looking as normal as I could, Stan's first question was a curious one: "Jesus, how tall are you?"

"Six-foot-seven."

"You play basketball?"

"Of course," I lied.

"You're hired. Go see the lady upstairs, fill out the paperwork, then come back and see me."

If he thinks I'm the great white basketball hope, this could get ugly. What have I gotten myself into? I just wanna drive a goddamn truck!

I finished up the paperwork and headed back down to the warehouse to see Stan. As I passed the tractor-trailer rigs in the yard, I knew I'd be driving one soon—if basketball didn't permanently ground me.

Shit!

I gave the school district ten days' notice. Leaving was a melancholic experience. I had logged a lot of miles behind the wheel of Bus 6, met Maynard, and watched many children grow into young adults.

I was now in the moving business—and the new basketball center for the LDM United Screwballs. My teammates were all operations guys, drivers and packers from LDM, and Stan was the op's manager. Basketball was his passion.

Why me, Lord?

When I reported to work on Monday morning, Stan gave me a few company shirts and told me to take a straight truck (not a semi) to Marin County. As I pulled into the northbound lane of U.S. 101, I felt the small diesel rumble under the cab. It was a relief not to have a bunch of kids behind me. I could relax.

The first basketball game was that Friday night. If I still had a job on Saturday morning, I'd be driving a semi for the first time. Pretty cool, I always wanted to give that a whirl, I felt up to the challenge,

The basketball game went better than I expected—by which I mean I didn't disgrace myself or the team. Once Stan realized that I wasn't anything to write home about, he rotated me in and out to rest the other players. Gene Koepke, a bear of a man, was the other center, as well as a foreman on the trucks. I don't remember if we won or lost that night, but I had a truck to drive the next morning. (Stan put me in a few more games after that, until he managed to recruit a decent center, and then he let me retire.)

Saturday morning I was off to Hollister to move the contents of a three-bedroom, fully furnished home to Palo Alto. The three helpers took a car, but Stan rode in the semi with me to evaluate my driving. I knew how to drive, but only forward. I had kept that little secret to myself. The truck and trailer were already hooked up, thank God, so I didn't have to make a fool of myself trying to connect electrical and air brake lines, not to mention hitting the kingpin with the fifth wheel, a precise exercise that takes mucho practice.

The truck had a ten-speed Road Ranger transmission and a shaky day cab, not meant for going long distances. The poor thing huffed and puffed all the way to Hollister, but I didn't care. The humming of the diesel exhaust stack was music to my ears, and I was having the time of my life. Once we hit San Jose, Stan told me I was a born trucker and laughed his ass off. It was nip and tuck staying at the speed limit going up the hills, but with enough shifting I got it done.

My next lesson was how to load a 45-foot trailer full of furniture—no small task. I soon learned that the driver is responsible for making everything fit into the trailer. The helpers brought it, but I had to put the puzzle together.

Damn, I just wanted to drive!

Stan was there to teach me how to load, showing how everything has to fit snug in linear tiers. As we worked together that morning, he wanted to hear my music business stories. I filled him in on Homer's and the early days with the Dead in Palo Alto. At first, he thought I was bullshitting, but the stories were too outrageous to be lies. My family was counting on me to succeed in the moving business, so I cut the fables short and focused on the task's at hand,

It took five hours to fill that trailer. By the end of that time, I was hot and sore, but the load looked beautiful, everything tight as a tick—strapped, padded, and ready for the road.

Wow, I did that!

Then we hit the road back to Palo Alto. The poor old underpowered Mack now had an added 9,000 pounds to pull. I shifted and shifted those gears all the way, and was worn out by the time Stan and I pulled up to the delivery address. My right arm ached like a sore ten-speed transmission from all the shifting.

The helpers were waiting for us out front, and the husband and wife were standing on the porch of their new home, happy to see their things arrive in what they hoped was good shape. I felt in charge as I climbed down with my clipboard and paperwork in hand.

But then Stan said, "We're in a cul-de-sac, Andy."

"So?"

He smiled. "You're gonna have to back out the way you came in, at a ninety-degree angle, pull forward, and then back into this street, again at a ninety-degree angle."

The fucker's testing me.

What I managed to do was jackknife the truck, with cab and trailer side by side—and blocking an intersection, to boot. It must have been something to see. Everyone, including the customers, were laughing hysterically.

Stan had sandbagged me: Backing up a semi is the skill part of the job, and you can only learn it from experience. Once the laughing stopped, Stan got behind the wheel, straightened the truck out, and put it where it belonged. Of all the lessons that day, the most important was that I was going to have to learn how to back that bitch up.

I spent the next two weeks practicing exactly that after work. Then Stan assigned me my own semi to drive and care for. I was the driver and manager on each day's job, responsible for all the paperwork, crew productivity, and good relations with the customers. I loaded delivered all over the San Francisco Bay Area.

Soon I was qualified to drive in all eleven western states for United Van Lines and was itching to spread my wings with some overnight runs. When I got my first long-haul assignment, it was to take a load of storage vaults full of furniture from our warehouse in Redwood City up to Carson City, Nevada. The route crossed Donner Summit on Interstate 80, with possible snow conditions.

Talk about trial by fire. This could be trial by ice!

My long-distance maiden voyage began at 8:00 on a Sunday morning in a twin-screw Freightliner cab-over with a cozy sleeper, a Detroit Diesel that had some guts, and a sixteen-speed gearbox with a splitter. Luckily for me, I didn't have to chain up, since the snow was light. What a beautiful ride! First up the western slopes of Donner Pass, a cruise over the peak, then back down the eastern slope, I cut over to Highway 389 and rolled into Carson City at sunset. Once in town, I parked in the lot of a small casino and went in for a buffet dinner. Afterwards, I returned to the Freightliner, got out my sleeping bag and my thermals, climbed into the bunk, turned out the sleeper lights, and slept like a baby in my down cocoon.

The unloading went fine the next day. I completed the paperwork, got a hundred-dollar tip for my efforts, and paid the local crew. I was back in the yard in Redwood City by 8:00 P.M., parked the truck, and headed to our mountain home and the baby.

The road is a funny thing; it creeps slowly into your being. For the next six months, I hauled furniture throughout the western United States, filling in with local work when not running the interstates. I quickly became the most reliable driver in United's west coast household goods fleet. I got along with the customers, had zero damage claims against me, and kept my equipment spotless. The Freightliner became my home away from home. I turned the sleeper into my shelter from the elements, wiring it for TV and music. My dispatcher was a nice woman named Charlene Vincent, who gave me all the VIP jobs. Every load was a personal challenge to exceed the client's expectations. I drove that Freightliner for eleven months, learning everything there was to know about the moving business. That would serve me well in the future.

Hot Licks and the Holy Grail

Robert Altman Archives
Chuck Berry

Rollie and I had a good running buddy named Spencer Bornes, a slick, bright fellow, who owned a small auto body supply company in Mountain View. He had a good income from his company, and we all

213

respected his obvious self-discipline. Spencer was also an accomplished keyboardist, favoring a Hammond B3 and, just like the rest of us, had dreamed of making it in music.

One day in 1976, he approached Rollie and me to see if we would partner with him to put on a concert headlining his idol, Chuck Berry. Spencer would put up the money, and we would provide the production skills. We had already done several shows at the Foothill College Student Union, but that only had room for five hundred people at most, and we knew that Chuck Berry would attract a lot more than that. The Flint Center for the Performing Arts at De Anza College in Cupertino, the same place we put on the Jerry and Nicky show, seemed the most logical choice. We applied to the District Board to put on the show at the 2000 seat venue. Since we had a good reputation with the Board from our previous production, we were quickly approved.

If produced correctly, Chuck Berry could be a joy to work with, and everyone would make money. I had seen him once at the old Fillmore, and again at Fillmore West. He always traveled alone, just him and Lucille, his red Gibson guitar. Supplying the backup band was the promoters' responsibility, and they damned sure better be astute enough to hire musicians who could follow Chuck's changes, or it would be a very short and humiliating evening. Many promoters across the country had taken financial baths presenting Mr. Berry.

One who did *not* take a bath was Bill Graham, who provided Steve Miller's Blues Band behind Chuck's first appearance at the Fillmore—and Michael Bloomfield and friends, including Nick Gravenites and Mark Naftalin, the second time. Chuck appeared to enjoy both shows immensely. In fact, Bill couldn't get him to leave the stage. Chuck thought they were all great players, but kept forgetting their names. Maybe all the white boys with long hair began to look the same after a while.

I had also seen Chuck Berry a third time, at a sold-out show at the Memorial Auditorium in Honolulu. The promoter prepaid a large deposit, flew Chuck over, and put him up in an expensive hotel. During the opening song, it was immediately apparent that the backup band was a bad choice—all union local boys who probably had never seen or heard of Chuck Berry. The drummer couldn't keep a simple 4-4 or 4-2 rock beat. Chuck went ape shit, actually taking a drumstick out of his hand and showing him a rock beat on the snare drum. Then he dressed them all down. It was humiliating, and the promoter was fucked. After a mere four songs, Chuck split, with all the money.

A. Bernstein Archives

Paul Butterfield and Nick Gravenites at Their High School Prom

"So, boys," I told Rollie and Spencer, "you think Chuck wants a lot of money up front to play? Guess what? He gets to walk and keep it if we don't handle this thing perfectly with the backup band. Your ass could be next, Spencer. So don't fuck around. Let's take our time and find the exact right fit."

They got the message.

I had been hearing from friends about a young Peninsula guitarist named Robben Ford, who was killing Bay Area audiences with his blues guitar and phenomenal band, so I drove out to Walnut Creek to see the Charles Ford Blues Band in action. I was simply blown away. Robben was—and is—a prodigy, the real deal. Whatever his band cost, it would be worth it.

Rollie and I set up a meeting with Robben at his manager's office in Redwood City, and when Rollie told Robben that we wanted his band to back up Chuck Berry, his eyes got as big as saucers. He couldn't have been more then eighteen at the time. When I told him about my experience in Honolulu, he smiled, shook his head, and said, "You don't have anything to worry about."

On the drive home, I was sure that we had made the right choice. Rollie kept his mouth shut, trusting me on this one.

After a brief media blitz, the tickets sold out fast. Robben's name on the bill drew many young fans in the area who might not have attended otherwise. This was a big night for Spencer. Although he had relied heavily on Rollie and me, we tried to fade into the background on the night of the show. He had paid for his role as promoter, and we wanted him to enjoy it.

At 7:45, Spencer introduced Robben's band. They played a solid 45-minute set and left the audience in a light lather, but they also left a lot in the tank for the star. During the break, I handed Chuck's set list to Robben. He looked at it and told me with a smile that he and his band had been practicing Chuck Berry songs for weeks.

"We know them upside down and backwards, Andy," he said, smiling.

When Spencer brought Robben's band back onstage, Chuck rolled out from stage right, slamming the opening chords of "Sweet Little Sixteen" as soon as the spotlight hit him. Chuck was the razor thin, hot shit rock 'n' roll messiah. Every single cell in his body exuded Chuck Berry. When he started strumming the second song, "Rock 'n' Roll Music," he turned and looked Robben straight in the eyes. The gauntlet had been dropped. This young white boy took a lead handed to him by Chuck Berry and set it on fire. The two of them traded licks back and forth, song after song. The place came unglued. The campus security officers had their hands full, keeping the kids from dancing in the aisles.

Chuck got down and did the duck town strut across the stage many times that evening—perhaps ten, but who was counting? He couldn't make this kid say uncle, no matter how hard he tried. Chuck would step up front, side by side with Robben, beam at the band, then smile back at the audience in recognition of these great young musicians. He appeared to be having the time of his life, as did Robben. Chuck might have gone on for another two hours if security hadn't told me that it was curfew time on campus, and pulled the plug.

That evening was like being around for the birth of rock 'n' roll, something Chuck Berry was able to duplicate every night, given the right set of circumstances. My bet is that Robben and the boys never forgot that night.

Autumn in March

While I was running the road, Lisa mastered glass cutting and design, and was soon producing magical work. She was always a force to be reckoned with when she was motivated. My craftsman buddy Glen Whear and I built her a stained glass studio when I was home. It took us a month, but we had a great time doing it. With the new baby coming, it was more important than ever for Lisa to have her own space. We cut a window in that had a view to the coast. The place was ready by the end of February, so we moved all of Lisa's equipment in. She loved that studio.

Soon, I was back to working locally again, three to four days a week, so I could be around as the day drew closer for our new arrival. As with Ode, the baby would be born at home. At that time, before ultrasounds, there was no way to know the gender, but by the position in Lisa's womb, the doctor thought it would probably be a girl.

June and Arthur were over regularly as we prepared for the birth. Late in the afternoon of March 3, 1977, Lisa's water broke. I was visiting our next-door neighbors when she called me to come home. The birth of our second child had begun. I called June and Arthur around 6:00 P.M., by which time the contractions were coming pretty quickly. I tried to sound calm, but I really wanted June on the premises as soon as possible.

Lisa's mother Dorothy and her good friend Holly were also there to witness the birth and help out.

If June doesn't get here soon, I'll have to deliver this baby myself!

The first thing June did when she arrived was take measurements of Lisa's cervix.

"This baby will not be putting the party off for long," she announced.

Holly and I traded off breath coaching Lisa as her contractions became longer and closer together.

With Ode sleeping peacefully in the next room, Lisa gave one last push, and all ten pounds of Autumn Rachel Bernstein slipped out—hand first, just like her brother.

Dorothy was crying and laughing, beside herself with joy, as were we all. The baby had a bruise on her face, which was at first a little alarming.

"Her arm was pressed against her face as she came through the birth canal," June said. "It'll go away in a couple of weeks. The important thing is, she's got ten fingers and toes, and is breathing easy."

Autumn decided to express her displeasure with her swollen nose by letting out a battle cry. But Lisa soon took care of that by putting her to the breast.

Our happy home was now blessed with a beautiful baby girl, whom her brother loved from his first glance at her the next morning.

Meeting Maynard's Mates

S ince Homer's, much had changed in my life, mostly for the better. Certainly, all the concerts and promotions had been a roller coaster ride of the first order, and seemed to be a great preparation for something—but I really had no idea what. I'd recently taken a new job, hauling sand over Highway 17 from Santa Cruz to the San Francisco Airport every day, a 165-mile round trip, twice a day.

My life was just a series of chapters, apparently connected by music, buses, and now trucks. How in the world they were related, I had no clue. I knew that dreaming was part of the mix, maybe even the main ingredient.

The one thing missing from my country life, with wonderful babies and a patient wife, was a sense of brotherhood. Sonny Terry's brief mentorship had been a turning point, and I often thought of the importance he placed on family. True brotherhood, however, seemed fleeting. I often thought of Maynard. We shared a love of the road, listening to Leon Russell on rainy days in the cottage in Dogpatch, dreaming about buying Kenworths, and hitting the interstates for one of the Van Lines.

However, the reality was that there were two babies and a wife who needed an income and security. My driving skills had carried me up to this point, and close brothers would have to wait.

My God, I'll be thirty in four months!

Now that I was the father of a daughter as well as a son, I reached out to Maynard's parents to relay the message to him, and to tell him that Lisa and I sent our love. Aside from missing Maynard, I missed his eclectic collection of vehicles. He loved my old firetruck, "Castro Valley," and I was just as attached to his World War II Dodge army ambulance. They were two of the coolest early '40s heavy-duty trucks to be seen anywhere. When we convoyed to the pizza joint or just cruised around town, it was awesome to hear those two old veteran trucks grinding through the crash gearboxes. Maynard and I never missed a double clutch shift, up or down. It was those old Gillig buses that broke us both in.

All I knew when I called Maynard's parents was that he was out running the road with Willie Nelson, who was making a dent in the pop charts with "Blue Eyes Cryin' in the Rain" and some songs with Waylon Jennings. I had seen Waylon open for the Dead at Kezar Stadium at some point and had enjoyed his set a lot. Jerry Garcia was a big fan of Waylon's, which drew in the Dead crowd.

I figured Maynard was probably living the life we had talked about years before. For now, I was driving a semi, riding on top of 50,000 pounds of sand every day and holding on for dear life. Back and forth, up and over, empty one way, then full coming back.

The morning one of my fuel tanks fell off the truck at dawn was close to being my last.

Either upgrade my truck, or I'm outta here.

I got the upgrade, which made a world of difference in the job, and I felt much safer about risking my life every day, running that damned hill.

But in the back of my mind, the number 30 kept me up at night. I was still so full of dreams, I could hardly control myself, and the time was running short to find my destiny. What I really wanted to do was explore the logistics of bands on the road. That had been a great curiosity of mine ever since the concert and club production days. Just a glimpse would do. Logistics seemed to be the natural progression for my life. Trucking was the low rung on the supply chain ladder. I wanted to work my way up to the top.

A few weeks after Lisa delivered Autumn, she was back to a normal routine. Her friend Holly was almost living at our house by this point. When my brother Rick called to invite me to visit him in Hawaii, I decided to take a short break from the action.

The very afternoon I arrived, my brother's wife, Linda, answered the phone and said it was for me. To my surprise and amazement, Maynard was on the other end! His parents had told him about Autumn, and when he called my home, Lisa gave him my brother's phone number. It was so good to hear my old buddy's voice again, that low, steady baritone.

"What the hell's goin' on, man?" I said. "What a surprise!"

"I'm on Maui with the band, restin' up. We're playin' a gig in Honolulu in a few days. Come on over and meet the guys. They've heard about you. Hell, you'll probably fit right in."

"I'll be on the first flight in the morning."

"By the way, Andy, does René Comeaux still live in Hana?"

"He does indeed. And I have his phone number."

"Is he still in the horticultural arts?"

"He sure is."

When I got to the Intercontinental Hotel on Maui, where Maynard and the band were staying, they had reserved a room for me for three nights. Once I had settled into my ocean view room, I called Maynard and invited him over. My brother had kindly given me three fat joints for the trip.

Soon, a gentle tapping of fingernails on my door signaled that my friend had arrived. When I opened the door, there Maynard was, dressed in a tee shirt that proudly proclaimed "TUBE JOCKEY" across the top of a cartoon bus. To complete the outfit, he had on cutoffs and flip-flops, with shades in place, and hair a-flyin'.

"You look great!" I said. "I've never seen you out of boots and jeans before. Look at those white legs!"

"Listen, Andy," he said, without missing a beat, "the band can't beg, borrow, or steal any weed around here. We even tried asking a few of the hotel employees, but no luck."

"Okay, tomorrow we'll drive out to Hana and see my buddy. But for right now, I've got three fatties to get us through."

Maynard's blue eyes melted.

As we sat on the balcony, talking and toking, I called room service, and for the next hour, Maynard and I watched the waves roll in, drank Primo beer, and downed a few plates of Maui onion rings. My brother's pot was "da kine," so we only smoked half of one joint.

"What's that bus all about on your tee shirt?" I asked.

"That's my office, Andy. A '58 GM Greyhound that Willie bought off Dolly Parton and Porter Wagner. Willie calls it 'The Tube' because it's nothin' more than a long steel tube, and I'm the primary tube jockey."

We both laughed.

"So how's life on the road?"

"Well, ya know, I'm a vegetarian, so that means a lot of grilled cheese sandwiches at truck stops. When I have a bad gas attack, I can clear the back of the bus from the driver's seat!"

We howled.

"Other than the menu, though," he said, "it's fun as hell most of the time, and Willie's a great guy.... I work with his stage manager, a guy named Poodie. He's originally from Waco, Texas. In fact, Waco's Chamber of Commerce dubbed him the prettiest baby born in Waco in 1948! Quite a character. Wanna meet him?"

"Hell, yes! I'll bring along what's left."

"That will be deeply appreciated by all."

Poodie Locke Archives
Willie and Poodie, 1977

He made a call to one of the rooms, and we headed out the door.

"Just like the good ol' days, buddy," I said as we walked out of the elevator a few floors down.

Maynard stopped in front of a room and gave the familiar fingernail tap he had made on my door. I could hear laughter and music inside.

When the door opened, a big man with long blond hair and a fuzzy face said with a broad crooked grin, "C'mon on in, boys!"

"This is Andrew, Poodie," Maynard said. "Andrew Bernstein from Palo Alto."

"Have a seat, son," Poodie said, handing me a can of beer from an ice bucket. "Make yourself at home. Maynard's told us all about ya. This here is Steve, and that's D.W."

Steve, who was a Jackson Brown look-alike, got up and shook my hand. "Take *my* seat," he said. "I'll sit on the bed. We're a little short of chairs."

I sat down, shook hands with D.W., pulled out one of the joints, and lit it.

"Time to burn one, big boy!" Poodie said. He had a big laugh and seemed to be the leader of the party.

"It's probably Maui Wowie," I said, "but I got it in Honolulu."

"It could be Detroit brown," Poodie said. "We'll take it!"

Steve turned out to be Steve Koepke (no relation to Gene), the drum roadie for the band. He was a 23-year-old Texan from Houston, who seemed very pleased to meet someone from Northern California. Steve was a warm guy, and I had the impression almost immediately that we would click. Maybe to impress me, he took the deepest tokes that I'd ever seen. I found out later from Maynard that Steve was Willie's brother-in-law.

"Hey, Kopeck!" Poodie called. "Leave some of that joint for us!"

At some point, I learned that D.W. was the guitar roadie, and had been the bus driver before Maynard. His full name was Daryl Wayne English, the stepson of Paul English, Willie's longtime drummer and best friend. D.W. had a hearty handshake, hair to the waist, and a big warm smile. I intuitively felt that, like Steve, he would become a friend.

Poodie Locke Archives
Paul English, ca. late 1970s

"You can call me Daryl Wayne or D.W.," he said, "but don't ever call me just Daryl."

With five guys puffing away, the fat joint was gone in no time.

As I pulled out the second one, I said, "Enjoy it, guys. This is it."

Around 8:30, we all migrated down to the lanai bar for food and drinks. Along the way, Steve and D.W. grilled me about San Francisco—the music, the women, and the intrigue that surrounded the '60s.

At the bar, we were soon joined by a few of the other crew and band members. Maynard introduced me to a guy named Chris Etheridge, and we soon fell into a conversation that went on for at least two hours—a nonstop who-do-you-know exchange about San Francisco musicians.

A. Bernstein Archives
My Good Brother Chris Etheridge

Chris was one of the two bass players in the band. He was originally from Meridian, Mississippi, but had spent a great deal of time in California, mostly L.A., playing as both a studio session musician and a band mate with some early folk rock groups. The best known ones were Gram Parsons' Flying Burrito Brothers and The Byrds, around the time they recorded *Sweetheart of the Rodeo*, which happened to be one of my all-time favorites.

Chris was a naturally nice guy, interesting, funny as hell, and completely without pretense. He was much more like someone I might know at home than what I imagined these Texans to be like.

The next morning, Maynard called my room to tell me that our rental car had arrived, and it was time to head to Hana. I had called René earlier to tell him we would be dropping in. When I met Maynard in the lobby, he said we were going to stop by Willie's room first, just to say hi. That, of course, was fine with me.

When Maynard did his finger-tap on the door, it was opened by a tall, thin young man with a head full of curls and a short black beard. Willie was sitting on a couch and stood up to greet me as I walked in.

"How do you do, Andrew?" he said. "Maynard's mentioned you many times."

We shook hands, and he introduced me to the curly headed guy, whose name was Mickey.

I had no idea why we were there, other than that I would be hanging around for a few days, and perhaps Maynard had told Willie about our horticultural expedition. In any case, Willie was very friendly. At one point, he asked my opinion about "Stardust," which was playing in the background.

Recognizing it as a Hoagy Carmichael tune that I guessed was being performed by Willie himself, I said, "It sounds great. My dad used to listen to that song all the time."

"It's from my new album, *Stardust*. Should be out in a month or two."

Mickey didn't say much, but was generally friendly. Before Maynard and I left, "Georgia on My Mind" was playing, and I wanted to hear it all the way through, since it was my favorite Ray Charles song. I guess it was one of Willie's, too. His rendition was meltingly good.

"Wow! That harmonica break's beyond compare," I said.

"I'll tell the harmonica player you said so," Willie replied with a smile. "Are you sticking around for the show in Honolulu, Andrew?"

"Looking forward to it, Willie. Hope to hear 'Georgia on My Mind.'"

With that, we did handshakes all around, and Maynard and I were off.

On the way to the lobby, Maynard said, "By the way, the harmonica player was Mickey."

"We're Not Gettin' Out for Shit!"

W hen Maynard and I got to the Avis counter down in the lobby, who should be waiting for us than D.W. and Steve. Standing with them was a gorgeous blond, who was wearing a brown bikini top and a loose skirt. She was so beautiful that I barely noticed Steve and D.W.

"Andrew," Steve said, "this is my girlfriend, Babe."

I was already under her spell.

As we approached the car, Maynard said to me, "I'm not letting any of those others drive. So it's either you or me, buddy."

"Well, I'm on vacation from hauling sand up and down a mountain, so it's all yours, pal."

As Maynard took the wheel, I got in front with him because I needed the leg room, and Babe sat in back between D.W. and Steve. We pulled out of the hotel parking lot and got onto a two-lane highway that would take us to the northern side of the island. From there, we had to head east to Hana, which was at the northeastern corner. The whole drive was only fifty miles, but half of that would be through a tangle of curves and twists.

I soon discovered that Babe was as bright and spirited as she was physically dazzling. But Steve clearly saw her very differently, disagreeing with everything that came out of her mouth. If she said the ocean was blue, he would say it was green. And D.W. did the same thing with him. All three tried to get me on their side. I figured the best policy was to go with Babe or stay neutral, but the guys soon caught on to that, and stopped asking my opinion.

Maynard and I often looked at each other and said a prayer that we would make it to Hana without any blood being spilled in the back seat. For two reasonably laid back hippies from Palo Alto, these guys were like aliens on steroids—with Texas accents, yet!

Steve Koepke Archives

Babe and Steve: Who Needs Mushrooms with a Girl Like This?

Soon we hit the first series of curves, and the car got quieter. The views were truly spectacular, so the back seat was now full of oooohs and ahhhhs.

Not too far into the winding part of our journey, Mr. Koepke announced, at the top of his lungs, "The best shrooms in the world grow in the piles of cow shit dropped along the hills of the Hana Highway."

He claimed to have done extensive research on the subject, so we should all be prepared to devote a significant portion of our day checking piles of shit for magic mushrooms.

"Koepke," D.W. snapped, "shut the fuck up! We're goin' straight to Hana, see this René guy, and then head to the Seven Sacred Pools, and home."

"Steve," Babe said, "don't even *start* going down that mushroom road. We're heading to the Ponds…, and then we have to drive all the way back to the hotel. So we're not gettin' out for shit!"

But every time we passed a herd, Steve yelled, "Cows! Look! Cows and cow shit!"

"Koepke," Maynard said stoically, "I'm not driving this car in the dark tonight, so no shit expeditions!"

"Oh, c'mon, man! I'm tellin' ya, this shit is the real fuckin' deal. We'll all see God tonight. Stop the fuckin' car, Maynard!"

"Steve, I'm stopping for fifteen minutes, and we won't come looking for you. Got it?"

"Fuck you, Maynard! C'mon, Bibe."

Steve got out of the car, and Babe reluctantly followed.

"Andrew," Steve called, "you gotta come, too, man. I know you want some. Fuck those guys!"

I told D.W. and Maynard I would tag along to make sure we were all back in fifteen minutes. Steve seemed to be a little impulsive, but I was digging his energy. He was a wild and crazy guy with a very intriguing girlfriend.

Steve, Babe, and I set off on our shit expedition. I suggested we break off some small limbs from surrounding trees to use as poop probes before we got too far into the pastures—hopefully bull free.

As Steve raced ahead, I asked Babe, "Is he always like this?"

"Oh, Andrew, you have no idea. He's been talkin' about gettin' his hands on these mushrooms for *months*."

By now, Steve was forging ahead like a madman through dung heaps, some of them still steaming.

"There won't be any in new piles of shit, Steve," Babe hollered.

"Fuck you, Babe, start diggin'!"

Of course, the cow shit expedition went longer than we planned. There seemed to be an unending horizon of cow pies just over the next hill, with no shortage of next hills to conquer. I had to hand it to Steve, though. His quest for higher consciousness on these Maui hillsides knew no boundaries. He had his mind made up that we were not leaving shroomless. In fact, after an hour, we each had a shirt pocket full of tiny white caps, and Steve was beside himself. But it was yet unknown whether these little buttons were full of poison or smiling faces. Nobody, including dear Steve, was ready to start gobbling them down until we had a second opinion.

When we finally got back to the car, I was already tired, and we weren't even halfway to Hana yet. The dynamics between D.W., Babe, and Steve were wearing me down. The hormone-fueled bickering between them had me thinking about hitchhiking back.

But although Steve called out to us to "Stop the car!" whenever he saw a cow, we did eventually make it to our destination.

René had given me directions to his cottage, telling me to take a left turn onto a dirt road when I saw a sign to Waianapanapa State Park.

But when Steve saw another sign, which pointed to a "Black Sand

Beach Paradise," he yelled. "Drop us off at the beach, boys, and pick us up later!"

D.W. was pissed. "Shut the fuck up, Koepke! We don't even know where the beach is. We're not losing you out here. We're going to René's."

Once again, all manner of "fuck you's" sprang forth from the back seat, but Maynard and I just rolled our eyes and headed further into the bush along the dirt road that hopefully would take us to René's.

When I saw a man standing on the porch of a cabin at the end of the road, I recognized my good old 'coon ass brother from Palo Alto, René Comeaux. The Ragin' Cajun himself.

I wanted out of that car as fast as possible. As René was passing out beers to everyone on his porch, Steve started drilling him with questions.

"What's with the cow shit and mushrooms around Hana, René?"

"No mooshrooms, Steve," my friend said. "T'ain't none till da rain cumin, Bro. 'Bout tree munts, Bro. Only da teeny weenie now."

We showed René the tiny white caps we had picked.

"Dem only makes you'all sick, not hiiiigh, Bebe."

With that, Babe and I handed over all our caps to Steve, and he shut the fuck up about cows for the rest of the day. "I'll be back in the rainy season, man" was his final comment on the topic.

Birds were squawking and singing nearby, creating a pleasant atmosphere to relax in after the crazy road trip. As we sat around eating René's *pupus* on paper plates, he told us he was expecting a visitor. Sure enough, within five minutes, one arrived. Standing about my height, but carrying an additional 150 pounds, a "local boy" showed up on what had to be the hardest working Honda 50 I'd ever seen. It was apparent that René, after only a year on this island outpost, had made friends with the natives.

The big Muke was not much interested in us, but we sure as hell were impressed by him.

Big Muke and René excused themselves and headed over to the Honda, which had little saddlebags draped over the back fender. I watched as the big fellow handed René a brown paper bag. My friend looked like a flea talking to an elephant as the two of them spoke indecipherable pigeon, slapped each other's backs, and planned to go lobster diving that afternoon (I could make out that much). Then off the big Muke went on his Honda, with the little engine spewing out smoke from the tiny exhaust pipe, straining to get up to speed—without much success.

The aroma preceded René—a pungent sativa cloud drifting in on the breeze. That brought a smile to everyone's face, including the usually stoical Maynard. The bag held enough for everyone back at the hotel to have a little baggy full and enjoy the local flavor. Because of the smell, and the fear of it reeking up the car, René sealed the bag in an old tee shirt, then wrapped that in a towel, and put two huge rubber bands around the bundle. We eventually put it in the trunk for the ride back to the hotel.

But first, it was off to the famous black volcanic sand beach, just a short distance from René's house. All of us, including René, piled into the rental car and drove the half mile to the coast. Sinking our toes into the warm black sand, totally high from the bud, was an amazing feeling. We all wandered off more or less toward the water, which was way too rough to swim in, and took in the beauty of Maui, a wild and unsettled place. But alas, we needed to keep the show on the road, so after half an hour, I rounded everyone up, we drove back to the cottage, dropped off René, and headed to the Seven Sacred Pools for a brief dip. On the way, we drove through "downtown Hana," blinked, and were back in the countryside.

The pools were beautiful, but packed with people.

How in the hell did all these tourists get out here?

Apparently, in rental cars.

"We have to be on the road in no more than one hour," Maynard told us as we walked from the car to the pools, about a quarter-mile away.

"Fuckin' aye, Maynard," said an obviously bummed Koepke. "Shit, man, I ain't leavin' till me and Bibe been swimmin' in ever one of them fuckin' pools."

"Well, Steve," Maynard said, "then you and Babe better have taxi money, 'cause I'm *not* gonna come look for ya."

D.W. laughed and shook his head. "Did ya hear that, Kopeck? Maynard gave you an ul-tee-*may*-dum. I'd love to have the back seat all to myself, so why don't you and Babe relax and take a nap in one of them pools?" He burst out laughing.

Babe pulled a little camera out of her purse and took a few shots of us posing by the ponds. Then we all changed into the swimsuits we had brought with us and splashed around in several of the ponds.

After forty-five minutes, Maynard showed up, found each of us in a different pond, and said, "The car's leaving for the hotel in fifteen minutes, whether you're in it or not."

We were all in it.

On the drive back, there was no mention of cow shit. The back seat was mostly quiet.

As we zigged and zagged our way through the twisters, I asked Maynard about the upcoming show in Honolulu. He told me the guest artists would be The Charlie Daniels Band, Bonnie Raitt, Pure Prairie League, and, of course, Willie.

"That's a great line-up, no shit. Bonnie Raitt..., really? Where are all those folks staying right now?"

"Probably still recovering from the party in Honolulu a few nights ago," said D.W. from the back seat. "Bonnie was table dancing!"

Sorry I missed that one!

"Andrew," D.W. continued, "Willie invites all his friends to play at his picnics in Texas, and this was no different. I've been along for the ride since the beginning, and the guy just has a charm about him that makes his contemporaries adore him and wanna be around him."

Getting Acquainted

The next morning I slept in, finally getting up about 11:00 A.M. The phone light was blinking, telling me that I had some messages. When I pressed the button, I listened to a recording from Chris Etheridge, asking to meet me for breakfast. I called his room, but he wasn't in. There was also a message from Maynard, asking me to call him. When I did, we arranged to meet for breakfast in half an hour, down at the patio dining room.

Just as I was about to step in the shower, there was a knock at my door. When I opened it, Poodie walked in without waiting to be asked.

"Got that horticultural artwork from Hana, big boy?"

As I handed him the bundle, he gave me a brand new white tee shirt with blue piping that had Willie's picture on it over the words *Willie Nelson and Family.*

"This is from Willie, big boy. Thanks for helpin' out."

When I got down to the patio in my new tee shirt, everyone was sitting at two long tables, having breakfast. Chris had saved a seat for me, and waved me over.

As I sat down, he said, "Where the hell'd ya get that cool tee shirt, Andrew? I've only seen it on Willie and a few other folks."

I could tell that some of the guys were mumbling about this.

Politics. Better be careful here.

"Poodie gave it to me a little while ago."

Chris and the others let it go at that.

There were many new faces at the tables that morning, and a lot of them were checking me out, both because of the tee shirt and the fact that I towered over everyone else. Besides that, the tropical humidity had turned my hair into a giant Brillo pad. I must have been a sight.

After breakfast, Maynard drifted over from the other table, where he had been sitting, and introduced me to some of the folks I'd just broken bread with. One of them was the second drummer in the band, Rex Ludwig, and his wife, Cricket. When she mentioned that she was from San Jose, we immediately became allies. She told me that some of the group would be on the beach in an hour or so if I wanted to join them.

After Cricket left with Rex, a tall thin guy came up to me and whispered in my ear, "You earned that tee shirt, man. Pleased to meet ya. I'm Snake, Willie's personal assistant."

I've never met a snake before…, but, yes, I can see the resemblance.

I stood up and gave him a firm handshake. "Pleasure, Snake, I'm sure."

"Two things arrived in Willie's room at the same time this mornin'," Snake said. "An old tee shirt from Hana, and a bunch o' new ones for the band from Scooter Franks, who just arrived from Austin with his wife. Willie just swapped you a new one for the old one."

He gave me a wink and walked away smiling.

Maynard said, "Snake's the key man around here…, an ex-Marine, who helps out with Willie's security."

Snake just told me he's Willie's assistant, but he's really the chief of security?

"Seems like a nice guy," I said.

"Oh, he is. But don't forget, his name *is* Snake."

Maynard and I decided that the beach sounded like a good idea, so we agreed to meet at the lobby bar for a drink after changing into our suits.

The bar wasn't far from the check-in counter, so a lot of new arrivals from the family drifted in. One of them was a husky guy in a cowboy hat and boots, who immediately recognized Maynard and sat down next to us.

"What's up, Mister Lutts? God, I need a beer! Maynard, you look absolutely ridiculous! Where's your clothes, man? Bartender, a Budweiser, please…, and one each for my two friends here…, or whatever else they want."

"Michael Jean Schroeder," Maynard said, "this here's Andrew…, Andrew Bernstein, my old friend from California."

The cowboy put out his hand, which was half a ham shank in size.

"Heard some stories 'bout you, Andrew. Are they all true?"

"Maynard don't lie much," I said.

"Unless he's had too much to drink," Schroeder shot back. "Which ain't often."

This brought a smile and a chuckle from Maynard.

I soon learned that Schroeder was the guitar tech—although he was responsible for keeping *all* the instruments in tune.

"I barely got my ass out of Dallas yesterday," he said. "They had to hold the plane for me."

"Yohhhh, Schroeder!!!" a voice boomed from across the lobby.

Pushing his way through the hotel guests as if he were the President of Maui, Poodie rushed up to the bar and threw an arm around Schroeder's shoulder. Then, looking over at the bartender, he shouted, "Hey! Four shots of tequila here! Cuervo Gold!"

After the beer and the shot, Maynard whispered in my ear, "Let's get the fuck outta here."

When we got down to the sand, there was a Hawaiian boy at a kiosk handing out towels to the guests.

The entourage of pale-skinned folks from the Lone Star State wasn't hard to find. We could hear them before we saw them. When Cricket spotted me, she motioned for us to join her and a couple of other ladies. All the chairs were taken, so Maynard and I sat down on our towels.

Cricket introduced me to the gals, who turned out to be the wives of Scooter and Bo Franks, the tee shirt barons.

"That shirt looks like it was *meant* for you," one of the ladies said.

"Would you like a drink, sir?" a voice said.

I looked around and saw a lovely Hawaiian girl, dressed in white, just like the towel boy, with a tray of drinks in her hands for the ladies.

Maynard ordered a Coca-Cola, and I ordered a Mai Tai.

"Make his a double," Cricket said, pointing to me, "and put it on my bill."

With beer, tequila, and rum floating around in my blood, I was soon swapping tales with my new friends—while Maynard slept. I probably heard damning stories about everybody in the band, but it was all in good fun. I have no memory of any of it now, since the sun and booze boiled it out of me. I just remember laughing so hard that I actually cried a few times.

When I saw that Maynard was starting to turn hot pink, I woke him up.

"Time to get off the sand, buddy," I said, "before we get deep-fried."

As I walked into my room, the phone rang.

"Yo, Andrew!"

It was Steve.

"You *are* goin' to the show tomorrah, ain't ya?"

"Hell, yeah. I'll even be on your flight."

"Fuckin' cool!"

The next day, a Saturday, I was up early to make reservations at a hotel in Honolulu for that night, planning to fly home on Sunday. I had been thinking about my new friends, and the world they inhabited. It was a glimpse, nothing more, into a lifestyle that had a very strong pull on me. I was also aware that I was an invited guest and needed to play it very cool. Keep my trap shut and smile a lot.

While I was packing up, Chris called.

"Y'all comin' to the show today, Andrew?"

"I'm packing up right now, Chris. Do you have the name of the hotel in Honolulu where you'll be staying? Steve was supposed to give it to me, but I guess he forgot."

"The Sheraton Waikiki, man. Ya can bunk with me if you need ta. We can get a cot in there if there's not two beds. Also, I'll get ya a backstage pass from Poodie."

"Cool, Chris. Thanks. I'll ring your room when I get there."

"I want ya to meet Marty Grebb, Bonnie Raitt's sax player…, great guy and an old friend o' mine. He's from Boston. You guys will really get along. He'll love your stories."

"Can't wait. Thanks for everything."

I called Maynard to see what he was up to. Like me, he was packing. We agreed to have a quick breakfast before heading out, he in the band shuttle bus, and me in a cab.

When I got down to the lobby restaurant, Maynard was already there.

"Being on Maui a few days," I said, "has reminded me of why I left Hawaii six years ago…, island fever."

" I know what you mean, man. It's back to the interstates for me. My home is the road."

It's your reality and my dream, brother

"There's high hopes, Andy," Maynard said, "that this new album, *Stardust*, is gonna really launch Willie's career. He's been so good to me. God, I hope he's right about this one. The guy deserves it. He works so hard, but he's just missed the big time by inches. Been overlooked by the labels and mishandled by more than a few promoters and managers."

"Well, if the rest of the album's as good as 'Georgia,' he's got nothin' to worry about."

Just then, Poodie appeared at our table.

"Andrew," he said, "here's your backstage pass. Stick it on your pants and don't let anything happen to it. Security will be tight as hell."

"Thanks, Poodie, I'll guard it with my life. If Chris asks you for—"

"Chris already called me. So, have fun. See you in Honolulu, big boy!"

"I think you've made a good impression with the top Texans, Andy," Maynard said with a trace of sarcasm. "They're not usually so accommodating to a Yankee outsider. But I guess you and René saved our collective asses."

"Really?"

Your timing couldn't have been better."

"My timing? Hell, you called *me*, remember? I had no fucking idea you were even here."

"Go with it, partner. These guys know how to have a good time, and you're included."

I made my way to the airport and flew out with the gang. I was already seated and reading a newspaper when Steve and Babe boarded, looking like they just rolled out of bed, hands full of carry-on luggage and bags of potato chips and pretzels. They didn't seem to have too much patience with each other, so I held my paper in front of my face as they approached. I didn't want to have to pick sides in the "family feud" of the morning.

It was a short flight, maybe an hour, and soon I was in a cab headed to my hotel. Since I already had my backstage pass, I thought I'd enjoy some time to myself and head over to the stadium in a couple of hours. By now, it was only 9:30 in the morning.

I checked in with Lisa, who told me that a house had become available in Loma Mar, near Pescadero, by the coast. She sounded very excited.

"It's at the top of Dearborn Park Road," she said. "I haven't seen it yet, but it sounds like it's big enough for the kids to run around! When will you be home?"

"Tomorrow. Man, that sounds great about the house. I can't wait to see it…, and you and the kids. Is everybody okay?"

"Your son misses you. He keeps saying, 'Dadda! Dadda! Dadda!' every time the phone rings."

"Well, tell him I'll be there tomorrow night. I'll call you as soon as I get to the airport. I've got a lot of stories from this trip. What a cast of characters!"

Under the Banyan

I stepped out of the cab at Aloha Stadium around noon. The gates were open, and people were heading in with their tickets in hand. Taped music was blasting over the public address system. After all the music I had heard and produced in my life, I could feel that familiar old adrenaline kicking in. Although I had absolutely nothing to do with this production, and was only here on a whim, I set forth like a man on a mission to hear my new friends play music.

I circled the stadium on foot, looking for an entrance that would honor my pass. The ticket takers kept telling me I had to find the artists' entrance, but they didn't know where it was. After forty minutes of this nonsense, I saw some small trucks going back and forth, and figured I had found the backstage area. This time, when I showed my pass and said, with all the authority I could muster, "I'm with the band!" no one stopped me, and I walked right past two cops.

It was a beautiful day in a gorgeous setting. Puffy white clouds drifted across the bluest sky imaginable. Trees lined the backstage area. One in particular was the biggest banyan I had ever seen in my life. Its monstrous canopy provided shade to a large part of the stage beneath.

As I wandered around, I spotted Chris in the distance. He took me to the dressing room area, where the rest of the gang was mingling with musicians from the other three bands.

Willie saw me and greeted me with a handshake. Craning his neck to look up at me, he said with a smile, "How ya doin', you tall drink o' water?"

"Just fine, Willie. Thanks so much for your hospitality on Maui. I had a great time getting to meet your family."

Taking a vial out of his pocket and popping the cork, he said, "Put out your index finger, Andrew."

When I did, he poured out a heaping dose of brown powder on my fingertip.

"Don't spill any o' that," he said. "And I suggest you chase it down with a beer. It don't taste very good." At that, he let out a hardy laugh. "We gonna see ya in Tahoe next month? Isn't that your neck o' the woods?"

"You bet, Willie, I wouldn't miss it."

Tahoe? Nobody said anything about Tahoe.

As usual, Willie had a gang of people wanting a piece of him. As he turned to talk to one, I felt a tap on my shoulder. It was Steve and Babe, both with eyes the size of Eskimo pies!

"Willie's mescaline, man!" Steve said. "He's targeted everybody backstage."

"I guess we're all gonna be stoned to the bone today," I said.

"That's the way Willie likes it."

Babe laughed. "I like you, Andrew," she said with a big smile.

"I'm gonna check out the stage," I said. "Poodie gave me an all-access pass."

"I'm goin' with Andrew," Babe said.

"Hell y'are!" Steve growled. "I gotta go to work in an hour. Stick aroun', Bibe."

I took off, heading for the stage. When I climbed up the stairs under the huge banyan tree, I was blown away by how much equipment was up there.

This place is chock full o' gear! Check out the logistics, big boy! This ain't the Stanford Music Hall.

The names of each of the four bands were stenciled in white on the rolling equipment cases—perhaps a hundred of them, stacked four-deep to the back of the stage. It was clear that as each band completed its set, the stagehands would come up and move everything out for the next band.

Three semis, which were parked just outside the gates, had obviously brought all this stuff from the airport. This operation had to have been expensive and a logistical nightmare. That's probably why this was the first and *last* of Willie's "annual" Aloha Picnics.

Pure Prairie League would be opening the show, so their stage manager was giving orders to the stagehands and the sound techs to check lines and monitor volumes. Through all this, I did my best to stay out of everybody's way.

By the time I walked back down the stairs to get some water, thirty minutes later, I was feeling like a rainbow, my skin was tingling, and I was smiling ear to ear.

Thanks, Willie! Enlightenment is now mine for the taking.

I wandered out into the audience, and for the next hour, before the music started, I was an amateur anthropologist, studying the enormous ethnic variety of the people—especially the female kind.

Promptly at 2:00 P.M., Pure Prairie League kicked into one of their up-tempo country rock tunes, and the party was on. I was thoroughly enjoying their harmonies and acoustic guitar work, but it soon got too hot for me in the sun on the football field, so I headed to the backstage area and found a shady spot onstage under the banyan tree.

When the League broke into "Amy," their big hit from the year before, the crowd started singing along. I was slapping my thighs to the beat when I saw Willie coming up the stairs with Snake. Since Willie didn't want to be seen yet, he walked behind the speakers and equipment cases to a spot at center stage where the guitar stands were. Then he strapped on his guitar and walked out front while the band was still singing "Amy." When the crowd went wild, the band didn't know at first what was happening. Then Willie walked up to one of the microphones and joined the band for the last verse and chorus.

This was the first time I ever saw Willie perform. The man could play! He picked out leads and strummed softly while adding vocals in a unique style.

While Willie was playing with the League, Snake walked over to me and said, "Willie's fixin' to sign these guys to his new label, Lone Star Records."

"No shit! I had no idea Willie had a label."

"He's takin' a stab at it. Willie's that way. *Can't do it* ain't in his vocabulary. He's a real music outlaw, not a manufactured one."

"I'm beginning to understand that."

After another number or two, Willie put his guitar back on the stand and left the stage for the League to do their encore numbers. As he and Snake walked past me, I noticed they were both pretty smiley—even glazed. At the end of the set, the first change got under way. I stood there fascinated, watching the whole shift take place. Charlie Daniels' gear was moved up as the League's went off in the opposite direction, then down a ramp, and onto a semi that had pulled up a few minutes before.

I decided to look around for some food, but before I got too far, I ran into D.W.

"Andrew, you comin' to Tahoe in a couple o' weeks to hang?"

Been invited twice now.

"I've coming, D.W. Thanks for asking. I'll be there with bells on."

"Fuck the bells! Bring some good Humboldt if you run across any..., something along the lines of what René gave us a few days ago."

"I'll keep that in mind."

"I told my old lady that I met one of Maynard's friends from California in the music business. She'll be at Tahoe and wants to meet ya. She lived in L.A. for a spell, doin' record promotions. Ya'll may know some of the same people, she figures."

"What's her name?"

"Pamela..., Pamela Brown," D.W. said.

"Don't know her, but I'm lookin' forward to meetin' her.... Do you know where I can get any food around here? I thought this was a picnic."

"You got here too late for lunch this morning, Andrew. We had a big catered barbeque with Hawaiian pork and all the trimmings. Now you'll have to find something out front at one of the stands."

Too much hassle. I'll just get some water.

I had seen some coolers backstage, so I headed toward those. Poodie and Chris were already there, taking out bottles.

"Hey, Andrew," Poodie said. "A stagehand gave me a joint. Let's head over to one of the bathrooms to smoke it."

As the three of us headed for the backstage men's room, we saw a cute redhead in the distance.

"Hey, Bonnie!" Chris called. "Come on over." Then to me, he said, "She's an old friend of mine. I've known her for years."

As the redhead came closer, I realized it was Bonnie Raitt.

"We've got a big fat local one here, Bonnie," Chris said. "Wanna join us?"

Her face lit up. "My pleasure, boys!"

The four of us walked into the men's room without Bonnie batting an eyelash. We crammed into one stall, Poodie lit up the joint, and we passed it around the toilet bowl.

The pot was excellent, so by the time we tried to get out of the stall, we all tripped over each other, and the scene dissolved into pure slapstick as we got stuck in the tight space.

Poodie decided that the moment was right for him to direct traffic.

Wanting to be a gentleman and let Bonnie out first, he said, "Move the fuck out of the way and let Bonnie through."

The problem was that the door swung in, so there wasn't enough room for us to open it.

Finally, we were able to squeeze Chris out, since he was the skinniest. That eased the pressure, and the rest of us were able to escape.

Bonnie was howling with laughter as she made her way back to her dressing room.

"Thanks for the smoke, Poodie," I said. "I'm gonna catch Charlie's set. See y'all later."

I was starting to pick up some of the Texas twang.

Back under the banyan, I enjoyed Charlie's homegrown blend of southern-flavored, shit-kickin', fiddle-fueled country rock. Charlie was hot back then, and shredding his fiddle bow, he got the crowd fired up from the get-go. I dare say, I couldn't have enjoyed Mr. Daniels and company more.

Eventually, Willie came on for a few tunes, giving me an opportunity to learn more about his range on the guitar, which this time was a jazzy take on normally boring country licks.

After that set, I simply couldn't wait to hear Bonnie and more Willie.

In the meantime, I wandered down to the truck to watch it being loaded. The load-in/load-out roadie for Charlie's band was instructing the stagehands about which case numbers to bring first, since the fit had to be tight.

Same damned thing as loading furniture!

After my close inspection of the logistical techniques, I came across Steve and Babe sitting backstage with Maynard and D.W.

"Well," I said, pulling out one of the Hana joints I had rolled that morning, "here we all are together again. Let's celebrate!"

"Fuck, Andrew!" Steve bellowed, looking at Babe, D.W., and Maynard. "I don' wanna share it with all *them*, man."

"Tough shit, Steve!" I shot back. "It's all or none.... Now, I don't wanna miss any of Bonnie, so let's just duck behind that wall and *burn* the fuckin' thing."

That's exactly what we did, and then I retired to the banyan tree to dig Bonnie Raitt from spitting distance. As she came up the stairs with her band, she poked me in the ribs with a *big* smile. I was in fine form to enjoy her set.

In 1977, Bonnie was well into her stride, just prior to her big Grammy year—red hot in every way. It was like the time I had watched Boz Skaggs at the Fillmore with nobody else in the house. She expressed each song with the sincerity and dexterity that just seems to exude from someplace deep inside her. Her genius was a perfectly natural expression of the blues from the greats of a bygone era. She alone, in my opinion, creates a mood with her blues that brings the message, stripped of flashy extras.

Bonnie swayed gently with the music while she sang and played.

The crowd simply couldn't get enough of her on that perfect afternoon, and neither could I. Her sax player, Chris's friend, whom I had yet to meet, played scorching leads, a real asset to the overall quality of her music.

At the end of the set, as the sax player walked by me to head down the stairs, I called out, "Great set, man, really dug your horn."

"Thanks, man. What a great day!"

Robert Altman Archives
Kris Kristofferson at the Monterey Pop Festival, 1970

Finally, Willie's roadies, including Steve and D.W., all appeared on stage at the same time. Everyone else's gear was almost removed, and the big stage would be Willie's to wander very soon. During the setup, Waylon and Willie's recorded music blared out of the PA system, broadcast by the sound guys in the mixing booth out in the crowd.

Once everything was ready, in the late afternoon, the band came up the stairs and headed for the center of the stage. As they passed by, Chris whispered something in my ear about seeing purple dragons, but said it would be okay, and smiled.

Willie opened with "Whiskey River." The "take my mind" verse seemed so fitting at the moment. Then he did a medley of songs by other artists, including "Me and Bobby McGee" by Kris Kristofferson, making them all his own. From ballads to spirituals, he just rolled. Mickey, the tall skinny harmonica player, wove the background rhythms and textures effortlessly into each tune.

At some point in the middle of the set, Willie said, "Got a few new ones for ya'. They'll be on my new album, *Stardust*, comin' out in a few weeks."

The songs I heard in the hotel room!

I stood awestruck as he opened the mini-set with "Georgia on My Mind." I was truly transfixed by every word and note in that song. Chris Etheridge could see me smiling and grinned back. Mickey stepped up to play his lead and just nailed it shut. I could feel the adrenaline rushing through me.

Willie also played "Blue Skies" and "Stardust" before moving on to his next mini-set, which featured songs from *Redheaded Stranger*. He opened with "Blue Eyes Crying in the Rain," a tearjerker of a love song. I wasn't familiar with the other songs from that album, but they all told a story of love, sadness, and a cowboy's code of conduct. I was touched by those songs, and promised myself I would learn more about the album when I got home.

Toward the end of this set, all the guests showed up on stage to join in for a few final numbers. Bonnie, Charlie, and the members of all three bands came onstage to do "City of New Orleans," and finished up the night with a rousing rendition of "Amazing Grace." By the time it was over, I was knocked out.

I was especially impressed by Willie's energy and professional presence. His vocal phrasing and guitar playing were his obvious trademarks. Maynard had landed himself a job with a future.

Steve Koepke Archives

Bonnie and Willie (Slim's in the tank top at the left)

I had an early flight the next morning, so I said my goodbyes on the run. Naturally, Steve insisted that I stay.

"Damn, Andrew, stick around a while! We'll be roarin' back at the hotel, man. Just gotta load this damned truck, and we're done."

Babe rolled her eyes at the mere mention of roaring. I was with her.

"See ya in Tahoe, buddy."

Although I hadn't seen much of Poodie that day, I made it a point to find him before I left. He wasn't hard to find. You could usually hear him long before you saw him.

"Yohhh, Andrew! What's shakin'? Comin' back to the hotel to party? I know the bartender. He promised free shots of tequila for me and all my friends."

"Love to, Poodie, but I've got an early plane in the morning."

"Who doesn't?"

"Yeah, Poodie, but they won't carry *me* on. I've gotta get there on my own. But thanks for the tee shirt, the pass, and all your generosity. I appreciated the opportunity to hang out here the last couple o' days. And don't forget to express my gratitude to Willie."

"You're comin' to Tahoe, ain't ya, Andrew?"

"Any chance I can get to hang out with y'all, I'm takin' it!"

While I was flying home, I kept replaying the last few days in my mind. It felt like reading a really good book that I couldn't put down. As I thought of some of the scenes, I had to laugh—especially when I remembered Koepke out on the side of the mountain, searching for cow shit with the poop probe. Now that I look back on it, I was already formatting the first draft of this book.

At the same time, I focused on how I might push the transportation bar a few notches higher. For the immediate future, sand trucks were my ticket to paying the bills, plus I still had some bucks in my bank account from the producing days. But watching the logistics at the stadium in Hawaii, getting an insider's look at how all the gear of four bands was choreographed to be *where* it was needed, *when* it was needed, had made a big impression on me.

I could do that.

Before I landed in San Francisco, I had made the decision to go down both trails simultaneously. I would put in the hours and work hard with the trucks, and I would also find the time to chase those gypsies down the highway.

I was glad that I had fit in so effortlessly with my new friends. This was a great big dream come true. The fun and the opportunities were just too good to pass up.

By 3:00 P.M. on that perfect spring day, I was back on the La Honda mountaintop. When I pulled up in front of the house, Ode, who was two years old by now, ran out onto the deck, with Lisa right behind him, carrying one-month-old Autumn.

"Dadda! Dadda!" Ode called out. I scooped him up in my arms, tickled his fat little belly, and hugged him as hard as I could. He was so adorable, with his long blond hair, chubby cheeks, and big blue eyes.

"Oh, God, Andrew!" Lisa said as soon as she set eyes on me. "What a great tee shirt!"

She never looked prettier, and our little baby girl was perfect.

"How's Maynard?" Lisa asked. "How in the world does he fit in with a bunch of Texans?"

"Carefully, with some apprehension," I said, laughing.

"He must be a fish out of water. C'mon…, *Maynard?!* A vegetarian, with barbeque at every stop?"

"He's doing his thing, driving his dream…. Anyway, I made some pretty good friends over there, Lisa."

I gave her a thumbnail sketch of the group, especially a few colorful individuals, and the overall great vibe that Willie creates with his music and his personality.

"I'm going to Tahoe in a couple of weeks," I said. "The tour behind the new album, *Stardust*, is kicking off at Harrah's Tahoe."

"From the look in your eyes, I can see that you want to further your bus driving career and party across the country at the same time."

She knows me too well.

"Truth is, Lisa, I'm interested in learning more about the potential opportunities with Willie, and the training program seems to already be under way. In fact, from what I can see, I'm probably overqualified for most of the positions. I certainly have more experience in actually producing and coordinating concerts than any of that bunch. I'm not interested in being a professional hanger-on, but Willie's a special man, and I'm gonna take a second look, since he personally invited me to the Tahoe gig."

Lisa smiled. I knew she could tell there was no way she was going to talk me out of this.

"My Little Corner of Heaven"

"Andrew," Lisa said to me the next morning, "That house in Loma Mar is ours if we want it. I guess we should have a look."

"How can it be ours if we've never met the owner or even seen the place?"

"Apparently, the owner is…, well, one of *us*."

"Why didn't you say so in the first place?"

"Anyway, it sounds like a great house. I've got the owner's name and number…, Bob Daniels. He lives on the mountain where the house is. Let's call him!"

I got up, showered, and called Bob.

After we talked a while, he said, "Come up now, man. Love to have ya as a neighbor. I think you'll fit right in."

"Great, Lisa and I and the kids will drive up this afternoon."

As I hung up the phone and walked to the glass doors that looked out over the expanse of sky and mountains as far as the eye could see, I knew I would miss the awesome northern view across the valley and the western view to the coast.

"I'll never forget this view, baby."

"Me, either."

The ride up to the top of the one-lane Deerborn Park Road was death-defying in its vertical climb and wealth of potholes.

"This is all gonna be mud in the winter, Lisa."

"We'll figure something out. We always do."

After climbing a quarter of a mile, rising three or four hundred feet, we saw the house. It was nestled up against a heavily wooded hillside, under a thick canopy of second-generation redwoods.

Lisa and I took one look at those trees, and said to each other, "Banana slugs!"

When we met Bob and told him our concern, he laughed. "The foundation is off the ground," he said. "Slugs need an earthen entrance, and this house is sealed from the dirt and moisture."

It was a nice old place, all redwood, with a section of the wall in the living room that rotated horizontally, opening into a hidden space where they used to hide booze during Prohibition. This had been a party house.

The place also had plenty of room for the kids and a small backyard for them to play in. Scattered around the mountaintop, there were seven or eight summer homes, which Bob also owned. He was building a house for himself next-door to us. Lisa ended up designing and making a stained glass window for his front door.

After I gave Bob a cash deposit, we drove down to Redwood City to buy Lisa a car. Because of the dirt road up the mountain, we needed something with four-wheel drive, and the only car that had that in those days was a Jeep, so we bought a brand-new Cherokee. I still had the old firetruck for myself, which could easily climb the mountain, plus my VW station wagon, which could make it on most days—if it weren't raining.

In the days leading up to my taking off for Tahoe, I became aware of a process going on in my mind. I couldn't really put my finger on it. It wasn't daydreaming exactly; more a kind of actualizing. In fact, I was visualizing how I wanted things to go on this new adventure, one step at a time.

No rush here. Enjoy the ride and use what's offered up to consider the next move.

With a lot of hours in the sand truck each day, I had a game plan pretty well sketched out by the time I was ready to hit the road to Tahoe. It came down to a simple mantra: "Use Common Sense and Don't Make Waves."

I planned to leave on Friday morning to get up to Tahoe well before the first show that evening. The night before that, just after I got home from work around 8:30, the phone rang.

"Hey, Andrew, it's Darryl Wayne. How the hell are ya?" D.W. was very polite when he wasn't giving Koepke a ration of shit. "Hope to see you this weekend, man. And could you maybe bring just a little up with you, please, if it's not too much trouble?"

Not wanting to be seen as the go-to guy, I said, "I don't know, man. Let me think about it."

"Okay, I understand. By the way, Pamela's flying in from Dallas. She can't wait to meet ya."

"Your old lady?"

"That's the one."

Harrah's Tahoe was one of the newer hotel casinos on the Nevada side of the lake. I reserved a room at an economy hotel down the street. I was not on a superstar budget, so $49.99 a night beat the hell out of $200 plus.

On Friday morning, I made a last-minute decision to pick up an ounce of Humboldt from my old friend Dickey Lee Jackson—not a big deal, just something to share. Dickey could always be counted on, even at the last minute.

As I left La Honda, I gave Lisa and the kids a hug and climbed into my VW.

"Say hi to Maynard," Lisa said. "Have fun, but be careful. Don't get carried away..., we need you."

"Don't worry, I'll see you Monday night. I told the boss I'd be back on the sand rig Tuesday morning."

It was a perfect spring day as I headed over the Bay Bridge toward Berkeley. The view was gorgeous, with the bay sparkling blue. I could see the Golden Gate Bridge as I looked over to the west. In no time, I had cleared Sacramento, gotten onto Highway 50, and was climbing the foothills of the Sierras, eventually cresting and dropping down into Lake Tahoe.

After checking into the Flea Bag Lodge and taking a little rest, I called Harrah's and asked for Maynard's room. He invited me over to join him for a meal, which sounded great, since I hadn't eaten anything since leaving home.

When we had done the light shows up here a few years before, we were living in Army Surplus teepees, so casinos had no appeal to me. Thus, as I walked into Harrah's, I didn't have the slightest idea what to expect. After five minutes, I was totally lost. Even finding the elevators was a challenge. People absorbed with gambling were a new and absolutely foreign experience to me. But eventually, I found my way to Maynard's floor.

When my friend opened the door, the first thing I noticed was the breathtaking view behind him. Of course, it was great to see my old buddy again, and we were soon headed down to the buffet for the first of many visits over the weekend. He had some little dated cards that were good for two meals a day for two people. But before we even made it to the restaurant, a familiar sound was once again floating across the airwaves in my direction.

"Yohhhhhhhh! Andrewww! What's up, big boy? Good to see ya! Got any good weed?"

At the sound of weed, Steve and D.W. pulled up behind Poodie to join our little circle.

"First, I've gotta eat, Poodie. I'm really starving. C'mon, join us."

Maynard seemed cool about that, although he didn't really have a choice.

As the five of us sat down at a big booth, I said to Poodie, "You're lucky. I decided at the last minute to bring a little along. But I hate driving with it."

D.W. smiled. "Thanks, man. We don't know too many people out here in California, 'cept y'all."

"It's good to have high friends in places," I said.

Everyone cracked up.

"Time to greeeze, big boy," Poodie grumbled as he stuck a fork into a bleeding piece of roast beef. "Texas rare. Just how I like it."

"C'mon, Poodie, knock it off!" said Maynard, the lifelong vegetarian.

Poodie ignored this, but I could hear Maynard thinking, *Fucking meat-eating heathen!*

I myself was thinking, *These two are polar opposites.*

As we walked through the casino with full stomachs, Poodie bellowed to Chris Etheridge, "Hey, Easter! We're gonna burn one in five-sixty-two..., Maynard's room!"

As we approached 562, Michael Jean showed up with a short grey-haired guy I'd never seen before.

"Andrew," Poodie said, "this is Bowman. He travels with us. Funny little fucker."

"Pleased to meet ya, Andrew. Poodie's an asshole. I'm not *that* funny. I'm a songwriter, not a comedian."

"Well, I'm a truck driver," I said. "At least for the time being.... What songs have you written?"

"'Wildwood Weed' was one of my hits. Jim Stafford sang it."

"How appropriate!" I said as I reached into my pocket for the bag.

"You can call me Cod, Andrew," Bowman said. "That's what these dickheads call me."

"Cod it is!"

What the fuck kinda name is Cod?

"What's in that bag, big boy?" Poodie asked.

"It's the shit, Poodie, La Honda cush…, fresh and seasoned to perfection. Check out them red hairs."

Poodie stuck his nose in the bag and said, "Andrew, this shit smells like two skunks in heat!"

"Shut the fuck up, Poodie," Steve chirped in, "and let Andrew roll one."

I was glad to see that nothing had changed in the three weeks since I'd last seen them. As the first joint was going around, Steve asked if he could roll the second one. He really just wanted to get his fingers dirty on the fresh resinous bodacious buds. I couldn't blame him.

Suddenly, there was a knock on the door and voices. It was obvious that a few others had been advised of what was going down in 562—or else could smell it through the walls.

Maynard picked up the towel he had placed at the bottom of the door, opened the chain, and in walked Willie's old friend Cooper. Next to him, there was a beautiful woman with long brown hair and bangs.

"Hey, guys," she said with a lovely smile, as she stepped into the room. "How ya'll doin'?" She had a sultry voice.

As Maynard replaced the towel, and Cooper sat down in a chair, the beauty walked over and kissed D.W. on the cheek.

"Pamela," D.W. said, "that's Andrew sittin' over there. He's the one from San Francisco."

She walked over to me and gave me a firm handshake. Her great big brown eyes were wide open, and her smile gave a hint of a beautiful soul inside.

"Pleased to meet ya, Andrew. I'm Pamela Brown."

"Where's that fuckin' joint?!" Koepke blurted out. "Sheeit! I already got the next one ready to burn."

"Nice to meet you, Pamela," I said, ignoring Koepke.

"I *love* San Francisco," Pamela said. "I've got so many friends there."

"I might know a few of 'em, Pamela. You never can tell."

"We'll have to hang out and talk when we get a chance."

"Anytime, Pamela," I said as the joint came my way.

Just then, Cooper whispered something to Poodie, who came over to me and asked softly, "Andrew, think Cooper could take a little o' this for the other rooms?"

"Of course. That's why I brought it."

I filled up a few empty cigarette wrappers with buds, and gave them to Cooper.

"I've got some more if you need it," I said. "Just let me know."

"Thanks, Andrew. I do security. Lemme know if *you* need anything."

And he was gone.

Snake and Cooper BOTH *do security?*

Eventually, it came time for the crew members to do a line check onstage.

As I got up to leave with the others, Poodie said, "Hey, big boy, where you stayin'?"

"A shit hole down the street."

"Fuck that! We got a few extras. And if we don't, we will. Give me that fuckin' phone, Maynard! I'm callin' Snake."

I'm gonna have a view of my own!

"Whaddaya mean, rooms are limited?" Poodie snarled into the phone. "Snake, we're talkin' 'bout Andrew here. He's an invited guest...." He winked at me. "That's better.... The last name's Bernstein." He threw me a big grin. "You're stayin' here, Andrew. Git your shit from down the street and check in."

"Poodie, I can't take this from you. Are you sure?"

"Don't argue with me, Slim. Go get your shit. See you at the early show. I've got two backstage passes for ya. Don't forgit to remind me..., call my room."

I left some weed on the table.

"Thanks, Poodie," I said as I closed the door behind me with my baggie a third gone.

The 7:00 P.M. cocktail show would be Willie's first appearance ever at Harrah's. Then at 11:00 there would be the dinner show. The next five nights would kick off the tour for the *Stardust* album. This may have been

just another gig for the guys, but for me it was like being on top of the mountain. Hell, I was barely able to keep my composure. But I did keep it, and would soon be acting like I was just another one of 'em—the tall one.

California Slim, if you please!

I checked out of the fleabag and into a clean lake-view room on the twelfth floor.

It's pretty early in the game, I thought as I sat in a comfortable chair overlooking the water. *But these Texans sure are nice to their guests. I have no idea how to carry on…. Use mom's common sense and don't make waves.*

I took a short nap, showered, and waited for the phone to ring—which it did at precisely 5:30.

"Andrew, it's D.W. What's shakin'?"

"Hey, man, just enjoying the view and thinkin' 'bout burnin' one."

"Cool! Some of us are gonna have dinner in one of the restaurants. Why don't you join us? We can reminisce about Hana." He laughed.

I could hear Pamela laughing in the background.

"The gear's all set up," D.W. said, "so we don't have to be onstage till six-forty-five…. Gonna all meet up at the Sierra Room in fifteen minutes. It's on the top floor, I think. Check the brochure in your room. We'll see you there in fifteen."

"Ten-four, man!"

I called Lisa to let her know what was going on.

"How cool it must be," she said, "to have a room with a view of the lake. Are you excited about seeing Willie tonight?"

"I sure am…. How are the kids?"

"They both miss you…. Andrew, we should be ready to move by next weekend. I'm gonna pack like crazy the next few days. I have a sitter who can watch the kids. I can't wait to move."

"Listen, babe, I'm about to have dinner with some of the guys. I'll call you back a little later."

At the entrance to the restaurant, Pamela Brown, D.W., Poodie, and Steve were waiting for me, along with a good-looking short guy.

"Andrew," Poodie said, "this here's Buddy, from Dallas. We call 'im 'Budrock.' He's the lighting director for us on this tour. Works for SHOWCO. Buddy's run the lights for everyone from David Bowie to Lynyrd Skynyrd."

I bet HE'S got some stories.

Poodie Locke Archives
International Man of Mystery, Buddy "Budrock" Prewitt

Maynard showed up a minute later while we were still waiting to be seated.

But then we learned that there were *no* seats—for us.

"Tee shirts are not proper attire for the Sierra Room," said the manager. "Sorry."

"Listen, man," Poodie said, "we're the crew for the Willie Nelson Band, and we've been told that our dress is fine by people more important than you."

"Well, they're going to have to call me," the manager said. "I can't risk losing my job."

"How 'bout we go change into our *dress* tee shirts that we keep for just this kind of occasion?" Poodie said with a straight face.

"No tee shirts."

"You'll be hearin' from your boss!"

I can't wait to see that guy's face when he has to seat us all in tee shirts.

As we all headed to the elevator, Poodie said, "I'll have that motherfucker's ass fired. We've sold this place out for the next five days, two shows a night. This is bullshit!"

That night we ate buffet. Afterward, we rendezvoused in Poodie's room to smoke a joint before the show.

"Hey, big boy, come on over here," Poodie called as the joint was going around. "The stage crew mostly wear dark colors onstage. Here's a couple o' black tee shirts…. And here's your *Stardust* pass. It's good anywhere for this tour."

The pass was blue, with the *Stardust* album cover on it and "ALL ACCESS" written across the bottom. I rushed into the bathroom to change into my new *Chrome Trailer Hitch* tee shirt with *Willie Tour '77* on the back. I didn't have a chance to look at the other one, so I left it under Poodie's bed to pick up after the show.

Once we were well glazed, we herded ourselves to the elevator and got on the service unit that went directly to the kitchen, with a few stops for waiters going down. It was a big freight elevator, so we all fit. I asked Pamela if she would like to have coffee or lunch in the morning. She said sure, we could talk later in the dressing rooms.

The door of the elevator opened into a huge subterranean kitchen with dozens of chefs cooking and waiters filling trays and running drinks out to the house. It was general mayhem, like a scene out of *Goodfellas*, the backstage entrance to Tuddy's bar and nightclub. But instead of mobsters, we were the couldn't-walk-straight gang, laughing and oblivious to the chaos.

After passing through three guarded doors, having to show our passes each time, we were finally *somewhere*. But I had absolutely no bearings, and wouldn't have been able to find my way out if my life depended on it.

"Andrew, follow me," Steve said. "I'll show you where the dressing rooms are."

Around a few more corners, and we came to a door with a sign on it that said "Mr. Nelson."

Steve opened the door and walked in. I didn't feel comfortable, barging into Willie's dressing room, but Steve had no problem with that.

"Hey, Andrew," he called. "C'mon in. There's some mighty fine food in here."

I walked in and saw that the room was empty, aside from Steve. It was a huge suite with leather sofas, fine artwork, crystal glassware, dramatic lighting, and bowls of food with Steve's fingers in them.

"Help yourself, Andrew!"

I don't wanna be gorging myself on food when Willie walks in.

"I'll be back, Steve," I said. "Gonna check things out."

"Yer missin' somethin' special, man. This here's some *good* shit!"

I wanna be anywhere but here!

Down the hall, I saw Michael Jean in a small dressing room, tuning guitars.

"Hey, Andrew, c'mon in. You play guitar?"

"I'm a hack, but I love to play. Do you?"

"Yeah, I got a little band back in Dallas. We jam and have fun."

"Is that Willie's Martin you're stringin'?"

"Yup. It's an ornery gut string guitar, but Willie ain't Willie without it. Name is Trigger. New strings every night. God forbid he breaks one, it's my fault more than likely. He don't like much slack in these strings, and he knows how far he can stretch 'em."

"Sounds like a pressure job, man."

"It's not just Willie. I got *all* of 'em after me if I fuck up their instrument."

Guitar tech. Not the job I'm looking for.

With Mork and Mindy on the TV and a Bud in my hand, I was quite happy to sit with Michael Jean and let the invited backstage guests mingle. There were well-dressed cowboys, record executives, and famous actors milling around.

I may be the only bottom dump driver in this crowd, but not tonight, baby, not tonight!

Everybody stopped in to say hi to Michael Jean and shoot the shit a little.

When Poodie rushed past the door, he did a double-take and backed up.

"Hey, Andrew! Follow me!"

"I'm right behind you, Poodie."

He led me to the stage—the biggest one I'd ever seen in my life. The curtain was down, so I could hear the audience, but not see them. It was surreal. After all the nights at Homer's and the Stanford Music Hall, this was overwhelming.

Poodie led me across the immense stage to a spot at stage left just behind the second tier of scrim.

"Listen, Andrew, if you just stand here, nobody will fuck with you, ya big yahoo. Then I can relax about this area. Stay behind the scrim. If any chicks jump onstage to grab Willie on this side, help ol' Shorty out. Normally, we'll be there first. But just in case. Okay, Andrew?"

That isn't really a question.

I nodded.

"Bowman opens for Willie…, then a short break, and the band comes on."

"You can count on me, Poodie."

"I know."

From the other side of the stage, Bowman went out in front of the curtain to a mike that had been set up for him next to a guitar on a stand.

"Ladies and gentlemen," came a voice over the loudspeaker system, "please welcome Mister Don Bowman!"

After the audience gave him some mild applause, Cod told some off-color and politically incorrect jokes about songwriters in Nashville, got a few laughs, picked up his guitar, and sang his hit song, "Wildwood Weed."

Steve saw me in the wings and came over. "Good place to watch the show, man. If ya see any good lookin' chicks in the audience, lemme know and I'll go talk to 'em. Set us up, man."

"Okay, Steve."

Does this guy ever NOT think about pussy?

When Bowman finished up, the band casually came onstage behind the curtain, plugged in their instruments, and waited for Willie. Easter was on my side of the stage and walked over to say hi. I didn't know the other bass player, although I had seen him around, and heard his name was Bee.

Willie soon came out of his dressing room and mingled and laughed with some friends and guests at the side of the stage. He had on a guitar strap that was red, white, and blue macramé, very cool. Trigger was on a stand on the front line. Willie walked over to it, strapped it on, turned to the musicians with a smile, and gave a thumbs up.

Right fucking in front of me, the curtain rose, and Willie launched into the first chords of "Whiskey River."

As the crowd erupted, a huge Texas flag dropped right behind the drummers, just in front of the black curtain backdrop.

Mickey was blowing his harp, just downstage left a bit from Willie, not far from me. The piano was on the other side of the stage, set back a little, with Willie's sister Bobby at the keys, pretty as a picture, playing her heart out. I hadn't met the guitar player yet, a handsome well-dressed singer and picker named Jody Payne. He sang harmonies with Willie and played rhythm guitar. I was taking mental notes and feeling my oats.

The area where I was standing seemed to be off-limits to guests, who were all on the other side, by the dressing rooms. Poodie stopped by after "Whisky River" to check on me. He had to travel behind the flag and scrim to get there. I was happy to see him, but happier when he left. I was in my little corner of heaven.

Willie shot me a smile a few times. Even Mickey nodded when he saw me. From where I was, I could see the far third of the house and the first ten rows up close.

Directly across the stage from me, I could see a guy I didn't know, who was mixing the sound onstage so the musicians could hear themselves. He was wild-eyed, with shaggy curly hair, and looked like a mad version of Leon Trotsky. I wondered what part of Texas *he* came from, since he didn't look like anybody else in Willie's family.

I'll ask Poodie who he is.

At the beginning, Willie stayed with pretty much the same set that he had played at the picnic in Hawaii, but cut into the *Stardust* material a little sooner, opening with "Blue Skies." Although the album hadn't yet been released, who from that generation didn't know a standard like "Blue Skies"? Willie's first chord strums to this tune made a new classic of an old beauty. The audience was eating it up.

"Want some water, Andrew?" Poodie said as he handed me a small bottle.

"Thank you, Poodie…. This is amazing. Willie and the band sound *great!*"

"He's gonna be bigger than the Beatles, big boy. This album's gonna put him on the big map, the world stage."

"I don't doubt it…. Who's that guy on the monitor board over there?"

"Another SHOWCO guy, Pete Stauber. We call him 'Pee Hole Pete.' He's the nastiest man in show business." Poodie laughed. "You'll meet him…, crazy sonovabitch."

I can hardly wait.

"I gotta take a leak," I said. "I'll be right back."

"Okay, but be careful walking behind the curtain. If you trip, you'll be the star of the show."

I walked into Willie's dressing room, which was full of people I didn't know.

Why would anyone want to stand around and talk to each other, eating potato chips, when they could be out THERE?

Willie's bathroom was tastefully elegant, with a marble floor and granite counters. I had the feeling that more than one rendezvous had taken place in that shower.

When I got back to my "post," Willie was just starting "Georgia on My Mind." I really appreciated the interplay of the band, particularly Willie and Mickey, on what was now my favorite song of his. From the looks on the faces in the audience, I could see that they were enthralled. Mickey's rousing solo on the harmonica stamped this song as a hit for the ages. There was no question about it in my mind. This *Stardust* material was pure magic.

Once the first show of the evening was completed, and Willie did his usual fan appreciation stroll across the front of the stage to sign autographs, the curtain dropped and the house lights came up backstage. I watched for a minute as the house photographer snapped a few shots of Willie posing with high rollers and other VIPs.

As I drifted toward the dressing rooms, Maynard was standing just offstage.

"Hey, man," he said, "I think I was right about this album being a launching pad for Willie. The audience fucking ate it up. 'Georgia' may become his new signature song, don'tcha think?"

"You okay, Maynard? You seem a little pale."

"Well, there have been a few changes that may have an effect on my gig. Can we talk about it in private?"

"Of course. Wanna go to my room?"

"Good idea."

Fortunately, he knew the way back through the three security checkpoints and the underground kitchen, still bustling as much as ever. I just followed—left foot, right foot.

As I rolled a joint in my room, Maynard opened up:

"Willie's leased two new buses. They're already out in the parking lot. Willie's got one of 'em, and the band has the other."

Probably Eagles. I wanna see THOSE *fuckers!*

"What's wrong with that?" I said. "Sounds like fewer people on your old Tube."

"What's wrong with it is that Poodie's in charge of *my* bus now. That means I've gone from being Willie's driver to Poodie's lackey."

"Oh, shit, Maynard!"

"Shit is right. That's how he treats me. It's gonna be a challenge, I can tell you that."

"Not what you expected."

"I had a feeling there was gonna be a new bus, but I didn't think it would be *two*. You know, I'm glad you're here, Andy. I can imagine you fitting in with this bunch, and it sure as hell would make life easier having you around."

"Thanks, man. It's a little early to speculate on that. But I'm here for you anytime."

"I might be taking you up on that. Willie's gonna be *big*. Once Poodie gets a full head of steam working for a superstar, he's likely to take no prisoners, including bus drivers. I'm replaceable."

"That's not gonna happen. You've always told me how close you and Willie are."

"*You* wanna be Poodie's chauffeur?"

"I didn't sign up for it…, but probably not."

"Andy, you've already made an impression on these guys. I think you're probably as much a stray dog as any of 'em. Willie tends to gravitate to that breed."

"Maynard, you represent the positive, sober energy field that Willie appreciates so much. He holds you in high esteem for your curiosity and inner peace."

"Living so close to these guys is making me irritable, Andy. I mean, there's a bunch of family members…, Willie's family. I'm proud to be one of 'em, but I feel like the fuckin' *weird* one!"

"It's all relative. Take it as it comes and don't change shit. Would you rather haul fuckin' sand?"

An hour later, back at the dressing rooms, it was a lively scene, with everybody well lubricated.

I guess the early show is just a warmup.

While I was mingling with the guests, I felt a little nervous, always being the giant in the room. I found a beer and headed to the stage, where Harrah's crew were tweaking away. It was quiet there—only the low hum from the gathering crowd out front, with some soft background music on the P.A. system.

I walked up to the monitor mixer where Leon Trotsky was getting his board ready.

"Pete," I said, putting out my hand, "I'm Andrew. Poodie told me your name. I'm a friend of his."

"Saw ya today," the grizzled bearded face said to me. "I'm Pee Hole Pete, the nastiest man in show business. Pleased to meet ya."

We shook on it.

"That's quite a name and a helluva distinction, Pee Hole."

"Thanks, Andrew. Got any weed?"

"I've got a little, yeah. In my room."

"Let's burn one after the show, okay?"

"I'll find ya, Pete, and we'll git 'er done."

"What's up, Slim?" Poodie said, coming up behind me. "I figured ya might be gamblin' with us between the shows. Koepke called your room and left a message."

"I was hangin' out with Maynard, just catchin' up."

"Maynard Lutts from Palo Alto," he growled softly. "Gonna watch the left side for me, big boy?"

"I was planning on it, Poodie. My pleasure."

"Thanks, Andrew. It's really the crew's job, and we keep a close eye, but you're big enough for backup. I appreciate that…. By the way, there's gonna be some guests on your side for the second show…, several players from the Raiders…, but we won't leave ya alone with 'em."

"No problem, Poodie. Are they drunk?"

"A few of 'em are pretty buzzed."

"Can I go hang out in the dressing room instead?"

"You'll be fine, Andrew. Either me or Koepke or Schroder'll be there."

Poodie was right. Just before the curtain went up, after Bowman's set, six or seven behemoths arrived, ready to enjoy Willie. Poodie was with them, so I stepped aside to make room for the herd.

"Andrew, this is The Ghost, David Casper, an old friend."

David had to look up a little at me, and, by God, it *was* The Ghost, along with Lyle Alzado and a few others.

"Pleased to meet you, Andrew."

"Same here, Dave. I'm a fan of yours, but a forty-niner faithful…, born and raised."

"I won't hold that against you. We both love Willie."

Very well spoken. He has a future after football.

The band was ready, the curtain was raised to the sound of Willie's unaccompanied voice, singing "Whiskey River, take my mind… (*big guitar chords*)… don't let her memory torture me."

The best way to enjoy being backstage with six Raiders standing next to you is to not budge an inch.

Feet in cement…. You're an immovable object.

Eventually, the players headed back to the dressing rooms to party, even Dave, but he stayed the longest.

It's a miracle, drunk as they were, none of 'em fell through the scrim.

"Dave's a great guy, Andrew, a fuckin' good human being," Poodie said, obviously relieved that the boys had gone.

"Willie draws a real cross-section of friends and fans, doesn't he?"

"Yeah, but David's a special friend of ours."

The energy of the crowd was much higher for the second show, and it clearly fed Willie, whose *Stardust* set was stronger and crisper. It's a funny thing about energy in live performances. I'd seen that when I was producing shows. The audience fires up the artists, no doubt about it. That's why band crews, who see hundreds of shows a year, can tell a good night from a run-through. It's all about the electricity between the house and the stage.

I was developing a deep appreciation of another song Willie featured that night, "Crazy," the Patsy Cline smash hit from the '50s.

"Poodie, Willie sings this one like he wrote it."

"He did."

"You're shittin' me!"

"You need to do some homework, big boy. Willie's written more songs than you can imagine."

"Poodie, this is *American* music. I guess you can call it country, but it's no more country than the Dead performing "Sing Me Back Home" by Merl Haggard, for Chrissake."

"That's why his star is finally rising, Andrew. He's the consummate American singer-songwriter. I agree with you, big boy, he has more in common with the Dead than probably anybody else."

The next morning, eager to see the new buses, I called Maynard.

"Time to check out the equipment," I said.

"How about the breakfast buffet first, Andy?"

"Meet you there in thirty minutes. Don't forget the breakfast tickets!"

I got out of bed, opened the double set of drapes, and was about knocked over by the morning view of the lake. I really had to pinch myself.

Is this real? C'mon, Andrew, this is another day in Paradise.

At breakfast, I didn't want to continue our conversation about bus politics, and neither did Maynard. It was too beautiful a day.

After we ate, we took a long walk out to the far reaches of the back parking lot to see the new tubes.

As we got closer, I said, "Hey, Maynard, remember when we almost kissed mirrors on Page Mill Road every morning at sunrise in our Gilligs?"

"These babies are a big step up from those old road hogs, Andy."

Three coaches and one semi were lined up next to each other, clean as whistles, the chrome wheels of the buses sparkling in the Tahoe sunshine. The two new buses were Silver Eagles, the Tube was an old single-deck Greyhound, and the semi was a Kenworth cabover tractor pulling an air ride Great Dane trailer. The Eagles were painted in two-tone schemes without any graphics. The old Tube, Maynard's bus, was a standard silver side. At one point, it had "Porter Wagner and Dolly Parton" on both sides, but the paint had been removed. However, you could still see the outline of the letters.

Looking at the Tube, which I had never seen before, I said, "I'll bet *this* old bus has some stories."

"It's amazing this bitch has survived, Andy. I've been told Koepke and D.W. drove this thing like it was a pickup truck, grinding the shit out of the gears. Mickey found me just in time." He laughed. "Saved Willie a shitload of money on repairs, I can tell ya that."

"She drive anything like the Wheels' old double-decker job?"

"Not a thing. That old scenic cruiser, when it was healthy, was a joy to drive. This one is more like a Gillig school bus."

Maynard gave me a tour of the Tube.

"Smells like a boy's locker room," I said.

"What do ya expect, Andy? There's five smokers on this bus and a great deal of flatulent activity."

"I can smell every single fart."

Maynard didn't have keys for the Eagles.

"They're with the drivers," he said, "Big Jim, who we call 'The Singing Bus Driver,' and his stepson, Allen Johnson, who we call Big Al."

"How about the semi?" I asked. "Leased as well?"

"Yeah. The driver's named Rick. Nice guy. You'll meet him later."

"Let's go see what the guys are up to."

We no sooner reached the entrance to the hotel than Poodie and some other guests were getting ready to board a minibus.

"Hey, Andrew…, Maynard…, get your asses in gear. We're goin' out on *Miss Tahoe* for a private tour of the lake."

"Have fun, Andy," Maynard whispered to me. "I'm on vacation from Poodie right now. Not interested in being trapped on a boat with him."

As I walked over to the minibus, Poodie shouted, "Where's Maynard goin'?"

"Said he was gonna call his old lady."

"Time to roar, Andrew. Phil Harrah loaned us his boat for a two-hour cruise around the lake, skipper and all."

"All aboard, Captain," I said, taking a seat next to the driver of the minibus.

"Close the door and head to the wharf!" Poodie barked.

Looking around, I saw that he was the only one from the band.

Five minutes later, eight of us were boarding the fifty-foot yacht and felt her power as the Captain opened up both engines and headed northwest toward Crystal Bay.

Poodie and I settled into a couple of comfortable lounge chairs with cold beers at our disposal from a cooler a few feet away.

"How in the hell did all you guys end up working for Willie?" I asked. "I mean, this is the damnedest bunch of wild asses I've ever met. I'm somewhat of an expert on the subject, but you guys far and away take the cake."

"Willie likes family, Andrew. It all starts with his roots…, his sister Bobbie, and his grandparents, who introduced 'em both to music. But Willie's had his share of ups and downs. Hell, try bein' a songwriter in Nashville, competin' with the very best."

Poodie was opening up, and I loved it.

"Slim, do you believe I ever thought that workin' for Willie would end up with me cruisin' around Lake Tahoe, enjoyin' a beer with an old friend of the Grateful Dead, and seein' nothin' but million-sellin' albums ahead? Shit, no, big boy!!"

"But how did all these guys get here? I mean, did they just drop in one day and get hired? Damn, *I* just dropped by one day. Is it that fuckin' easy to join the club?"

Poodie's belly laugh could be heard at the other end of the lake.

"Shit, Andrew! That's not too far off. Each one of us has a story. In my case, I just had a way of makin' Willie laugh, and that was it. We're probably a little top-heavy, to be honest, but we're a family. Let me tell ya somethin'…, you're a curiosity to these guys, includin' Willie."

"How's that, Poodie?"

"You were part of that San Francisco hippie scene. Maynard told Willie and all of us about you. Back then, Willie was tryin' to make it as a songwriter in Nashville the traditional way…, writin' love songs about pickup trucks and three-legged dogs. The music machine in Nashville ripped off some songs from him for peanuts, which went to make millions… for *them*. Then, along came the music scene in San Francisco…, Janis, The Dead, and it lit a spark that became a bonfire. For Willie, Waylon, and Chris, it was transformational."

"From the left side of the boat," the Captain announced over the loudspeaker system, "you can see Crystal Bay and the teahouse on the island."

As Poodie and I got up to look, he said, "Just hang around, Andrew. You're always welcome until you're not…, and that's not likely to be anytime soon. Enjoy the ride, big boy, it's just begun."

When I got back to my room, I called Lisa.

"I heard 'Stardust' on the radio today," she said.

"No shit! Really?"

"Yeah. And it wasn't on a country station, either. It was on KSAN! I loved it and listened for the harp break you told me about. I turned it up and enjoyed it so much. Talented guy."

"That must mean the album's been released. Or at least the single."

"I guess so, Andy. It looks like Willie's gonna kick some ass."

"Poodie says he's gonna be bigger than the Beatles!"

"Well, you're pretty damned lucky to be up there. Don't blow it."

All I had eaten on the boat was a few hors d'oeuvres and beer, so I was hungry. Some of the boys were bound to be in the twenty-four-hour buffet, so I figured I'd head over there after I washed up in my room. Sure enough, when the elevator door opened, there was Steve with two eighteen-year-olds (I hoped) in cowboy hats and Levis with big belt buckles.

The bigger the belt buckle, the smaller the brain.

"Yo, Koepke! What's shakin'?"

"Not a thing," he said, rolling his eyes. "What are *you* up to?"

"Gonna greaze."

"Andrew, this is Holly, and this is Patty. They're from Fresno."

"What do *you* do, Andrew?" they said at the same time, probably hoping I was a musician.

"Stage security."

"Wow, that's so cool!" Patty said.

"I'll bet no one messes with *you*," Holly chimed in as she craned her head back to look up at me.

"Ya'll wanna join me for lunch?" I asked.

"We're goin' to Holly's parents' cabin," Steve said. "Why don't ya come along?"

"Where is it?"

"Kirkwood, just a short drive."

I knew where Kirkwood was, and it was way more than a short drive.

"I'm gonna pass, Steve. But thanks for the invite. Don't be late for the show."

When I got to my room, I called Pamela to ask if she wanted to join me.

"I'd love to, Andrew. D.W.'s down workin' on the stage, so I've got plenty of time."

As we sat down among a group of people who looked very irritable, probably because they had just been cleaned out in the casino, I said to Pamela, "How does a Boston Yankee like you wind up sounding like you were born and bred in south-central Texas?" I laughed. "Not that I'm an expert on accents or anything."

"Ya'll will be soooon, Andrew."

"Well, I guess if a Bostonian can put on a drawl like that, there's great hope for me."

We both cracked up.

"Why would ya'll ever wanna leave San Francisco if it's yerrr home? Ah mean, really, it don't snow there."

"You have a good point, Pamela. And I have a family there as well. But I've been screwing with this music business for a bunch o' years, and, by God, I think Willie's rocket is about to launch, *big*-time. My wife heard 'Georgia' on the radio just this mornin'."

"I know. The album's comin' out in a few weeks. Very exciting, Andrew. Ah hope they can cope with it. I worry 'bout a few of 'em, but I love 'em all."

"I'm just gettin' to know them, plus I've been needin' some new male friends, to tell ya the truth. And along come the Willie Nelson family, kerplunk, right into my lap."

Pam started laughing so hard, I thought she would pee in her pants.

"Don't ya git it Andrew? The same thing happened to *all* of us..., me, Snake, Poodie, Chris, all the way up the line. There's in-laws, friends, even a few friends of friends, and some that nobody knows *where* the hell they came from."

"It does feel like a family, Pam, it really does."

"You've made an impression on them. D.W. told me Willie called you an original hippie from San Francisco."

"I've been called worse."

"Seen Kopeck?" Poodie asked as I arrived backstage. He looked pissed.

"I saw him leave for Kirkwood this afternoon with two young chicks from Fresno."

"He better not be late, or I'll have his ass. The show's startin' in *fifteen minutes!*"

Still not feeling totally at home backstage, I headed for a friendly face.

"Hey, Michael Jean, back to Trigger again, are ya?"

"New strings every night, Andrew. By the way, you seen Steve? Poodie's been lookin' for him."

"Nope. Bowman's about to go on, though, so I'm hopin' he'll show up. He was hangin' out with two teenage cowgirls this afternoon."

"That be Steve. Oh, well."

At that very second, looking calm and collected, with both girls in tow, there he was.

"Where the fuck is Poodie?" he asked. "I need a couple o' passes."

"Where've you been, Steve?" Michael Jean asked. "Poodie's hot."

"Ah checked the drums this mornin', before I left. What's the fuckin' big deal?"

"You're late, Koepke, that's the fuckin' problem, asshole!" said a red-faced Poodie, who appeared more than a little agitated. Then he noticed the girls. "I'm Poodie, ladies, Steve's boss. What the hell did you do with him all day?"

"Fuck you, Poodie!" Steve snapped. "Ya ain't my boss. Gimme two passes for my guests here. Hurry up, I gotta go to work."

"Get goin', Koepke. I'll take care o' the girls."

"You fucker, these are *my* friends!"

At that point, I decided to head across the stage to check things out. As I passed Willie's dressing room, I noticed a few familiar patches on the backs of some of the guests.

Hells Angels!

The Oakland and San Jose chapters were well represented.

Déjà vu.

From the left wing, thinking of who might show up, I stared straight ahead at the curtain, feet in cement once again, until Bowman finished and it was time for the flag drop and "Whiskey River." Then I looked around. Fortunately, I was alone. Poodie was probably busy taking care of business with the cowgirls. I had to laugh. The politics of the backstage scene were right out of central casting. I'm sure Poodie had his eye on the same prize that Steve did, both eager fans of the ménage à trois.

"Yo, Andrew! Some of our friends are gonna be watchin' from this side."

"Lemme guess…, Hells Angels?"

"They're right behind me. Snake's bringin' 'em over. You may wanna watch the first show from the other side tonight. Snake thinks it's best."

"So do I."

Once Snake arrived with the boys in tow, I headed over to the other side and decided to spend some quality time in Willie's dressing room, hobnobbing and munching over a few beers. My old Tony Lama truck driving boots were this evening's fashion statement. I'd cleaned much of the funk off them before I'd left from home. On this particular night, I was six-foot-eight, and totally enjoying it. There was a live telecast of the show in the dressing room, and speakers for sound. I'm not sure who I met, but Bowman and Pamela were there the whole time, along with a steady stream of their friends from Austin. The cowgirls were in and out, with Steve often on their tails. Bowman's blue humor, aimed straight at Steve every time he passed through, was lightning quick and funny as a crutch.

"Andrew," Pamela whispered in my ear, "Bowman's such a sweetheart, ain't he? But he's got a razor tongue and takes no prisoners. Goes after loudmouths and braggers first, then women and children."

"Fortunately for me, I tower over him, so he's left me alone..., other than calling me a tall sumbitch."

Pamela laughed.

"He's probably too intimidated to jump on your case. But that will end when he's comfortable with you. Just when you think it's safe to open your mouth, he'll make you pay..., the little shit."

"Why do the guys all call 'im Cod?"

"Nobody's told ya?"

"Nope."

"Take a look at his bottom next time he walks by..., he's got none. Willie nicknamed him Cod, short for Cod ass. Now ya know."

After the second show, everyone headed over to the casino to gamble and hang out. Not being a betting man, I hung around the main bar with a few of the guys and a couple of Hells Angels who were with them. I thought I recognized one of them, but couldn't be sure.

Maybe at Homer's?

"We Hardly Know Ya, But We Love Ya"

"Hey, Lisa, I'm home!" I called as I walked into the house. "*Anybody here?*"

Ode came running into my arms, chanting his Dadda, Dadda mantra.

"How's my big boy?!"

"Trinny! Trinny!" he squealed as the dog came to greet me.

"I'm in the bathroom!" Lisa shouted. "Giving Autumn a bath. Come on in."

"Wow, look at my big baby girl and her mama!"

Ode was tugging on my sleeve. "Outside, Dadda! Outside, Dadda!"

A. Bernstein Archives
Ode and Trinity, 1977

Trinity was also insisting that I go out and toss a tennis ball until my arm fell off. Every time she headed into the bushes after the damned thing, Ode laughed his head off.

When we went back inside, Ode ran to his room to play with his trucks and buses, and I headed to the kitchen to make a sandwich. There were packed boxes everywhere.

"Wow," I said, when Lisa appeared with Autumn wrapped in a towel. "Nice pack job. I'm very impressed."

A. Bernstein Archives
Autumn, 1978

"Are you really gonna drive a twenty-six-foot truck up that hill, Andrew?" Lisa asked. "You could easily kill yourself. You know that, don't you?"

"I'm not trying to be macho, Lisa. And I don't want my kids to be fatherless. I just know I can do it."

I think.

"By the way," Lisa said, "speaking of driving, how's Maynard doing?"

"Oh, shit, it's getting a little iffy at this point. He may be approaching a fork in the road. Not immediately, but Willie's rocket is taking off, and I'm not certain Maynard will survive. I know he and Willie have become great buddies, but the pressure of that bubble may frustrate Maynard into making a move. He's been talking about trucking again."

"Yeah, he's a little low-key for that life…. Did you have fun?"

"I stayed sober, took it all in, and made some new friends. Casino life's a trip…, and not always a good one. But I have to laugh every time I think about some of the crazy shit that went on. I'll tell you, though, I think Willie's gonna be playing these big rooms on a regular basis. The shows were all sold out, two a night."

"Something tells me you're gonna be going back for more. Please don't abandon us, okay?"

"I promise. But it's a bright flame, you know. I'm just a hardheaded helpless moth."

The next morning, I was back in the sand truck at an ungodly hour. The company was really hard up for drivers, so if I showed up at 5:00 A.M., I was assured a truck for the day. However, the new commute from Loma Mar was going to be an hour and a half each way, adding a full hour to the total round trip. I didn't look forward to making that drive day after day; I needed something closer to the coast.

A. Bernstein Archives

The Loma Mar House at the Top of Dearborn Park Road

"I'm fucking exhausted, Lisa," were my first words as I dragged my sorry ass through the door that night. "But I saw a small fleet of Peterbilts parked out on Pescadero Road. Maybe I'll stop by in the morning and see if they're looking for drivers. It's a hell of a lot closer than San Jose."

"Lookin' for drivers, sir?" I asked the next morning, walking up to a man behind a desk in a small office."
"Ever pull a set of doubles before?"

"Yeah, I'm pulling bottom dumps out of San Jose right now, but I'm moving to Loma Mar, and the drive's a killer."

"Sand don't count. These trucks go to the L.A. flower markets…, real truck drivin'."

Flowers were one of the primary crops from this part of the coast.

"Well, does it pay better than sand?"

"It does, but its hard physical work, and these trucks have tiny sleepers. A big guy like you won't sleep very well. I got a load goin' down in two days if you wanna give it a try. The first few trips are tough, particularly if you don't know the L.A. area."

All of a sudden, those two trailers looked awfully long. I wasn't quite ready to drive that damned monster around L.A.

What was I thinking?

"Let me talk to my wife. I'll get back to you."

"Well, it better be pretty damned soon. I need a driver in two days."

I climbed into "Castro Valley" and drove back to La Honda.

Not ready for that much excitement.

"Lisa, I'm gonna try and get back into the moving business. I'll just do local work outta Redwood City…, if they'll have me."

"It's probably a good idea. I know they'll take you back."

I called LDM United that afternoon. "Hey, Stan, it's—"

"I know who this is. What's up, stranger?"

"Will you have me back for local work?"

"This time, yes. God knows, I need class A drivers for locals in the worst way."

"One thing…. I wanna be able to come and go. I'm still a ramblin' man."

"I think we can work something out."

"See you in a couple o' days. Can I have my old rig back?"

"It's been waiting for you. It's your hot rod, brother." He laughed.

Three days later, I climbed up into my Mack for a long day of office moving for the Stanford Research Institute in Menlo Park. It was hard work, but I knew the great shape I would be in after a few days.

That weekend, I rented a twenty-six-foot bobtail truck for the big move. I loaded that motha as tight as a tic, using all my bed bugger skills. It was a busman's holiday of sorts. When I locked the back doors, there were 7,000 pounds onboard.

I knew I only had one run at the hill in Loma Mar. Success would depend on keeping the truck moving. If I stopped on the grade, I'd better have a good escape route.

Lisa and Bob, my new landlord, directed traffic. Nobody could come up or down until I had the truck safely in my driveway. It was scary as hell, but I pulled it off, even surprising myself.

When I came home from work one night, about three weeks later, Lisa said, "Someone named D.W. called…, wants you to call him back tomorrow morning before ten. He left a phone number at a Holiday Inn in Michigan somewhere. Said his last name is English."

I wonder what he wants.

The next morning, I called him before I left for work.

"Hey, Daryl Wayne, what's up?"

"Shit, man, *Stardust* has taken off. We're sellin' out every show. C'mon out and join us on the road for a week. We got plenty o' room."

"Where the hell are ya?"

"Big outdoor amphitheatre…, Pine Knob in Clarkston, Michigan. We got a day off tomorruh. Then we're playin' the next day. It's pretty close to Detroit…, not sure exactly how far away, a cab ride maybe."

"Okay, so if I fly out the day of the show, I can catch a taxi from the Detroit airport and hook up at the gig around showtime, right?"

"Absolutely. It'll be great to see ya. We could use a little sunshine as well, okay?"

"Shouldn't be a problem."

My next call was to Dick Jackson.

"Hey, Dickey, how ya doin? I'm gonna need a single ozer tomorrow afternoon, alright?"

"No problem. See ya after work."

I called United Air Lines and booked a one-way flight to Detroit for Saturday morning.

The night before my flight, I stopped by Dickey's cool farmhouse on twenty acres in San Gregorio.

"Hey, Marge," I said, as Dickey's girlfriend opened the door.

"Come on in, Andy. Dickey's out back. I'll tell him you're here."

Richard Jackson was well known and liked out in coastal country. He had a Red VW bus/camper with a white pop-up top. Everyone knew that bus. I originally met him at René's house in Palo Alto. He had been a driver for Allied Van Lines before he hurt his back and went on permanent disability. His moving days were well behind him.

"The movin' man!" he hollered as he came into the house.

"Takes one to know one, buddy. Movin' is groovin'."

He tossed an ounce on the coffee table as he sat down next to me.

"Roll one up. You're gonna love it!"

"I will. Aroma test first. Don't rush me."

Marge let out a loud laugh at our interplay.

"This is for a few new friends of mine. I'm gonna hook up with them in Michigan tomorrow."

"Oh, yeah? Are they from La Honda?"

"Nope. Texas."

"Lemme guess. Musician friends o' yours."

"You gotta keep it cool, okay?"

Marge took a sudden interest.

"Of course, man. Shit, how many years have we been friends?"

"Willie Nelson's crew."

"No shit!" Marge said. "This stuff is goin' to Willie Nelson? Fuckin' cool!"

I opened the little bag, took a sniff, and zipped it shut.

"Smells great. I'm not gonna smoke any now. I gotta get home and get packed."

I paid Dickie and split.

With an early flight, I was out the door before Lisa and the kids were even up. The good news was that a full breakfast was being served on the plane. The bad news was that I was in a middle seat in the smoking section.

Fucking last-minute ticket!

On my right, a black woman was smoking menthol cigarettes nonstop as she talked to a girlfriend across the aisle.

On my left, a properly dressed businessman introduced himself.

"Good morning, sir. Going to Detroit on business?"

Shit! My hair's out to here, I've got a full beard and moustache..., what kinda business does he think I'm in?

"Well," I said, "I'm gonna meet some friends who are currently working there. Gonna pitch in and help out a little."

Please shut up!

"Wow, must be an important job to fly to Michigan from California. What kinda work are you in?"

Bullshit time!

"I'm a logistics manager for a small freight forwarding company in San Francisco. Gonna oversee a big de-install."

As I spoke, I pulled a *Sports Illustrated* out of the seat pocket and opened it to give the guy the hint that I would now be reading. Fortunately, he got the message, so I read or slept all the way to Detroit.

"Excuse me, officer," I said, after collecting my bag and walking to the curb. "Can you tell me where Pine Knob is?"

He looked at his fellow officer and smiled. "About a hundred miles from here."

"Are you kidding me?"

"Nope. Willie Nelson's playing there tonight. The place is sold out, so good luck getting in."

I pulled my *Stardust* backstage pass out of my coat pocket.

A. Bernstein Archives

"I'm with the band. Just running a little late. Can you direct me to an honest cabbie?"

They looked at the pass, then one of them ran across the parking lot about a hundred feet to a limo. In sixty seconds, it was in front of me.

"He's only gonna charge you two hundred bucks. He's our buddy."

"Shit, boys, how can I thank you?"

Wanna burn one?

"Say hi to Willie from us, his two biggest fans."

I shook hands with them both, thanked them from the bottom of my heart, and rolled to Pine Knob in style. I knew we were getting close when the two-lane country road started to be lined up with cars parked on both sides.

Pushing the button to lower the privacy window, I asked, "Are we there?"

"Yes, sir, headed to limo parking out front."

"Try the backstage entrance first, where the trucks and buses go in. I have a pass."

"Cool. Hand it up here and we're in."

I gave it to him just as we were approaching the chain link gate.

He rolled down his window, but before he could say a word, the cop asked, "Is this Andrew Bernstein?"

"Yes, sir, he's in the back. I have his ID."

The driver showed my pass to the cop.

"No problem. They've been asking about him for hours. I'll radio 'em you're here."

Those fuckers really are hurting!

I could see the buses at the top of a little knoll, which we reached in no time. By now, it was 7:15, and I could hear Willie playing onstage. As I got out of the limo, D.W. was already waiting for me.

"Yo, man!" he drawled. "We was startin' to give up on ya."

We half-hugged and then D.W. pulled out a wad of hundreds and settled up with the driver.

As the limo pulled out, I had a vision of me smoking a joint with those two cops back at the airport.

D.W. was riding with his dad on one of the new band buses, so we headed over to an Eagle, and I parked my bag on an empty bunk.

"As ya can hear," D.W. said, "the band's playin', so let's burn a quick one and head to the stage."

The fine buds were everything Dickey had promised.

D.W and I then floated through the backstage area to a set of stairs.

When we got to the top, there was Willie and the band, with thousands of people in front of them.

Poodie and Steve spotted me from across the stage and smiled as if the Red Cross had just arrived in a war zone.

They both walked over to where we were standing and gave me big hugs and slaps on the back—all in clear view of the audience, which I found a bit daunting.

"Andrew," Poodie said, "we ain't never seen these kinda crowds up north before."

"Fuck, Poodie, out on the main road, the cars are lined up for miles."

Steve blurted out, "You and fuckin' D.W.'s high, ain't ya?"

"Nice to see ya, Steve."

"Fuck you guys!"

Maynard appeared with a big shit-eating grin on his face.

"Hey, brother," I said with a one-arm hug.

"Great to see ya, Andy." Glancing toward the crowd, he said, "Do you believe this? It's like someone turned on a switch. The last tour was nothin' like this."

"I believe the switch is named *Stardust*, Maynard. It's all over the radio."

"The boys have been waiting for you all day. All I've been hearing is, 'Where's Andrew? Where's Andrew?'"

We both laughed.

As I looked over at Willie and the band, they were playing with great enthusiasm. The *Stardust* material was drawing the heaviest applause.

Hoagy Carmichael had had huge successes with *Stardust* and *Georgia on My Mind* forty years before. Now these American classics were Willie's to claim as his own. It was stunning. The heartland was eating this stuff up.

The outdoor stage was big, but not too big to hide six-foot-seven me. Chris was the first musician to spot me. He tapped Willie on the shoulder, and they both turned around, looked at me, and started laughing. Willie gave me a thumbs up.

Welcome to Michigan!

"Now that Willie knows you're here, big boy," Poodie said in his smoke-ravished baritone, "I expect he'll pick up the tempo considerably." He laughed. "We love ya, Slim. We hardly know ya, but we love ya."

"It may be harder to get rid of me than it was to invite me, ya know that?"

"Willie calls all the shots, Andrew. He's a pretty good judge of character…, just look at *us*." He winked.

I looked around at the motley crew and nodded in agreement.

"A pretty good judge indeed, Poodie."

They look like they all rolled out of a boxcar.

"Where are we rollin' to tonight?" I asked.

"An all-nighter to South Bend. Probably get there about ten A.M. Just enough time to shower, eat, and head to the gig."

As the show wound down, Willie did a few encore numbers. Big Jim, the singing bus driver, joined in on "Will the Circle Be Unbroken," and the show ended to grand applause. Willie tossed his last bandana of the night into the front row, people dove for it, and it was a wrap.

The same Kenworth tractor that I'd seen in Tahoe had already backed the equipment trailer into position for the load out that night. I felt the urge to help—the trucker in me was alert and alive. But I kept my mouth shut and just observed for a few minutes. Everyone else was headed for the buses.

"You're ridin' with us tonight, Andrew," Willie said, walking up to me with a big smile. "See you on the blue bus in fifteen minutes. Don't be late."

"Okay, I'll get my stuff and be there in a few minutes."

Shit, I wanted to watch the whole load out.

As I climbed onto the band bus to get my suitcase, Bowman and Chris were in the front lounge. Just as I was coming back from the sleeping area, Bowman said, "Where the fuck *you* goin', Slim?"

"Ridin' with Willie tonight."

"Well, just a goddamn minute there, Andrew," Bowman said. "I believe you've got all the California weed in this county on your person right now, and we *want* some before you get on anybody else's bus!"

"He's tellin' the truth, Andrew," Easter chirped in. "No weed, you don't get off this bus."

I happily doled some out to soothe the savage beasts.

"See you in South Bend, boys. Don't smoke it all. I doubt it's gonna last long."

"Let's catch up tomorrow, Andrew," Chris said. "I've got some things I wanna talk to you about.... Personal stuff, okay?"

"You got it, Chris. I'll see you before the gig tomorrow, for sure."

Before I got off the bus, I introduced myself to the singing driver, Big Jim.

"I'm Andrew, an old friend of Maynard's from California. We used to drive buses together."

"You don't look *that* old," he said with a smile, extending his hand for a shake. "I'm Jim. Talk to me later if you're lookin' for a bus drivin' job. I own the lease company."

"I will. Thanks, Jim. I'm riding with Willie tonight."

"Allen, my stepson, is driving his bus. Introduce yourself when you get aboard."

As I walked over to Willie's bus, the air was thick with Diesel fumes, as all the drivers were warming up the rigs for the long ride.

As I stepped onto Willie's bus, Allen reached out his hand and introduced himself. "My stepdad just radioed me that you were on your way over. Can ya lock that door, please? Appreciate it."

"No problem."

As Allen put the bus in gear, he said, "Please zip up the privacy curtain from the inside. I'm looking forward to getting to know you, man. Come on up and sit in the co-pilot seat a little later. I'd love to hear some stories. Maynard's mentioned you plenty around here."

"Hey, Andrew," Snake said as I walked into the front lounge after zipping up the curtain. "There's a couple empty bunks in the back. Find one and put your bag up. We got a bottle o' Jack goin' 'round. Willie's a new grandpa."

I smiled down at Willie, who was sitting at a table. "Congratulations, Grandpa. I've got something to help along the ceremony."

"Take your time, Andrew," Willie said. "The bathroom's to the left if you need it. Go ahead and get settled. We ain't goin' nowhere."

I dropped my bag on a bunk, brushed my teeth in the tiny bathroom, and took a seat on one of the couches in the front lounge. Snake was sitting at the table, across from Willie, with the Jack Daniels bottle between them.

I was finally where I had dreamed I might be someday: in the Jackson Brown road album *Runnin' on Empty*. For this old driver, it was a pleasure to leave the driving to someone else.

"Are we celebrating a grandson or granddaughter, Willie?" I asked as Snake handed me the bottle.

"Grandson, Andrew..., my first. Snake, give Andrew your seat." He threw a pack of papers on the table. "Please, Andrew, feel free to roll one or two up. We've been eagerly awaiting your timely arrival."

I took a small swallow of bourbon, and passed it to Willie. "I don't drink this stuff often, Willie. Not much of a drinker, I'm afraid."

"I'm not much of one anymore, either, Andrew.... Please keep on rollin'."

As I was twisting up a big one, Willie's sister, Bobbie, came up front from the back lounge.

"You must be Andrew," she said with a warm Texas accent. "Welcome to our little rolling home."

Poodie Locke Archives
Bobbie and Willie

Bobbie didn't share in Willie's recreational activities, so she politely excused herself after a short while. The celebration of the new Nelson family member continued for an hour or so, and then folks started heading to bed. I excused myself and went up front to hang with Allen.

When I unzipped the curtain and looked out the windshield, I saw that rain was coming down in sheets, with lightning strikes across the plains as far as the eye could see.

"Holy shit, man!" I said as I sat down in the co-pilot's seat. "It's really coming down."

"Predicted to be off and on all the way..., nine hours o' this crap.... Your old buddy from California's a good driver, probably the best out here. The crew all say he gives the smoothest ride. A lot of these guys don't really get Maynard. They think he's weird. But Willie loves him, a real New Age man, who somehow found his way into this very set-in-their-ways bunch.... Except for Willie, of course. He's totally open and always lookin' for the next big thing. How long you out with us for, Andrew?"

"A week or so, give or take. These guys really love the California bud. Plus it gives me a chance to see the logistics of touring. Truckin' and movin' stuff is my life back home."

You're a truck driver, right?"

"Well, a mover, yes. I've done some long-haul bed-buggin', too."

"Have you met Rick, our truck driver? Really a nice guy. You should talk to him. He used to drive for North American Van Lines."

"Thanks, man, I'll speak with him...."

Allen and I talked for an hour or so. But then the storm got worse, and I could see he needed to concentrate, so I called it a day.

"Okay, man," Allen said. "Don't be a stranger. It gets lonely up here."

I was soon under the covers of my bunk and sound asleep.

The Smell of Diesel in the Morning

I felt like I had slept for ten hours when a gentle shoulder tap woke me up. "We're at a Holiday Inn in South Bend, Andrew," Snake said. "You can sleep on the bus, or go up to your room, whatever you wanna do."

He handed me a room key and a room list. I noted that my own name was on it. Now I knew why some of the guys had been calling him the "key" man.

ANDERSON DAVID 516
ARONSON JOE 402
BOWNAN DON C O DASS 407
COOK COY 409
ENGLISH B W 410
ENGLISH PAUL 514
ETHERIDGE CHRIS 412
GARVEY MICHAEL 413
HUGHES WILLIAM 502/504/506 503/505
KOEPKE LEFTY 415
KOEPKE RIGHTY 416
SPEARS BEE 421
GORHAM LARRY 422
LOCKE POODIE 423
MARTIN GRADY 424
NELSON BILLY WILD BILL 425
NELSON BOBBIE JACK FLETCHER 334
LORD BRAXTON 427
PAYNE JODY 428
PRUITT BUDDY 429
COOPER BILLY 502/504/506 521

RAPHAEL MICKY 430 506
SCHROEDER MIKE 431
SMITH DESI 433
SNAKE T ROBERT HENDRICKS 434
STAUBER SLIM 435
JOHNSON ALLEN 507 515
LOVE DANNY 510
INOVATIVE AUDIO 511
FRANKS BO 512
FRANKS SCOOTER 513
FOWLER GEORGE 521
BERNSTIN ANDY 523
HOLIDAY JIM 525
ROTHBAUM MARK 527 507
SPARE TOM 528

A. Bernstein Archives

"The crew's bus call is at noon, Andrew," he continued. "Just enough time for a shower and a few phone calls. Lemme know if you're gonna be riding another bus tonight. You're welcome to stay on this one. We don't take Willie to the arena until just before showtime, so you can stick around here and wait, or go on the crew bus to the gig early."

"Thanks, man. I'll probably go over on the Tube."

I grabbed my bag, put on some clothes, and climbed off the bus.

Everything looked totally unfamiliar except the blue sky and the Holiday Inn sign. As I walked by the counter in the lobby, I glanced at the clock. It was already 10:15.

Another day, another town. This could get exhausting.

From my room, I could see that the semi was down in the parking lot. I wanted to make sure to introduce myself to Rick, the driver.

Just as soon as I got undressed for a shower, the phone rang.

"Where the hell'd you go last night?" Steve bellowed through the speaker. "Sheeet! We was fixin' tuh party on the bus with ya. Had some tequila, too. And then you fuckin' split, mannn!"

"Willie told me I was riding his bus last night after the show."

"That figures. C'mon and ride with us tonight, Andrew. Sheeet! He gits everythin' he needs. What the fuck about *us?*"

"I was honored to be invited, Steve. What was I supposed to say? 'Sorry, I'm ridin' with Kopeck tonight'?"

"You're startin' to sound a lot like us, Andrewww. That could be dangerous. We may not lit ya go home."

"I'll see ya on the Tube at noon, Steve."

I cleaned up, called Lisa and the kids (it was early back home, so the babies were groggy), and headed down to the Tube to park my bag and catch up with Maynard, who was at the wheel of the bus, with the engine running.

"You've been driving for eleven hours, Maynard. When the hell are you goin' to sleep?"

"Just as soon as I drop you all off. I'm beat. How do you like the road?"

"Ask me in a week."

He laughed.

"I'll be joining you tonight for the drive to the next show. Where is it, anyway?"

"Cleveland. Not such a bad drive. Plus we have a day off tomorrow."

The concert site was a twenty-minute drive away. When we got there, Maynard parked on the street, by the side entrance. The arena was an old memorial auditorium in a totally unpicturesque neighborhood in manufacturing rust-belt South Bend.

The semi was already there, backed up to the loading dock. The driver was standing outside, next to his truck, so I walked over and introduced myself.

"You seem to have a dream truck-driving job," I said. "My name's Andrew. I'll be riding along with the band for a couple of days. I'm a truck driver, too…, in California."

"It *is* a good dream alright, Andrew. My name's Rick. Your friends are great guys to work with. There's a real sense of family…, not like some others I've driven for."

"Heavy metal outfits?"

"You got it. Bunch o' egotistical assholes!"

"I can only imagine."

We both laughed

"Maybe we can talk some more tonight, Andrew. I'm pretty bushed from last night."

"Follow my orders, and nobody gets hurt, gentlemen!" Poodie's voice boomed behind me. "Fuck this thing up, and I'll personally kick your ass! Everybody got it?"

Nods and murmurs of acknowledgment from the local stagehands were all he got.

I'll bet they love it when Poodie comes to town.

The back doors of the truck opened, and the stagehands unloaded the trailer under Poodie's dictatorship.

The road cases, which contained the cables, monitors, amplifiers, and mixing boards, were all on wheels, but the piano had to be moved the old-fashioned way: enclosed in a piano-shaped padded case, with five or six guys lifting it onto a four-wheel dolly. When they got the case to the stage, they took off the door, and there was the piano, waiting to have its legs screwed back on. Then all the crew needed to do was tip the piano into place. Schroeder was in charge of all this.

When the crew had completed the setup, which took two hours from start to finish, I found my way back to The Tube and pissed the rest of the day away until showtime. That meant watching TV and playing P-I-G, which involved tossing two small plastic pigs out of a dice cup, and getting points for them landing in various sexual positions. You got the most points for a full rear mount, otherwise known as "makin' bacon."

By 7:00 P.M., the old auditorium was buzzing as the crowd started to gather outside.

Just as I was about to get off the bus, a man got on, whom I recognized as the second bass player.

"Bee Spears, Andrew," he said, putting out his hand. "We've not been formally introduced. I'm the choreographer and lead dancer with the band."

Alright! A musician with a sense of humor!

"Gotta love the dancers," I said. "Is your second job, by any chance, being a bass player?"

"It is. The dancin' thing ain't been workin' out that well."

A few minutes later, the other standup comedian in the band, Don Bowman, got on The Tube, and he and Bee started one-upping each other. After thirty minutes of bone-chilling character assassination, Koepke came on board to announce, "Dinner's served, gentlemen!"

Sorry, none of you come close to the Sonny definition.

We followed Steve to a room backstage, where people were already scooping food onto paper plates. There was a vegetable I had never seen before, but immediately spit out as soon as I tasted it.

Everybody laughed.

"What the hell *is* this, Poodie?" I asked.

"Food of the gods, Andrew. Fried okra."

"It tastes like shit!"

"Well, ya better get used to it, 'cause you're gonna see it every night."

I'd rather eat snake ass.

After dinner, Steve and I went to The Tube to burn one, and then headed to the stage stupidified.

"Yo," Poodie whispered in my ear. "I want ya to stand next to the monitor board, by Pete. Keep an eye on things. Okay, big boy?"

"No problem. Will I have a little backup if required?"

"Ain't nobody gonna fuck with you, Andrew. You're too big."

I walked across the stage and took up my post next to Pete's board.

"Hey, Andrew," he said. "Ya still got some weed left? Seems like I keep missin' out."

"I'll catch up with you on the Tube after the show, Pete."

"Cool."

After Bowman did his fifteen minutes, the band went out onstage and put on their instruments with the stage lights off. Then Willie rushed out, strapped on Trigger, the Texas flag dropped, and the sermon was on:

Whiskey River, take my mind, don't let her memory torture me.
Whiskey River, don't run dry, you're all I've got, take care of me.

The love and adoration in the house was obvious. This was the heartland, and these were Willie's people.

I was totally focused on the audience reaction to each of the songs. They hung on every word of the ballads, jumping around to the fast ones and swaying to the slow ones.

As the show was coming to a close, just before he had to tear the drums apart, Steve came up to me.

"Don't tell me you're ridin' with Willie tonight, fucker! You're ridin' with us to Cleveland."

"Don't worry, I'll be around."

Rick the truck driver was watching the guys load up, so I walked over to say hi.

"You look well rested, Rick."

"Oh, man, I was so whipped from ten hours of rain last night."

"So, tell me, does this pay about the same as driving a truck for North American?"

"You really are interested in this, aren't you? You wanna ride to Cleveland with me tonight? We can shoot the shit about this business. Be nice to have a rider."

"If you don't mind, I'll take you up on that. I promise not to talk your ear off. Be back in a minute."

I went over to The Tube, where Maynard was sitting behind the wheel, warming up the bus.

"I'm riding with Rick tonight," I said. "Gonna try and learn something about entertainment trucking. See you in the morning. Tell Steve I'll see him later."

"Rick's a good guy, Andy. He'll tell you how things really are."

As Rick and I rolled onto the interstate, heading toward Cleveland, I asked, "Aren't there some big hauling outfits that just do road shows, stage plays, and all that?"

"There are, Andrew, but Willie's still getting used to having a fleet of vehicles to deal with. The big guys in this business get a lotta money. Entertainment trucking is a relatively new business, so there's still a lot of sorting out for smaller companies that don't have ten trucks or more. Willie seems to prefer working with smaller outfits right now, like Nashville Coach and my boss's little company."

"I'm sure he's keeping a close eye on his costs. He just seems like that kinda guy."

"Yeah, he's no rookie at this. He knows how to make money and lose money in this business."

"Is it difficult to keep your logbook up to date, with all this jumping around?"

"By the book, we schedule real tight to make sure it's all legal. As you know, the highway patrol can shut us down…, not a good thing in this business."

"When's the last time you didn't make the show 'cause your rig broke down?"

"Good question. With Willie, never. But it happened one time when I was driving for Michael Jackson. We had to airfreight all the instruments on a private charter."

"Bummer."

We talked most of the way to Cleveland. When we were about a hundred miles out, I took a nap.

Around 3:00 A.M., we pulled up in front of yet another Holiday Inn. The buses were already there. I was exhausted, so I immediately checked into my room and hit the hay.

The phone rang with an insistence that would have awakened the dead.

"Wanna have breakfast?"

It was Maynard.

Thank God, it's not Poodie, extending a wake and bake invitation.

"Meet you downstairs, Maynard. Gimme fifteen minutes."

At breakfast, I said, "You know, man, we should pool our money, buy a couple o' trucks, and get into hauling band equipment around."

"I know. It pisses Willie off how much it costs. He's talked about buying a Peterbilt, but the upkeep scares him."

"It would be a great gig for us, my man."

"You've gotta have really deep pockets for that kinda thing, Andy."

"Well, let's think about it."

"You riding to St. Louis tonight? Steve's been shitting a cow."

"Poor Koepke! Yeah, I'll be on the bus tonight. But I'll be flying home in the morning. Hopefully, without a hangover."

It was another sold-out show in Cleveland, this time outdoors. After the performance, I walked across the front part of the stage as the crews were loading out.

"Hey, buddy, down here!"

I looked over the edge of the stage and saw a young man about my own age, sitting in a wheelchair. He was wearing a cap that had the words *Vietnam Veteran* across the front.

"Sure would mean a lot to me if you could get Willie to sign this cap," he said.

"I'm sure he'd be glad to. I'll be right back. What's your name?"

"Jim, sir. I'm his biggest fan."

I reached down and took his cap.

"I'll be right back, Jim. It might take me a few minutes."

I knew the rule—I wasn't supposed to ask for autographs—but I figured every rule has an exception.

Big Al was standing outside Willie's bus door, smoking a cigarette and keeping an eye out for drunks, who tended to migrate around the buses.

"Hey, Andrew, ridin' with us tonight?"

"Nope. Goin' home in the morning. I just need to see Willie for a second."

I opened the door and got on the bus. Willie was sitting at the table, with his back to the wall, talking to somebody across from him.

"Hey, Willie," I said, "I'm taking off in the morning. Thank you once again for your hospitality. I really appreciate it."

"Okay, Andrew. Hope to see you again soon. You're always welcome."

"Willie, this cap belongs to a fan…, a vet in a wheelchair, who asked me if he could get it signed. I'm sorry to ask."

"Of course, I'll sign it."

"His name is Jim."

He picked up a pen from the table and wrote across the top of the cap's white bill, "To Jim, thank you! Love, Willie Nelson."

"Thanks, Willie. Take care."

I went to the floor level in front of the stage area and found Jim.

"Oh, man!" he said, with tears in his eyes. "Thank you so much. I'll treasure this. I really will..., forever."

"It's my pleasure, Jim. And thank you for serving. I'm Andrew. Pleased to meet you."

After that, I went behind the buses to have a good cry. This guy had lost his legs, and a little signature on a hat meant so much to him.

Willie and Leon

I fell into a routine during the end of 1978 of working long hours during the week on the moving trucks, and taking weekends off to be with Lisa and the kids. Autumn, who was a year and a half old by now, and Ode, who was three, were the most beautiful children in every way. She loved taking walks on the mountain trails, strapped to my back, and he loved riding in "Castro Valley" up and down the hill or out to the beach to chase waves with Trinity. The sound of the gears and the smell of the engine, plus the bumpy ride, made Ode giggle with delight. Fatherhood was everything I had hoped it would be.

Lisa and I would take the kids on outings to Pescadero Beach, and then have dinner at Duarte's Restaurant, where the old ladies, including Al Capone's sister, would pinch Ode's and Autumn's cheeks red.

The guys were playing Tahoe on a regular basis now, which was an easy jump for me on a one-hour flight out of San Jose. Tahoe had become a kind of home away from home for the band. Phil Harrah was such a generous host, and he and Willie had become close friends. The casino audiences embraced the music, selling out every show in advance.

On just about every flight up to the lake from San Jose during those months, there was a guy I recognized who would hang around with the band, and seemed to be a friend of Poodie's. We would nod to each other, but never spoke. He was a Hells Angel and seemed to want his space, so I gave it to him. But one night up at the lake, at a party in Willie's dressing room, I found myself standing next to him.

"It appears we have the same travel agent," he said with a smile. "I'm Larry Gorham."

"Andrew Bernstein. Glad to meet ya."

"I guess you've known these guys a while," he said. "You seem to be part of the family."

I nodded. Then I suddenly realized from his voice that I had met this guy once before.

"I *knew* you looked familiar," I said. "You and Denny helped me out, one Fourth of July, when things were getting out of hand at Homer's Warehouse."

"I remember that night. Beer bottles were flying, and somebody lit off a cherry bomb. You were one of the owners, right? Wasn't Dan your doorman?"

"He sure was. A great guy. Man, were we lucky to find him."

"You guys really cleaned that dump up. We respected what you were doing."

"Thanks, Larry. I'm sure we'll be seeing each other again, off and on."

Just then, Maynard came up to us.

"Got a minute, Andy?"

"Of course, man."

We grabbed a couple of beers from Willie's bar and found an empty dressing room.

"What's up? I asked.

"They've turned my bus into a fuckin' chuck wagon!"

"You're kidding!"

"No. And to make it worse, the crew now has their own Eagle, so I got a new madman on board..., the cook!"

"What's wrong with that?"

"He's worse than Poodie. Everybody calls him Le Beast! And I have to go vegi shopping with him every day. Ya know? Push the cart and buy the groceries."

"Why?"

"'Cause I fuckin' talked Willie into becoming a vegetarian, and now he wants to convert all these red-meat-eating road dogs! No more catering at the shows. The Beast makes everything. And to keep Poodie happy, we gotta find okra all the time, even when we're in fuckin' Poughkeepsie!"

"Oh, shit! So it's beans and shoots for the boys, eh, Maynard?"

He frowned.

About a month later, Willie teamed up with Leon Russell to record *One for the Road*, another album of classics, this time done as duets. The first hit was "Heartbreak Hotel," a great crossover choice that was an instant success with both country and alternative hip FM stations. I was crazy about that album, feeling that it brought out the best of both men. It was also an upbeat collaboration, with songs like "Don't Fence Me In" and "Sioux City Sue," which were from a far more innocent era.

Once the *One for the Road* tour got under way, it wasn't long before Maynard called to ask if I'd come out.

"The Beast has turned me into a bagboy and a waiter, Andy. I don't think I can do this much longer."

"Tell me the good news."

"Well, from a musical perspective, this is the best tour I've ever been on. Leon brought his whole orchestra on the road with us, including his wife, Mary."

Oh, my god! I've gotta see this. She's brilliant!

"He's got his conga players, his horn section, his backup singers, the whole deal!"

"Where are you now?"

"Indianapolis. But we've got tomorrow off in Lexington, Kentucky. We'll be playing there Friday night, and then heading to Atlanta. Come on out for a few shows. Leon and Willie are magical together, and I need a little moral support. You got me into this. I could use some brotherly advice just now."

"Shit, Maynard! Who woulda thought it? Remember listening to Leon in the cottage in Los Altos? I'll see ya in Lexington in a day or so. Tell the guys I'm coming, okay?"

"We're staying at the hotel on top of the Rupp Arena…, same place we're playing."

"Okay. See ya soon."

Of course, I stopped by Dickie Lee's on the way through La Honda to the airport early the next morning.

"Say hi to Willie for us, Andy," Marge yelled to me as I headed out to the driveway.

It was a pain in the ass getting to Lexington. Thanks to storms that made me miss my connection in Atlanta, I didn't arrive at my hotel until midnight. But the lobby was buzzing, even at that late hour.

When I got to my room, I called Maynard.

"Hey, Mister Lutts, I'm here. You awake?"

"I'm kinda dozing, man. Enjoying a chance to sleep when it's dark outside. You're late. Everything okay?"

"It was a motherfucker getting here…, a little plane from Atlanta in a big storm. But I'm so ready for Leon!"

"Go party, man. The guys are expecting you. I'm goin' back to sleep. Call me not too early, and we'll have breakfast. The groceries are all on the bus, or in the hotel freezers. We shopped today for the next two gigs. I'm pooped."

"Sweet dreams, buddy. I'll call you in the morning."

"Oh, one more thing, Andy. Larry Gorham's become head of security. This is his first tour."

While I was talking to Maynard, the light on my phone started blinking. As soon as I hung up, it rang.

"Hey, Andrew," said Steve, "glad you could make it. There's the most beautiful fuckin' chicks at the lobby bar. C'mon down. Ya ain't met my baby brother Kenny yet neither. He's runnin' with us now. Poodie calls 'im Kenpeck. It's catchin' on."

In the background, I suddenly heard Poodie yell, "Git yer ass down here, big boy!"

"Tell Poodie I need a drink, Steve. It was a sonovabitch flyin' in here in that goddamn storm."

I glanced at the radio clock next to the bed. It was 1:00 A.M.

When I walked off the elevator, I could hear the bar noise clear across the lobby. Well-dressed women and tied down gentlemen were strolling across the floor, sipping colored cocktails with flowers floating on top.

"California Slim! Git over here! What are ya drinkin'?"

"Nothing pink or green, Poodie. A beer would be fine."

"This is our friend Andrew from Palo Alto, Californ-eye-aye," Poodie announced to anybody in listening distance.

The guys were mostly shitfaced, dripping in Willie swag with a captive audience of fifteen or twenty young Kentucky sweet things. Poodie was buying, so the girls were drinking with gusto. Their boyfriends were watching from the perimeter with gloomy faces.

"How ya'll doin', sweetie?" one of the belles asked me. "I've never been to Californ-eye-aye."

I flashed a big smile and gave her a hug.

"Good to see ya, man," Steve said. "C'mon over here and meet Kenny.... Andrew knows everybody in Frisco."

"Hey, man," Kenny said, standing up to extend his hand. "Heard lots about ya. Really good to meet ya finally."

Kenny was very tall, almost as tall as me.

"You're a lot bigger than Steve," I said. "Do you kick his ass when he has it coming?"

"Fuck *no*, he don't!" Steve cried out. "*Never*, Andrew!"

"I kin kick his assss with one arm tied behind my back, Andrew," Kenny drawled.

"Just checking, Steve," I said. "Don't get excited."

Very soon, the three of us were carrying on as if we had been mates for twenty years. Kenny was a sweet guy, only twenty-one, five years younger than Steve and a polar opposite in personality—as laid back as his horny brother was laid forward. Kenny reminded me of myself: the baby of the family, with a hardheaded brother a few years older who loved to hear his own voice. I immediately recognized his plight, which required him, like me, to have the patience of Job.

"This place is noisy as hell," I said. "I have some to burn in my room. Let's go."

Over a few La Honda joints and some cold beers on a warm southern night, the three of us talked for hours on the little deck off my room. Kenny was fascinated to hear my Homer's stories, from Jerry Garcia to Sonny Terry to Asleep at the Wheel.

"Well, Andrew," Kenny said at last, "my own road's been a lot shorter than yours. But I saw all those names pass through the record distributing company in Colorado where I've been working."

"Really? What did you do there, Kenny?"

"Oh, it's behind me now, but I drove a forklift and moved shit around the warehouse.... It's hot and boring work, so I decided to take Willie up on his offer to try the road. Hell, I've known him since he married my sister when I was fourteen. Guess it's kinda a family thing."

Smart move, Kenpeck.

The next morning, when I called Maynard, he sounded refreshed and ready to go.

So what happened last night, Andy?"

"Just the usual.... Poodie holding court, young ladies swooning, and boyfriends trying to figure out which one of these loudmouth Texan assholes needed to get his ass kicked."

"You crack me up, Andy. It's the same story every night. Poodie's party..., it never ends."

Later that morning, down in the bowels of the Rupp Arena, I watched three truckloads of gear being unloaded by an army of stagehands.

"Leon travels heavy," Poodie said to me. "He has so much gear with him, it's an all-day job now. Willie really loves Leon..., told him to bring the kitchen sink if he wanted to. But Willie forgot to tell *us*!"

"Yeah, I can see he brought *several* kitchen sinks..., and a bathtub to boot."

"That's right, big boy. And it all has to come down after the show tonight, and be in Atlanta by morning for tomorrow night's show.... I can't wait for the reaction when Willie sings 'Georgia on My Mind' for the first time in that beautiful new outdoor amphitheatre they just put up.... Listen, Andrew, don't tell anybody I told you this, okay? Hell, you're one of us now anyway.... We're doin' a movie. The deal's in the bag."

"No shit, Poodie! I won't tell anyone, I promise. Who's playing you?"

"*I'm* playing me! Hell, *you* might be playin' *you*!"

I took a nap in my room until I had to check out around 4:00 P.M., and headed to Maynard's bus with movies on my mind.

As soon as I got on, the entire interior was totally unrecognizable. Up front, where the couches had been, there were now five or six two-person restaurant-style booths on either side of the aisle.

"Jesus, Maynard, what a setup! They've completely rebuilt the Tube."

"You talkin' 'bout my chuck wagon, stranger?" he said. "We even have a dumbwaiter from the kitchen to the storage bays down below. C'mon in back, and I'll introduce you to the chef."

He led me to the middle of the bus, which was now ovens, grills, and an industrial-size refrigerator, where a heavyset, wild-eyed man was sweating over a large boiling pot.

Before Maynard even had a chance to introduce me to him, the Beast looked up, nodded to me, and said, "Welcome to my kitchen, Andrew. Maynard told me you were coming."

"Pleased to meet you, Beast."

I knew he wouldn't be insulted by this name, since he was wearing a tee shirt with the name right on it in big bold letters.

"There's still bunks in back, Andy," Maynard said. "Find an empty one, and toss your bag on it."

When I went through the door to the bunk room, I saw that there were only four bunks left of the original twelve. The room for the other eight had gone into the kitchen. Fortunately, one of the bottom bunks was open, so I put my bag down.

A real fuckin' chuck wagon. Where's Gabby Hayes?

Maynard told me that dinner was served between 6:00 and 7:00 every night, so while he and Beast prepared a meal for twenty, I headed over to the crew bus with my little bag of herbs. All the usual suspects were there, and happy to welcome me onto their new Eagle.

This is gonna be one high-flying bird!

"No more Tube, Andrew," Poodie said, as I walked on. "We travel in style now."

Eventually, someone came onboard to tell us it was dinnertime.

The meal was good, if a little gaseous from all the soybeans and black beans. The fried okra was edible this time because it had some garlic on it, which neutralized the sour taste.

Bowman wasn't opening on this tour, since Willie and Leon together were already a show and a half.

I took a place out front, in the middle of the audience, where the mixing platform was, and sat right next to Mike Garvey, the sound engineer from SHOWCO. He had the best seat in the house, but he tended to look down on Willie's crowd as a bunch of hillbillies. Poodie didn't take kindly to that, so whenever he saw Garvey approaching, he would say, "Boys, the Mike Garvey show is coming our way!" It's true that Mike was a bit egocentric, but pleasant enough to me, since he loved the taste of my bud—the old equalizer.

Willie opened the show that night, joined by some of Leon's musicians, so it was a bigger sound for the Family band, but they pulled it off just fine. I enjoyed watching Garvey work the mixing board. He had thirty or forty microphone inputs to balance, instead of the nine or ten he usually needed for Willie. When Leon and Mary came on, they and Willie jumped around from song to song in their enormous repertoires, which drove Garvey crazy—and the same for Budrock on lights. The chatter between them on their headsets was nonstop, with Garvey cursing into his mike, "What the fuck are they doin' now?" Pee Hole added to the chaos, screaming over his set from the stage, "More on the congas, Mike! Bring it up, asshole! Louder!"

Poodie Locke Archives
Willie and Leon Somewhere on the Road

When the show ended, Garvey was cool and collected—just another night at the office as he turned off all the equipment.

"So how long you out for this time, Andrew?"

"Just a few days, Mike. Leon's a personal favorite. Had to catch some of this."

"Tomorrow in Atlanta's bound to be the best night on the tour. I know that new venue. It's a natural bowl, like Red Rocks…. Hey, gotta a little extra bud?"

I reached into the bag in my pocket, pulled out a few beauties, and discreetly put them in his hand.

"Thanks, man. Here, I made two recordings of the show tonight. This cassette's for you." He wrote the name and date of the show on the case with a magic marker. "Don't tell anyone, or I'll be fired."

"Thanks, Mike. Don't worry."

You can have buds every night, my man.

That was the first of many cassettes that Mike gave me.

Although leftovers were available on The Tube, there were no takers, so Maynard, Beast, and I put the food away, and Maynard aimed the bus for Atlanta.

As Beast headed for his bunk, I climbed into the co-pilot seat next to my buddy.

"Nice show tonight," I said. "Do Willie and Leon change it up like that every night? Garvey was goin' nuts."

"Shit, Andy, think of all the material between them, and they love playing together. Each one of them sort of walks into the other's set every night, maybe twice, and God only knows what's gonna come out."

"Well, I'm lookin' forward to Atlanta."

"No shit, Sherlock. It's why I called you."

"Wake up, Andy, we're here!"

"What time is it?" I asked, turning over in my bunk.

"Almost eight," Maynard said. "Snake dropped off a room list and your key. The crew bus call's at eleven. Even though we don't have to shop, I'm going over earlier, as usual, to start setting for a big meal tonight. I'll come back later and sleep, then see you at the gig tonight."

"Thanks, man."

Since I wasn't on any schedule, I slept in and ordered breakfast from room service around noon.

As I was finishing my grits and gravy, Chris called.

"Hey, man, what are ya doin'? Have ya eaten?"

"I have, Easter, but I'm fixin' to burn one."

"Are you in two-twenty-seven?"

"Yup. C'mon over."

As we lit up a fat one, Chris told me that he was experiencing a rough patch with his wife, and being constantly on the road didn't help.

"I really love my kids, Andrew. It's eatin' at me somethin' bad."

"I can relate, Chris. I only leave my family behind from time to time. I don't think I could do what you do."

"It's my life, Andrew. The only one I know."

"Why don't we go down to the pool?" I said. "It's hot as hell in here. This air conditioning's for shit."

When we got down there, most of the band members were lounging around.

Chris and I got right in the water.

David Anderson, Willie's personal manager for the last few months, walked by with Larry Gorham. They waved and sat down at a table with Mickey, Jody, and some people I didn't know, who were all wearing dark sunglasses and styled hair.

Chris and I felt a different vibe in the air.

"Hollywood has arrived," Chris said. "Those are studio folks."

As we floated in the pool, making snide remarks to each other and mimicking the faygelahs in dark glasses, we looked at Mickey, who knew what we were up to and had to work hard to keep from cracking up, but nevertheless seemed enthralled by these folks.

"They make me nervous, Andrew," Chris said. "They've been hangin' around a lot. I worry a bit about their intentions. Willie's such a good guy. I hope he's ready for this. I've been around the L.A. scene. They're piranhas when there's fresh blood in the water."

I was at the amphitheatre by 4:00 and headed straight to the crew bus. All the gear had already been set up, so the guys were hanging out in their air-conditioned Eagle. As usual, my little bag was a welcome sight.

"Have you been working hard, boys?" I asked as I climbed aboard. "It's hotter than hell in this town. I've been in the swimming pool all afternoon."

"Up yours!" Steve shouted. "Roll a joint and shut the fuck up!"

Poodie was holding court, as usual. "Yo, Kenpeck," he said to Kenny, who was sitting across the table from him, "roll one for Andrew. Stay busy, son!"

Kenny looked at Poodie a little cross-eyed, then smiled at me and winked. I don't think he much liked being Poodie's poodle.

"By the way," I said, as I sat down on the couch, "Dickie Lee's girlfriend, Marge, wishes everyone well. She sure would like to see ya'll sometime."

"Well, thank her for us, big boy," Poodie said. "She's welcome anytime. Be sure and tell her to bring her girlfriends along, too."

"I'll do that, Poodie," I said with my tongue bursting through my cheek.

"Andrew," Poodie asked, "you see any of them movie people at the pool today?"

"Lots of sunglasses and pimping goin' on," I said, "with hair gel and fake tans aplenty."

Poodie burst out laughing. "And I'll bet Mickey was right in the middle of it, wasn't he?"

"He was seen in the vicinity."

I'm not big on gossip, so I headed over to the chuck wagon to sample the evening's vegetarian meal, and Kenny came along.

"So, what do you think of these guys, Andrew?" he asked. "You've known 'em a couple o' years."

"This is a pretty special little sideshow, Kenpeck, with some very unique freaks. I'm just an observer." I said this with a snicker. "I've come to love them."

"Well, you mind if I learn from ya? I mean, you've been around the music business for years. Anything you can tell me will help."

"You don't need my help. Treat them the same way you treat Steve. That's what they understand. You have nothing to be worried about, man. You're a great guy and will do just fine."

As we got close to the chuck wagon, the food smelled delicious.

"Beast," I said, "if it's half as good as it smells, I'll kiss you!"

"The hell you will, you Frisco homo!"

Enlightened.

He grunted something about the meal being ready in fifteen minutes. As I sat down at the table across from Kenny, I whispered, "Don't follow this guy's lead, Kenpeck. He'll find himself out of step eventually and will rage that the world ain't fair. Let's have a cold Bud and burn one."

"Sounds good," Kenny said. "But Beast don't allow no pot on his bus."

"Damned right, I don't!" snapped Beast from the stove.

"Willie can, if he wants," Kenny whispered. "Sometimes he does it just to piss Beast off."

Out of nowhere, Maynard appeared and sat down in the booth across from us as we dug into the beans, yams, and okra

Mmmmmmmmmmm, dinner!!!

"Boys," he said," I had a good sleep and am really lookin' forward to the show tonight. Think I'll join you guys…. Beast's roadside fruit salad looks great!"

"Maynard!" shouted Beast. "Set up the outdoor tables. Hollyweird is here tonight…, all the bastards. Set up the extra chairs, too."

"After my grits, *sir*."

"I'll help you set up, Maynard," I said.

"Hey, man, you don't have to do shit. That's *my* job."

He finished his meal and went outside to pull folding tables and chairs out of the back bay of the bus, making a hell of a racket, which totally irritated Beast. I imagine that was Maynard's intention all along.

Kenny and I sipped our beers until he had to run off for line check onstage. He had a lot to learn under the tutelage of the Great Pooh-Bah.

I went outside, where Maynard had already set up four or five tables, and helped him put out paper tablecloths and napkins, salt and pepper shakers, plastic cups, and ice tea. Beast was pleased, and even gave me a "thanks."

After that, I headed back to the crew bus.

As soon as I walked on, Poodie called out, "Jew on the bus!"

All the guys laughed.

My elegant response was a simple "Fuck you, Poodie!"

"Big boy, where the hell ya been? Got a few things for ya."

"Helping Maynard and Beast. They're expecting to be busy tonight."

"Shit, man, you don't need to help them, for fuck's sake! I been carryin' this tee shirt around for ya. It's SHOWCO's shirt for this tour, a beauty. I also got a 'Heartbreak Hotel' key fob for ya. The record label made them up. Here's your tour stage pass, too."

"Thanks, Poodie," I said, and immediately put on the cool new *Two for the Road* tee shirt.

As the hot Georgia sun began to set and the air cooled, security opened the gate, and the audience streamed in to the sounds of Bo Diddley playing over the P.A. system.

Nice choice, Garvey.

As the concessionaires turned on their deep fryers, the air became thick with the smells of hot dogs and fried chicken.

Since the buses would be locked during the performance, I went to The Tube to get my sweatshirt. The guest tables next to the chuck wagon were full of the folks I had seen at the pool that day.

Maynard was slaving away, busing the tables.

"Hey, Buddy," I said to him, "I'm gonna find a place out front to watch the show from tonight. When I find a good spot, I'll come back and get ya."

"Thanks, man. The further away from here, the better."

I headed out into the crowd to search for the best place to watch and listen. There were some off-limit knolls to check out. One, about seventy-five feet from the stage, had a great view, just to the right of the mixing board.

The area was roped off, and a guard was keeping people away.

"Hey, man," I said, "one of the crew and I would like to keep an eye on the stage from here. Is that okay?"

Looking at the all-access pass around my neck, he said, "Shit, you can stand or sleep anyplace you like."

After Maynard finished his chores, we made our way back to the knoll, where the poor guard was having a helluva time keeping people off the little rise. He seemed relieved to see us.

"Hey, can you guys kinda help if anybody gets through?"

"We're here for ya, man," I said. "Not to worry."

When Leon opened the show, it was just him and his piano singing and playing "Tightrope" from the *Carney* album. He followed that with a ripping version of "Pisces Apple Lady," slowly bringing up his band, one section at a time. Soon the entire band was rocking, including Mary, the percussionists, the horn section, and finally the backup singers. The sound was as clear as a chorus of silver bells on a gentle breeze. Leon played for a solid ninety minutes, covering all his hits and lesser known gems that

Maynard and I knew from being committed fans. I think this must have been the first time in weeks that Maynard just relaxed and took in the music.

Finally, Willie made his appearance with Trigger. He just kind of eased into whatever Leon was playing at the time, and the crowd went nuts. When Willie and Leon broke into "Heartbreak Hotel," the audience roared its approval, and all bets were off.

"Maynard, check out Willie making a perfect night into a more perfect one."

"He's a trip, alright. Only Willie could pull off something like this."

The remainder of the show was awesome. When Leon took a break, Willie did a great set, with Leon's musicians weaving soft accents into his tunes. It was the best Willie set I had ever seen. After an hour, Leon came back for a rousing medley of tunes by Hank Williams, who was a favorite of both men. Leon had even recorded a tribute album called *Hank*.

Before the end of the last set, Maynard and I made our way to the stage, ten feet behind Leon's piano. It was a thrill to be on the stage with a musical genius like that. When he and Willie ended with "Hey, Good Lookin," I could barely hear the music over the screams and whistles.

After the amazing performance, Maynard and I headed back to the Tube. While he put away tables and chairs, I went onboard to get out of the chill. There was a full pot of hot coffee on the counter, so I poured myself a cup. As I was sitting alone, looking out the window from the back of the kitchen, the door opened and three people came in: Willie, Leon, and Sydney Pollack.

Jew and a half on the bus!

"Andrew," Willie said, "is there any hot coffee by chance? It's cold out there."

"There is. Everybody want some?"

"We sure do, thanks," said Willie.

"Black okay?"

They all nodded.

I poured three black coffees and set them down on the table.

"Thanks, Andrew," Willie said. "This is Leon and Sydney. Andrew comes out to help us from time to time."

"Pleased to meet you," I said, shaking hands with Leon and Sydney. Then, to give them some privacy, I returned to my seat at the back of the kitchen.

Every once in a while, someone opened the door to come in, but Willie always said, "We'll be just a few minutes, thanks a lot."

I couldn't hear what he and the others were saying, but I figured it had something to do with the movie that was in the works. There was also a lot of laughing.

Suddenly, they were gone as quickly as they had arrived.

Beast was the first one on the bus.

"Who the fuck left dirty dishes on the table?" he complained, looking me squarely in the eyes. "Did you let them leave without washing these cups?"

This jarred me out of my historic moment back to reality.

"I wasn't paying attention, man. Sorry, I don't know the rules of your café."

"My rules are that everybody cleans their own!"

"I guess Willie didn't get the memo," I said as I dashed out the door, and headed over to the crew bus, where I found Maynard hanging out.

"My bus open up yet?" he asked. "Willie tossed me off ten minutes ago."

"It's open. And Beast is living up to his name. What an *idiot* that guy is."

"Now you know what I have to put up with."

Clipboard Jockeys

When I got home from the Leon tour, Stan, my boss at the moving company, was happy to see me. In fact, business was so good that he said he would give me a significant raise if I would make a full-time commitment.

A. Bernstein Archives
Home from the Tour with the SHOWCO Tee Shirt

"Stan," I said, "I'm not quite ready to give up the side trips, but I deeply appreciate your offer. I've got a few more adventures ahead of me, I'm afraid. But when it's over, I'm your man."

By now, I had become an old hand at the moving game, so Stan's appreciation was well deserved. I made the company money every day, didn't break things, and got along with the customers. What more could they ask?

"I had a feeling money wasn't gonna keep you home," Stan said with resignation. "But Ted asked me to make the offer anyway." (Ted Tanner was the owner of the company.) "What's it gonna take?"

"Once my research is done, Stan. It won't be too much longer."

"How in the hell did I end up with my best Class A driver being a researcher on the side?"

"Something to do with basketball, if I recall."

"Don't remind me. Get to work, Bernstein. You have a ten-thousand-pound local in San Francisco today. Oh, yeah, there's also an upright piano that needs to come down a spiral staircase. Be careful."

"Fuck you!"

When I returned to the office late that afternoon, I hung around to chat with Charlene Vincent, my dispatcher and good friend.

"Charlene," I said, "I really wanna find a place in transportation that's not behind the wheel, breaking my back every day. You know what I mean?"

"You're a bright guy, Andy. You excel at the job you're doing now, and the customers love you, so I see no reason why you can't move up the ladder in the moving industry…, none whatsoever."

I liked Charlene a lot. She could be testy as hell when she was dispatching on busy days, but I respected her opinion and appreciated her belief in me.

One Saturday morning, Lisa walked into the living room while I was lying on my back, juggling Autumn.

"Andy, one of your Texas friends is on the phone."

Holding my one-year-old daughter under my left arm while I tickled her with my left hand to distract her attention, I picked up the phone in the kitchen. The voice on the other end was instantly recognizable.

"Hey, D.W., how ya doin'?"

"Good, man. Whatchu up to?"

"I'm just enjoying some time with my family. At the moment, I'm the Tickle Monster..., with a victim in my arms." I gave Autumn a kiss on top of her head. "What's shakin' with you?"

"Well, we're fixin' to start shootin' the movie in San Antonio, and we got room for one more extra."

"You're inviting me to come down and begin my acting career? Is that what you're telling me?"

"That's *exactly* what I'm tellin' ya. We got a bunch of concert footage to shoot. We could really use a hand, Andrew."

"When's the fun gonna begin?"

"The minute you get here."

"I doubt that, but I'll come anyway."

"Can you be here in three days? That's the first evening of shooting."

"A star is born, D.W. I'll see you Tuesday night."

I gave Dickey a call right away. When I told him about the movie being shot in Texas, he said, "Fuck you, man! I'm goin' this time. Who's in the movie, aside from Willie?"

"Me!"

"Aside from that."

"Hell if *I* know. But I'll be finding out in a few days."

When I checked into the Hilton San Antonio, late in the afternoon on Tuesday, the clerk handed me an envelope addressed to "A. Bernstein." Inside there were directions from D.W. about how to get to the shoot location. I needed to be at the HemisFair Arena, under the Tower of America, ASAP. There was also a pass that would get me onto the movie set.

I showered and caught a cab to the HemisFair. When the driver dropped me off out front, I didn't see anyone around aside from some ticket sellers in a box office.

At one of the windows, I asked, "Where are they shooting the Willie Nelson movie?"

"You gotta go all the way around to the back."

I soon found myself wandering around in a parking lot filled with trailers, portable bathrooms, cables all over the ground, and a small army of people rushing around—but not one familiar face. I was totally lost.

Just as I was about to approach a guy climbing out of the back of a truck with some cable wrapped around his shoulder, someone grabbed my arm from behind.

"What took you so long, Andrew? You're holdin' up the whole fuckin' movie!"

It was D.W., with a look of desperation in his eyes.

"How the hell was I supposed to find you in all this chaos?"

"Well, never mind. Let's head over to Willie's motor home for a minute."

When we got there, D.W. knocked on the door, and Willie let us in. His face lit up as soon as he saw me.

"Welcome to the movies, Andrew. Glad you could make it. This here's Emmylou. Andrew's an old friend." He tossed me some papers. "Emmylou and I are shootin' some scenes together tonight. We've been lookin' forward to your appearance."

I rolled up a fat one, just the way he liked them, and passed it around.

After a while, there was a knock on the door. When Willie opened it, someone said to him, "It's time for you and Emmylou to be on the set."

Emmylou looked pissed. "Where's that goddamn babysitter?"

"Where's the baby?" I asked.

"She's asleep in the other room."

"How old is she?"

"Nine months."

"I've got a year-old girl myself. I could help out, if you need."

"It shouldn't be long, Andrew. The babysitter should be here any minute."

At that precise instant, the baby started to cry.

Emmylou went to get her.

When she brought the baby in, she said, "Her name's Meghann."

D.W. looked at me as if I were crazy.

"I'm a father, man," I said. "It's the least I can do."

Two minutes after Emmylou and Willie left, a woman in her mid-twenties walked in, panting as if she had just run a marathon.

"Oh, my god! Where's Emmylou?!" she said.

"You just missed her. She's not too happy with you."

"Oh, it's a long story."

"Well, I don't wanna hear it. Here's Meghann."

I gently handed her the baby, and D.W. and I were out of there.

As we climbed aboard another motor home, Kenny called out, "Yo, Andrew! Are we ever glad to see *you*! Have a seat. Wanna beer?"

"Of course, I do, Kenpeck, I've been wanting one for hours."

Kenny gave me the background about the movie.

"It's a kinda road flick, Andrew. Syd Pollack's version of the Willie Nelson band on tour..., except that Willie plays a character named Buck."

"They got a title?"

"Not yet. But Willie's crankin' out a couple o' new songs for the movie, I know that."

"Who else is in it, aside from Emmylou?"

"Dyan Cannon..., Amy Irving..., Slim Pickens..., Poodie."

"Who the hell's Amy Irving?"

"Steven Spielberg's girlfriend."

"Okay."

"Some of us got teamsters' cards. We get to drive gold golf carts all around. Most of the musicians got speakin' parts, so they're all now members of the Screen Actors Guild."

"Cool. Kenny, are you gonna be a movie star?"

"Shit, I'll be damned lucky if the camera ever *finds* me. We're extry extras!"

Walking in from the back of the motor home, Poodie hollered for all to hear, "Yo, big boy! Got one to burn?"

"Hey, Poodie," I said. "Do these producers have any idea yet what they signed up for?"

Who would blindly sink millions into THIS operation?

"They're just now startin' to figure it out, Andrew. We call it Bull in a China Shop Productions! Let's burn one."

We burned two. Maybe three.

After a while, Poodie took me into the arena and led me up to the stage, where production teams were positioning cameras.

"They're gonna shoot several different scenes tonight, Andrew. Mostly concert footage."

A small army of clipboard jockeys was scurrying around, talking into handheld two-ways.

"The story is woven around a love triangle, big boy, featuring Amy, Diane, and Willie. It's gonna be a long evening, with everyone appearing in several scenes."

An audience of extras, perhaps three hundred in all, was seated in clusters around the auditorium so the camera could turn them into thousands of fans.

Poodie took me to the back of the stage, where a small group of his friends were standing. I didn't know any of them.

"Don't move, ya'll," Poodie commanded, "or every one of you will be kicked off the set…. And that goes for me, too."

The clipboard jockeys eyed us with suspicion, since we hadn't been there during rehearsal. All of us stood literally at attention. Not one movement during filming was allowed. Since I was the tallest one, most eyes were on me.

When Emmylou did her solo, it was breathtaking. In fact, she did three takes, getting better with each one. Then she did her duet with Willie several times. Just seeing her perform was worth the airplane ticket.

The major dramatic scene being shot that night had a pissed off Dyan Cannon storming onstage and kicking a guitar off the front into the first row of the audience. Unfortunately, she missed the stunt guitar and sent Jody's Martin flying. Jody gasped but had to suck it up until the scene was over. It turned out that the guitar was fine, but Diane felt terrible. However, I learned that night that Jody was highly capable of soothing beautiful movie stars.

When filming for the evening finally came to an end, it was none too soon for me, since I was tired of standing there like a statue. I was aware, though, that these scenes were part of cinematic history. I would be able to view them for the rest of my life.

Poodie gathered everybody up and loaded us onto a couple of shuttle buses headed for "the best tequila bar in San Antone."

"I bet the bartenders there all know you, Poodie," I said.

"Just like family, Slim."

As we headed to the watering hole, I asked Steve where Maynard was.

"He'll be comin' in tomorrah from Austin with his girlfriend."

"Oh, Susan…. Maynard's told me a lot about her. Shirt embroiderer to the stars!"

"That's the one. Cute little thing."

"She must have fallen for his deep blue eyes."

"Fuckin' Maynard. She's too good-lookin' for him," Steve said.

The bar was on River Walk, a beautiful commercial area on the banks of the Rio Grande. It reminded me a great deal of Sausalito.

At the Mexican restaurant, Poodie made his grand entrance with a sizable posse in tow. The wait staff were ready for us, with five tables already arranged into one large seating area. Within minutes, there was more Mexican food, beer, and tequila than I'd ever seen before in one place.

As the drinking went on, the stories grew longer, Poodie's voice got louder, and everyone, including guests with the good luck to be eating there, were part of the celebration. This movie was either going to be the best thing that ever happened to this bunch, or they'd all go down shitfaced. I don't remember going back to the hotel that night. I'm told I had to be carried to my room.

Pee Hole Pete was the first to call the next morning. He appeared to be in a normal state of mind, clear of voice.

"Good morning, Andrew. Remember that blond at the restaurant last night? The one with the really big tits? I sure would like to stick my tongue up *her* ass!"

"Pete, I'm already ill, and you're a disgusting pig for making me more nauseous. You prick! I'll get even with you if it's the last thing I do."

"Just fuckin' with ya, Andrew, don't get upset. Poodie just told me to make a wake-up call."

I could hear Poodie in the background, laughing and coughing.

"Get up here, Andrew!" he yelled into the phone. "Let's burn one! Fuck, it's ten-thirty. We gotta get to work pretty soon, big boy."

"*You* have to go to work, Poodie. *I* sure as hell *don't!*"

"You got the buds, Andrew. We'll see you in fifteen minutes in room ten-fifty-six. We got an open bottle of tequila goin' around." He started howling along with the other culprits.

"Fuck all of you assholes!"

When I walked into Poodie's room, Pee Hole said with a hairy grin, "Ya don't look well, Andrew."

"You don't look like anything I was hoping to see first thing this morning either, sweetheart."

Wake and bake, my least favorite way to start the day, was nevertheless how it began. Then it was off to the arena to shoot some daytime scenes. I was unsteady for the trip over in the minibus, but the weed actually took the edge off.

There was nothing for me to do but hang out in the backstage lounge while I waited for Maynard and Susan to show up. Most of the sound crew were also killing time in there.

"C'mon, Andrew," Pee Hole said, "let's go find Easter. I think he's done acting. He's got a trailer, and we can burn one in there."

As I got up to follow Pete, I should have known better. He was always a man on a mission, moving with reckless abandon. This time, he barged through the door ahead of me, never looking first to see what might be going on. Within seconds of me closing the door and entering the darkened auditorium, the klieg lights blasted us, and we heard "ACTION!!"

Pete had walked directly into one of Dyan's entrance scenes. At that point in the story, she was supposed to be on her way to kick the now infamous guitar. But Pete just kept waddling straight toward the camera.

The second unit director screamed at him, "What are you doing, you fucking idiot? We're shooting a scene here!"

Pete kept right on waddling.

Then there was a great deal of screaming, with Dyan louder than anybody else: "I'm not *doing* this anymore! These people are all stoned. I'm going home!"

I took that opportunity to sneak back into the dressing room, unseen.

The guys in the room were real quiet now.

Poodie jumped up from the couch where he had been beached. "Where's Pee Hole?" he asked me, looking terrified.

"He just kept on walking toward the camera, Poodie," I said.

They got a great shot of him!

"That dumb fuck is gonna cost us our teamster jobs!" Poodie yelled. "Walkin' into scenes is the one thing Willie said would not be tolerated."

Just then, Paul English walked in, obviously annoyed: "This is a movie set, goddammit! Do you guys understand what that means?"

"Yes, Paul, we do," Poodie answered in a humbled tone.

"Where's Mister Peter Stauber, gentlemen?"

Everyone looked at me.

"He kept walking, Paul," I said meekly. "I just peeked my head out the door and watched him walk towards the camera. And then the screaming began."

"Well, Andrew, perhaps you can remind Peter that this is not a rehearsal. Ya'll need to be careful. He just walked into Dyan's scene."

This was greeted by a bunch of nodding heads.

"If Dyan walks off this set, we are genuinely fucked, gentlemen. Do you understand?"

More nods of acknowledgment.

When Paul turned around and left, I decided to follow him, figuring that was the best way for *me* not to walk into a scene. When I got outside, I looked around for Maynard's bus. It was hard to see because the sunlight was so bright, especially after coming out of the dark arena. I finally spotted The Tube about two hundred feet away, parked over by a fence. And there was Maynard, setting up some chairs and tables.

"Maynard Lutts!" I shouted as I approached the bus. "How the hell are ya?"

"Great, man. Glad you're here. Go inside and introduce yourself to Susan. I'll join you in a minute. I gotta set up a little reception area here."

I climbed on the bus, and there were Pee Hole and Easter in a booth, sitting across from an angel of a young woman.

Maynard's doing just fine!

"Hi, Susan, I'm Andy," I said, putting out my hand.

"I'm finally meeting you, Andy! I feel like I've known you forever. You're so tall!"

"I know. It's kind of embarrassing around petite women."

"Not a problem. Just so long as I can reach up to hug ya."

I bent over and put my arms around her slight frame.

Then, as I sat down next to her on the sofa, I glared over at Pee Hole: "Dyan's scene was briefly interrupted, Pete. Paul's looking for you."

"Am I in trouble? You were there, too."

Easter looked sternly at Pee Hole.

"Paul's gonna kick your fat ass," I said. "He's really pissed. He didn't see me 'cause I ducked back in."

I had him now. Sweat was starting to form on his forehead.

"Fuck, I should've looked. Shit, what's Paul gonna do?"

"It could be your ass, Pee Hole."

But then I couldn't contain myself and burst out laughing.

Easter busted a gut when he realized I had been putting Pee Hole on.

"That's payback," I said, "for this morning's wake-up call. I won't repeat what you said in front of a lady, but don't ever say that to me again..., particularly first thing in the morning."

"I say *what* I say *when* I wanna *say* it! That ain't gonna change, Slim. Let's burn one!"

Just then, Maynard got on the bus. "Beast's not arriving for a few hours," he said, "so the smoking lamp is lit."

I threw the bag on the table between Chris and Pee Hole. Chris pulled out some papers and rolled a spliff.

"Andy," Maynard said, "I'll bet some of the techs and script people on this set must occasionally ask themselves, 'What in the wide, wide world of sports is goin' on here?'"

"By the way, Maynard," I said. "I haven't seen Slim Pickens around. Have you?"

"He drops in from time to time."

"Yeah, he's an old friend of Willie's," Chris added. "But his scenes don't start till next week."

"I can't wait to meet him," Susan said. "He was great in *Dr. Strangelove.*"

The second and last night of the San Antonio concert shooting wasn't a whole lot different from the first night—except that I kept my ass in the dressing room.

At some point, Mickey made an appearance between scenes he was in.

"Hey, Andrew! How long *you* been here?"

"Got in last night. I heard you're acting your ass off..., hardly any of it left."

He laughed. "Man, this acting business isn't much fun. You just sit around and wait an hour to do a scene that takes five minutes..., and then you wait another hour for the next one."

"I hear Willie's writing some new songs for the movie."

"Yep, he's already written a road song, and he's working on a couple of ballads."

"Will there be a sound track album?"

"Indeed. This is a musical, man."

"Where's Mickey?!" someone shouted in the hallway. "We need him for his next scene."

"Gotta go, Andrew. We got one more band scene to shoot. Good to see ya."

"Break a leg, Mick! Keep an eye on your ass!"

He gave me thumbs up as he headed out the door.

About a half hour later, Poodie burst into the room with his usual gusto.

"Hey, Andrew! Ya know, we're gonna shoot some outdoor concert footage up north a ways tomorrow. Come on up with us. You can hang out on Maynard's bus and just blend in."

I don't much feel like stomping around in a cow pasture for the next four days.

But to Poodie, I said, "I'd love to. I really would, Poodie. But you don't need another yahoo just hangin' out and gettin' in the way."

"Andrew, we love havin' ya here. You're not in the way. Hell, you're the only one we can depend on to *never* be in the way."

"Just invite me to the opening, Poodie. I'll be there with bells on."

"Just no name in the credits, Slim."

We all broke up at that one.

Picnic in Pedernales

Poodie Locke Archives

I guess I knew from TV that Willie had thrown a Fourth of July picnic over the last five or six years. I'd see the clips on the national news every Fourth. It always looked like a dusty, hot, uncomfortable beer fest in the middle of nowhere. Not my idea of a good time, but everyone seemed drunk and oblivious to the obvious unpleasant conditions.

When D.W. called in early June '79, and mentioned the picnic, I was prepared to tell him not *this* Fourth. Cow pastures, drunken rednecks, and dust devils were not on my agenda, no matter how much I loved my new friends. To my surprise, he told me this was to be a much more civilized picnic. In fact, it would be held at the new country club that Willie had bought from a bankruptcy court.

"Well, now you're talkin', D.W.!"

"It's a beautiful spot, outside o' Austin, with rollin' hills, a nine-hole golf course, and no dust devils. We're still workin' on the line-up. But, man, you gotta come. This'll be a slice o' Texas you'll be sorry if you miss. Everyone's comin', all our friends and thousands of fans from all over."

"Alright, D.W., you talked me into it. But what about security? I've been to these things, like Altamont, where it gets very sketchy pretty quick."

"Don't worry about that. Willie asked Earl Campbell to head up backstage security, and the local sheriffs seem to be onboard. The home owners association folks are havin' some ulcers about it. But tough shit! Willie's their landlord now."

"Alright, June is the busiest month at the moving company, so I'll be working my ass off the next thirty days. But I'll be there, man. Let me know about accommodations as soon as it's been arranged."

"You'll be hearin' from me, Andrew."

"Tell the guys I'm comin'."

"Oh, one more thing I almost forgot. The night after the picnic, we're playin' Caesars Palace in Vegas for the first time. It's a real big deal. Willie asked that you come along. He hates to hear no."

"I'm in, D.W. Vegas will never be the same."

I called Poodie a few weeks later and got the address of the hotels that had been arranged for the VIP guests and not-so-VIP guests. I was curious which one I'd been registered into.

"You're in the Hilton, big boy. All the swingin' dicks will be there. Shit, Bum Phillips and Darryl Royal are on your floor. You happy now?"

"Very happy, Poodie. Hell, the Holiday Inn's fine with me, you know that."

"You'll need to fly to Vegas on the morning of the fifth with the band, unless you want to ride the bus with us. We're leavin' right after the picnic."

"I'll fly, Poodie, thanks."

"Okay, Andrew, bring a little somethin' along to Austin to celebrate Humboldt County. My favorite county. Alright, big boy?"

"Of course, Poodie. Dickie Lee's already on notice."

"I hope we meet him someday, Andrew."

"You will, Poodie, I just know it. See ya in a week!"

Ode really wanted to see fireworks that year. We had talked about it, and I felt really bad about disappointing him.

"I'm gonna see Willie, Ode. I'm gonna bring back a special shirt from Texas for you and one for your sister."

"You go see Wilwee, Dadda?"

It broke my heart, but fireworks were waiting in Austin.

I arrived in the evening, around 6:00. It was really hot. When the plane door opened, the scorching wind circulated through the cabin. Stairs, not an enclosed Jetway, met us as we came through the door. The full force of the Texas wind and heat just about blew me over.

I'd no sooner gotten to the baggage carousel area than I walked right into Kenny and Willie, who had just arrived from Colorado.

"Nice timing, Andrew," Willie said, dressed in his disguise of the day—a cowboy hat, shades, and hair tucked up inside the hat. He looked exactly like Willie Nelson.

"I always try to be on time, Willie," I said as I gave Kenny a big hug and pat on the back. "What's up, Kenpeck?"

"Ohhh, not much, man…. Willie and me just got in from Evergreen. Ready to roar, that's for sure."

"According to Poodie, this train ain't stoppin' for a while," I said.

"We're done being stopped, Andrew," Willie said as Kenny smiled and grabbed their bags. Mine came around a second later.

As we walked out to the parking lot, Willie asked where I was staying.

"At the Hilton, Poodie told me."

"We'll give you a ride. Kenny knows exactly where the car's parked. Don't ya, Kenny?"

"Ahhhh haaa, yup, I do, Willie."

I followed Willie and Kenny as we wandered around the parking lot.

I hope he finds this fucking car quickly! I've got a big bag in my pocket.

"It's that Mercedes right there," Kenny said, pointing.

Fortunately, it was.

Kenny got behind the wheel, I climbed into the passenger seat, and Willie got in back. On the way into town, we all talked about the picnic and Vegas.

"You're comin' to Vegas, aren't you, Andrew?" Willie asked.

"I am, thanks. Really lookin' forward to it. Shit, Willie, *Stardust* and *Two for the Road* are burning up the radio. The movie's coming out sometime, and I've got a pocket full of Humboldt buds."

"May we please have a few, Andrew?" Kenny asked, speaking for them both. "We're plumb out right now."

I took a sock out of my carry-on, deposited a small handful of buds in it, and put it in the glove compartment. Nevertheless, the pungent aroma was stinking up Willie's Benz.

When we pulled up to the Hilton, I jumped out.

"Alright, Andrew," Willie said, "see ya in the mornin'. Come on up to the clubhouse when you get there."

"Okay, Willie, thanks. Kenny, give me a call later."

"Sure, man."

And off they drove to Willie's ranch, which was close to his country club.

After checking in, I headed straight to my room. It was pretty damned cool to have run into those guys at the airport. I had arrived on the night of the second, so there was a day to rest up before the big party on the Fourth.

After cleaning up and getting some room service dinner, I headed to the bar, where I immediately bumped into Steve as I walked off the elevator.

"Wheeere the fuck have ya been, mannn? Sheet, ah been waitin' all fuckin' day fur ya to git here. Let's go burn one in yer room."

Twenty minutes later, we were back at the bar. The place was jumping: cowboys and cowgirls of every description were drinking and carrying on.

"Hey, Koepke!" someone called from across the room. "Come on over here. I wanna talk to ya."

It was Rex Ludwig, the other drummer beside Paul. We joined him at his table.

"Hi, Andrew," Rex said, "nice to see ya. Glad ya came down for Willie's little party. Cricket's comin' in from the Bay Area tomorrow."

I soon learned from Steve and Rex that a woman named Red Deb was due to make an appearance at the bar sometime soon. Rex was of the opinion that this night was to be his and Red's chance to socialize, while Koepke held quite a different view on the subject.

"Fuck you, Rex!" he said. "Sheee's damned near my fuckin' girlllfriend."

"Koepke, you keep your ass away tonight. Me and Red are just gonna talk, and she's already agreed."

"Bullshit, Rex! You wanna fuck her. I know you do, you asshole."

In the middle of this argument, the two of them decided they had to go to the men's room at the same time.

"Andrew, save our seats. We'll be right back," said Steve.

They'd no sooner turned their backs and headed for the john when the lady herself showed up. She was a redhead alright, and there was no mistaking her.

Walking right up to my table, she said, "Hi, I'm Deb. Are Rex and Steve comin' back? I just saw 'em leave."

I immediately stood up. "I'm Andrew, Deb. Nice to meet ya. Yes, they'll be back in a few minutes. May I buy you a drink?"

"Thank you, Andrew, sure. Rum and coke, please."

I went to the bar and got Deb her drink, pronto.

"I've heard 'bout you, Andrewww," she said as I handed her the glass. "You're from Frisco, ain't ya? I sure hope I get a chance to visit that city one day. My gawd, it looks sooooo purty in the pictures."

Of course, I had the sexy answers to all her questions about my hometown and eagerly offered them up.

"Hey, Deb, I got something from California up in my room I know you'd like. Let's run up for a few minutes. The guys'll be surprised I'm not here…, kind of a little joke."

As the elevator door closed, Steve and Rex turned the corner and saw us from twenty feet away. They came waving and shouting. Deb and I both smiled as the door closed snugly in their wrenched faces.

I met Kenny for breakfast the next morning. Looking refreshed, he told me it had been an early night at Willie's ranch. He had the day off, since the SHOWCO production crews were doing all the heavy lifting at the picnic site.

"Andrew, remember Peter Sheraton?" he asked. "Willie's friend who used to be a bodyguard for Jackie Kennedy?"

"Yeah."

"Well, he's askin' some questions 'bout you."

"What kinda questions?"

"'Bout cockblockin' one of the musicians. But don't worry about it. He just makes a lotta noise. He won't really do nothin'."

"I take his threats seriously, Kenny, and he's crazy."

"Just tell Poodie if he fucks with ya. Willie will have his ass if he lays a finger on you, I promise. There's gonna be a party tonight out at the country club. Let's head out there in an hour or so, and don't worry about Peter."

We went to my room to burn one, and then split to Pedernales. At the entrance, Kenny showed his pass, and then we drove up the hill to the clubhouse, parking in front. There were workers everywhere. The production crews were putting the final touches on an enormous stage. Water trucks were coming and going, filling storage tanks. And other trucks were setting up enough Porta Potties for a small army.

When Kenny and I walked into the clubhouse, we saw Willie holding court, showing some friends where he planned to build his new studio.

"Hey, Andrew," he called when he saw me. "C'mon over here and take a look. This is where the mixing room will be…, vocal booths over there, a big open room here for all my musician friends. Whaddaya think?"

"I love it, Willie. Play golf, record, play some more golf, record. Shit, your friends'll never leave!"

"Well, I hope they don't. That's the whole point. Hey, are you comfortable at the hotel?"

"It's perfect, Willie, thanks."

"Good. I told Snake to make sure you have a room in Vegas, too."

"Thanks. By the way, how was the sock?"

"Mighty fine. Thank you. I mean that!"

Kenny and I took a little tour of the picnic grounds and ran into some of the guys from SHOWCO. Budrock was the first one to greet us.

"Glad you could make it, Andrew. Got one to burn?"

There seemed to be no end in sight for these four words to be aimed in my direction for the foreseeable future. Fortunately, I'd rolled five joints in my room for the July 3rd celebration.

At some point, late in the afternoon, bands started to soundcheck. I was sitting on stage by Pee Hole's console, just listening and enjoying. Toward the end of the soundcheck, Willie was still trying to get it right. He stepped up to a live mike, plugged in Trigger, and out came *"My heroes have always been cowboys, and they still are, it seems."* His voice was as clear as a mountain stream. He played the entire song, with cicadas singing backup and a Texas sunset providing stage lighting. It was a phenomenal moment. Then Willie packed Trigger back up and asked me, "Coming for supper, Andrew? We're barbequing on the patio."

"Wouldn't miss it, Willie. Ya nailed that sunset, by the way."

"It's gonna be a good one tomorrow. Let's go eat."

I kept an eye out for Peter Sheraton all night, but he never showed up. It was a wonderful party. Jerry Jeff Walker was telling tales at the bar, so there was lots of laughing and some serious swearing. Around 2:00 A.M., I caught a hotel shuttle back to the Hilton.

At 8:30 in the morning, my phone rang.

"What's shakin', big boy?"

"Poodie, are you actually awake at this hour?"

"I'll be out in front of the hotel in an hour. I'm in my Blazer..., it's green. I'll be there at nine-thirty sharp. Roll a couple for the drive out."

"See ya then."

When the two-door Blazer pulled up, a passenger got out—Peter Sheraton.

"Hey, Andrew," Poodie called. "Get in the back seat."

Without saying a word to me, or even looking me in the eye, Peter pushed his front seat forward so I could climb in back. Things were fine until we got halfway to the country club. Then Peter turned partway around and said, "So tell me, San Francisco, you pull that cockblockin' shit where you come from, too?"

"That's enough Pete," Poodie cut in. "No bullshit. I told ya, Andrew's a good friend. Leave it alone."

"You know the rules, Poodie. Keep lookin' over your shoulder, Frisco. It's gonna be a long day."

When we got out to the club, about 10:15, people were already streaming in for the first act, scheduled for noon.

Peter got out when Poodie parked the car, and immediately disappeared into the crowd.

"Wear this tee shirt, Andrew," Poodie said as he handed me one. "And use this stage pass to stay out of Peter's way. He only has a pass to get backstage, not a stage pass. You can only get onstage with one of these shirts, too."

A. Bernstein Archives
Slim's Stage Pass

"I'll be alright, Poodie. But thanks, man. I'll always remember this."

At noon sharp, local bands hit the stage. The day's line-up was still evolving as the show got under way. Late in the afternoon, Ray Wylie Hubbard brought the crowd to life. He was a local friend of Willie's and a wonderful songwriter and entertainer. I was blown away by his ballads and honky-tonk rock 'n' roll.

Fuckin' cool!

For most of the day, I stayed under the huge canopy that covered the stage to protect the musicians from the scorching sun. But a few times I did go into the audience to roam around, because folks—especially female folks—felt at liberty to take off as many clothes as they liked. Every twenty minutes or so, the grounds crew near the stage hosed down several thousand people. That reminded me of the free summer concerts in Golden Gate Park, especially those in the Panhandle, except with a lot more beer and cowboy hats.

At some point, Poodie came up behind me onstage and said, "Andrew,

Cooder Browne's comin' up next, then Johnny Paycheck. Cooder's a good friend of ours, great songwriter. Stick around, I want ya to meet 'im."

"Thanks, Poodie. When's Leon comin' on?"

"After Paymore. You haven't met Johnny yet, either. Stone fuckin' crazy. You'll love 'im. And he's comin' to Vegas to hang out."

Once Cooder finished up, Johnny's crew started to set up his gear.

"Johnny," Poodie said, "this here's our good friend Andrew…, from San Francisco."

A. Bernstein Archives
Slim's Picnic Tee Shirt

We shook hands. He looked up, then up some more, and smiled. I liked him right away. He was dressed to the country outlaw hilt, and rocked that crowd into hillbilly shit-kickin' heaven.

"He ain't much bigger than a popcorn fart," Poodie whispered to me, "but that little motherfucker can get 'em all stirred up."

Poodie had a nickname for all the stars he regularly came into contact with. Waylon was Waymore, Johnny was Paymore, Bowman was Cod Ass, and it went on and on.

Jerry Jeff Walker had started drinking early that day. He was supposed to go on in the late afternoon, according to his manager, who seemed fed up with trying to corral him. Jerry Jeff missed several stage calls, and I don't remember him ever going on for his set. I was pissed because he was one of my favorite songwriters, and I had been looking forward all day to seeing him.

A surprise last-minute addition to the show was Asleep at the Wheel. Imagine my surprise when Benson walked onstage.

"What the fuck are *you* doing here, Andy?" he said, giving me a big hug. "It's a long way from Palo Alto."

"Yes, sir, it is. But not that far if your bus driver is Maynard Lutts."

"Ahhh, now it makes sense."

As the sun began to set and the melting temperature slowly dropped, The Wheel kept the thermometer up with their blistering renditions of Bob Wills's music.

Old home week for me. Visions of Homer's.

After dark, the fun really began. With the sun down, Budrock started doing his usual magnificent job on the stage lights. He was especially brilliant when Leon came out—with deep blues for his ballads, and flashing reds and yellows for his up-tempo hits. When Willie joined Leon, it was as though the old tour just rolled into town. The audience, now revived by the cool evening, went nuts after each of Leon's gems. Looking out at the crowd, I thought about the soundcheck the night before, when I watched Willie singing to the empty fairways. Now there were thousands of drunk speed freaks swaying in the breeze, instead of a billion blades of grass.

Leon's performance that night was my favorite of the show. His haunting voice and poignant lyrics slayed me. The message in his love songs is often hidden by themes or settings, such as a carnival, in which the upbeat melody masks the deeper sadness of the words. I was riveted by Leon that night, moved to tears by several numbers.

When Willie and Leon ripped into "Jailhouse Rock" and other tunes from *Two for the Road*, the audience couldn't get enough, even though they had been there by now for nine hours.

As Willie's band gathered onstage to watch the end of Leon's set, and to prepare for the evening's grand finale, I noticed Rex lingering around the stage, giving me dirty looks. I was standing with Easter at the time and gave him the lowdown.

"Rex fucking told Peter Sheraton to kick my ass," I said, "because I cockblocked him last night with Red Deb. Can you believe that?"

"That's just Rex, Andrew, that's his M.O. Tell Cricket the story. That'll shut the little fucker up."

"Hey, Chris, there's a few minutes before you go on. Let's go burn one."

Chris and I sneaked off and smoked the last joint in my pocket.

"You're comin' to Vegas in the mornin', aren't ya?" Easter asked.

"Yep, I am. I'm on the same flight as ya'll."

"Well, I might need a hand. My wife's gonna fly home to Utah, and I'm gonna have the three kids to take to Vegas with me. The oldest one's only six. Do ya think you can help?"

"Of course, Chris. I'm a dad, too, ya know."

"That's why I'm askin'. Thanks, man."

When Willie performed his set, he and The Family Band were joined by all the various guests, dropping in and out. Jerry Jeff managed to get onstage and sing a few, but his manager was ever so careful to keep a watchful eye on him.

At the end of Willie's set, Ernest Tubb came out, and they sang a Jimmy Rogers song together, "In the Jailhouse Now." I could see the love that Willie had for that man—an original homegrown gentleman, who had dominated the country and pop charts when Willie was a youngster.

Poodie Locke Archives
Ernest Tubb and the Texas Troubadours

By the time Ernest's band was set up for the finale of the show, it was after 10:00 P.M. But no one was going anywhere. I stood with some of the guys on the side of the stage and watched the Texas Troubadour play many of his hits. My education in country music took a giant leap as "Walking the Floor Over You," "Waltz Across Texas," and "The Yellow Rose of Texas" rolled out, one after another. I knew all those songs, but had no idea who had written them. The guys could see in my face that I was blown away. Listening to this Country Hall of Fame original, I just about lost it.

After the set ended, I gave Poodie a warm hug and thanked him for the day from the bottom of my heart. Willie happened to see this as he stood nearby, and smiled and winked at me. I was literally overwhelmed at the kindness and hospitality of these wonderful people. I simply had no words to express my gratitude, not a one.

There were limos, minibuses, and hotel shuttles lined up backstage to take everyone to the hotels in town. There had been a fair amount of booze consumed by some of Willie's guys after his set, since Willie required them to stay sober until the set was over. I went into the clubhouse to pee before looking for a ride back to the hotel. Jerry Jeff was in the clubhouse, trying to break into Willie's office, drunk and demanding money. He scared the shit out of me. I ignored him and did my business in the john. When I came out, he was trying to beat down the door to the office. Apparently, his manager had had enough, and Jerry was on his own. On my way out, I let a security guy know what was going on.

Easter, who was now pretty tipsy, was standing near a limo, so I opened the door for him, and we got in.

"Hey, Andrew! *There* you are! Gimme a hug!"

It was Cricket, sitting between Rex and Marty Grebb, Bonnie Raitt's sax player, whom Willie had brought in for his set. Everybody was completely shitfaced except Cricket and me.

Rex looked surprised to see me, particularly with his wife at his side, hugging me. I glared at him, knowing he had tried to have me roughed up by Peter for interrupting his rendezvous with Red Deb. He looked stymied and drunk. Marty was really gone, and Easter was on the verge. Nevertheless, they all continued to drink and act like fools, while Cricket and I carried on a sober conversation.

When we had gotten about halfway to Austin on some expressway, Rex said that he needed to pee really bad. Then Marty chimed in that he needed to go, too.

"Hey," Marty said, "I'll show you guys how to piss in a bottle. We got a few empties here."

I looked at Cricket, and knew we had a problem. I lowered the vanity window and asked the driver if he could pull over for a highway pee break.

"No way, sir. I'll lose my license."

"Well, it's gonna come down to these guys trying to piss in long-neck bottles and making a big mess all over the floor, or we stop."

"I'll never do this damned picnic again," the driver snapped. "Shit! Okay, I'll pull over. But supervise them, please."

The guys were barely able to walk, but I herded them off the road, and they did their business, laughing and howling at the moon the whole time. Then, just as I got them all back in the car, flashing red lights lit up the limo.

"Shit, Andrew!" Cricket screamed. "We're all fucking goin' to jail!"

"Settle down, love," I said. "It'll be okay."

I closed the door and leaned against the car, waiting for the cop to approach.

"You know why I'm here," he said. "I don't need to draw you any pictures."

"Officer," I said in my softest tone, "there's a bass player, a drummer, and a sax player in there, and they're plumb beat after nine straight hours of playin' in the sun." *Don't mention that they're Willie's musicians!* "The limo driver will lose his license, and the band members will be fired if this moves forward. Please let us go. I'm not drunk and will take full responsibility for getting them back to Austin."

Amazingly, it worked.

"Get your asses outta here, *now!*" is all he said. And we were on our way home.

Cricket smothered me with kisses in appreciation. Rex and Marty just carried on, without even realizing what had just happened. But Easter was shaken. His wife was counting on him to take the kids to Vegas in the morning, so the thought of her bailing him out of jail for indecent exposure sobered him up fast.

Back at the hotel, safe and sound, Cricket told anyone and everyone that I'd pulled off a miracle and kept us all out of jail. She wouldn't shut up about it, which was fine with me, but Rex was shivering in his boots that I would bust him.

Fantasy Land

While Poodie's crew bus was driving to Vegas, I would be flying with the band on an 11:00 A.M. flight out of Austin. You can imagine what we all looked like that morning as we stumbled out of the hotel, after sixteen hours of playing, working, smoking, drinking, and carrying on at the picnic.

I don't know how they do it. This ragged bunch is gonna put on two performances tonight.

Somehow, we managed to get all our bags and ourselves, including Willie, into the vans for the drive out to the airport. Just as Chris had said, he had his three young kids in tow—and no wife. As we all headed to the gate, everybody just wanted to lie down. I'm sure the other passengers were highly offended (and justifiably so) by our language, our hangovers, our snotty crying babies, and our general "to hell with everyone else" attitude.

As we landed in Las Vegas that afternoon, we had no idea what Caesars Palace had in mind for the gang. At that moment, any bed in any room would have done just fine. Supporting each other, with Snake leading the way to baggage claim, we saw two Caesars employees waiting for us. They took our bags away, and then a third employee, this one dressed in a suit, led us to the taxis that we figured would take us to the hotel.

However, when we got outside, there was a long, long line of white limos at the curb, more than I'd ever seen before in one place, with security guards around to keep the curious away. Caesars had provided one limo for each hungover, longhaired, dirty-Levied one of us—including Chris's shrieking and blubbering babies. I hopped in with him to help with the kids and started talking like Donald Duck, which got their attention for at least twenty seconds.

On the ride into town, I saw that Caesars had plastered *all* the billboards between the airport and the hotel with Willie's picture from the back of the *Stardust* album. It was unbelievable—every damned one of them!

After a while, we faced a crisis: the kids had to go potty. *Now!*

Fortunately, we pulled up, about that time, in front of the grand, glittering portico of Caesars Palace and got out to the sound of Willie's music playing over hidden outdoor speakers.

Soon the whole check-in area was full of us, looking like something the cat had dragged in, with Chris desperately searching for a bathroom for his screaming kids. At first, a choreographed greeting team tried to wow us with gold keys and Caesars Palace baubles, but they soon realized that all we really wanted was a toilet for the kids, rooms with or without golden keys, and soft beds to drop onto.

No one else wanted to be around whining, so Chris and I and the kids had an elevator all to ourselves. It was a special one that went straight to our floor. When the doors opened, we stepped out into a hallway of swanky carpets and crown molding dripping in gold leaf. Willie's music was pouring down from the ceiling. All the rooms had double doors.

When we entered Chris's room, we stared in disbelief at what was in front of us. Everything was done in shades of red or pink: the heart-shaped bed on a pedestal, the heart-shaped hot tub at the end of the bed, and the satiny fabric draped all over the damned walls. There was French champagne in a heart-shaped bucket on one of the heart-shaped dressers, and two pink telephones. It was the damnedest thing I'd ever seen. I felt ill just looking at that junk. The colors certainly didn't help my sore eyes and queasy stomach.

I got out of there as soon as I could—which was when the first little tush hit the heart-shaped toilet seat.

"Good luck, buddy!" I hollered to Chris as I headed out the door. He had a forlorn look on his face.

My own room, several floors down, was in a totally different dimension—more like an upscale Holiday Inn suite in tones of soft blue—with not one heart in sight, thank God.

I took a two-hour nap, and then the phone started ringing. Kenny wanted to come up to burn one, so we did, and then we headed down to the Rosicrucian Room (or whatever the hell it was called) to meet Pamela Brown and D.W. for dinner.

On the way to the restaurant, we passed a long line of people who were waiting for the doors to open for the early show. They all looked like middle-class Midwestern American couples, very straight, and clearly excited to hear Willie sing.

At that point, food and drink and room service were all on the hotel. Later on, they realized that this policy didn't work with this outfit. But that night we took full advantage of the restaurant by ordering everything good on the menu.

"So, D.W.," I asked as the second bottle of Dom Pérignon arrived, "what color is *your* heart-shaped hot tub?"

"Andrew," Pamela broke in, "don't you like the Fantasy Suites?"

"More like nightmare suites," D.W. answered.

"I got a purple one," Kenny popped in.

"To match your silk underwear, Kenpeck?" I asked.

"Fuck you, Andrew!"

After dessert, it was time to head backstage. When we got there, Kenny and D.W. went to work, and Pamela and I got a drink in Willie's dressing room.

"Got yourself a new girlfriend there, Andrew?" said a familiar voice from behind.

"What's it *to* ya, Poodie? You just wish it was *you*, don'tcha?"

"Pamela Brown's the prettiest girl in town," he said.

"Whyyy, Poooodie Locke," Pamela said in her sexiest drawl, "I didn't think you ever noticed."

"Yeah, right!"

When Willie hit the stage, the crowd literally went nuts. I took my designated post, just behind the wing curtain, stage left. Willie played the opening chords to "Whiskey River," the Texas flag dropped, and the show was under way. The room itself was very impressive, with table seating in a luxurious setting and great sound and lights. Above the crowd, in the back of the house, Budrock was in a booth operating the lights, with Garvey next to him, mixing the sound.

At the end of "Whiskey River," Willie said, "I'd like to perform a couple o' new songs that I wrote for a movie we just did." Then he launched into "On the Road Again," followed by "Angel Flying Too Close to the Ground." Considering how famous these two songs became, the audience's reaction that night was only lukewarm. They wanted the hits. But I thought that "On the Road Again" perfectly captured Willie's lifestyle. I believe that was the first time he ever played it in public.

That first show was only a warmup, as Willie got a feel for the room and the acoustics. The dinner show was better. The audience had no idea that Willie and the band were burned out from the picnic and everything that followed. He actually sang "She's a Retarded Woman in Love with a Good-Timing Man," instead of "She's a Good-Hearted Woman," which evoked howls from all of us, especially Poodie, who happened to be standing next to me when Willie let that one fly. But the crowd had no idea.

This was the beginning of many runs for Willie and the band at Caesars. The brass at the casino told Poodie that Willie's first-night crowd had broken the record for money coming through the casino, previously held by an opening night featuring Frank Sinatra. For that honor, the hotel gave Willie, all the musicians, and every member of the crew a gold medallion.

Kopeck and Pee Hole immediately ran out to the nearest pawnshop and cashed in.

Bazeball

Willie was hot! He no longer recorded much with Waylon; his star was rising based on his own songwriting, singing, and guitar playing—not to mention his Willieness. At that point in his career, he had exclusive contracts with several of the biggest casinos, especially Caesars in Vegas and Harrah's in Tahoe and Reno. Everybody's favorite was Tahoe. It was gorgeous in every season, and we could ski in the fall and winter and go boating, biking, or hiking in the spring and summer—plus gamble and chase women all year round. But for Willie, the most important pastime was playing softball, with the hotel's stagehands against the band and crew.

It all began one night after a show at Harrah's, when the head of the stage crew approached Willie.

"Hey, man," he said, "we got a softball team, and we wondered if you guys would wanna play for beers sometime."

"Hell, yeah! Where and when?"

"Up about ten miles, on the Nevada side, by Phil's house, along the winding two-lane road that circles the lake. There's a first-class softball field up there. How about tomorrow?"

Soon we were playing the backstage crews at all the casinos, with lots of beer, plenty of smoke, and serious attempts to have fun. And *win*. Willie was competitive as hell. Whether it was chess, baseball, or making hit records, he was driven to excel. He wanted to win the games so much that he even recruited ringers when he felt we needed them. One was his good friend Dave Casper, "The Ghost." Willie and Poodie loved the guy in a big way. Willie also loved the fact that Dave could hit a softball as far as the eye could see. Poodie never tired of telling how, one day, Dave hit a softball over everyone's heads in the outfield, over the trees, and beyond the picnic tables. For all I know, that ball is *still* flying.

As for me, athletics had never been my forte, but softball was different. Not at first, though. I started in left field, but couldn't judge distance well and dropped fly balls on a regular basis. Paired up with Kenny at center, who was even worse, I was quickly becoming an embarrassment to the team—until Bee Spears suggested switching with me at second.

"In that position, Andrew, all you have to do is stretch out your long arms and legs and *stop* that fuckin' ball."

I was determined not to let anything get past me, no matter what it took. I would sacrifice my body for the team—and most of all, for Willie. Perhaps not with grace, that's for sure, but all six feet and seven inches of me flew in whatever direction the ball was going, and not much made it to the outfield. With Willie at shortstop, pretty soon we had double plays down pat.

One memorable afternoon, we played a game at Reno under cold, threatening skies against the Reno Harrah's team. The Tahoe crew had warned us that these guys were serious players, so that forced us to be at the top of our game. The casino paid professional umpires from the adult leagues in the area, who came for sober ball playing, and not to referee a bunch of drunk potheads. We had the new band bus, *Scout*, at the park that day, and one by one we disappeared to refresh ourselves onboard when our side was at bat.

A. Bernstein Archives
Scout

The Ghost was with us that day, so we were doing well. But the Reno team had a distinct advantage: *no* bus to freshen up in. Shortly after I made a trip to *Scout*, it was my turn at bat, but I had a hard time finding my way to the field, which was about fifty yards away. Willie, who was up right before me, smacked a double to right. I liked batting after Willie, because he just about always got on base. However, unlike most human beings, he could do anything just as well stoned as unstoned. This was not true for most of the rest of us, but since he set the bar, we tried not to make fools of ourselves.

At the plate, I had trouble tracking the ball, and quickly got two strikes on me. All I could see was Willie glaring at me from second base. Not wanting his hit to go to waste, I focused as hard as I could.

Crack!

The wonderful sound of wood against a big old softball snapped across the field. I had no idea where the ball was going, so I just lowered my head and headed to first base as fast as my legs could carry me. I heard Poodie yelling, "Faster, big boy! *Movvve*, Andrew!"

As I approached the first baseman, I prepared myself to take him out, if need be, to get a hit. Perfectly legal, but my THC-impaired vision made me focus on the wrong man. Instead of slamming into the first baseman, I knocked the first base *coach* out cold.

When I realized what I had done, I felt terrible. Play was suspended while I hovered over Budrock until he came around.

"What the fuck were you tryin' to do, Andrew..., *kill* me?" he yelled, with a huge scowl on his puss. "I'm on your *team*, you stupid cocksucker!"

Once it was apparent that he was okay, we all burst out laughing, but he continued to rail at me all afternoon. Poor Buddy, he's never let me live that one down.

The softball games became a big part of summers at Tahoe. As we played more and more of them, we honed our skills and got pretty competitive, led by Willie himself, who played every game as if it were the clincher of the World Series. Whenever we lost a game, he would insist that we play a second shorter one to try to tie things up. More beer, more refreshment between the games, and we would be back at it. If we got ahead, Willie would call the game, claiming that we had to make the show. We never did lose two in a row.

We had a few close calls for the 7:00 o'clock performance, notably on one absolutely perfect Tahoe day in August. The backstage crew at Harrah's had also improved their game, so we were tied until the last inning, when they scored to take the victory. Willie was pissed, blaming himself for striking out with men on, so we played a second game, starting at 4:30. We agreed to limit that one to three innings, and fortunately were ahead at the bottom of the third. We only had enough time for someone to take a group picture of all of us.

During the first game, a group of Hells Angels from the Oakland chapter had arrived to cheer us on, with the help of several cases of beer. When the hotel shuttle bus driver had come back to take us to Harrah's, we were still playing, so he parked and waited, a little grumpy because we weren't ready to leave.

Willie and the guys were happy because we had just won the second game, and the Hells Angels were happy because they were drunk.

A. Bernstein Archives
Softball at Lake Tahoe, 1979 (Slim's the tall guy next to Willie, top left)

As the rest of us headed for the minibus, Willie had a sedan driver take him to his digs at Phil's compound on the lake to wash up and change for the show.

"All you assholes on the bus!" Poodie shouted. "We gotta get back to Harrah's. We got a show to do."

Hot, tired, and loaded, we dropped into our seats.

Most of the Angels had come on their motorcycles, but Foo and Deacon had driven up in cars with all the beer and their old ladies. Now they decided to leave their ladies with the cars, and go back to the hotel with the band. As they headed toward the bus, they were joined by a very drunk Angel, appropriately named Dump Truck, since he weighed at least three hundred and fifty pounds.

Deacon, also a giant of a man with the girth of a Viking, was drinking a beer from one hand as he carried a cooler in the other.

The cranky driver, however, announced that no alcohol was allowed on the bus.

Deacon just offered him a beer and proclaimed in his booming voice, "Free beers on the bus, boys! The Angels are treating."

As the driver began to protest, Deacon grabbed his keys.

"Call a cab, buddy! *I'm* drivin' this bus!"

Shit! Now what?

"Hey, Deacon," Poodie called. "Back off. This is a recipe for trouble."

But it was too late for that. As Deacon climbed up the steps, the driver wisely started walking.

When Foo and Dump Truck came aboard, Deacon put the bus in gear, and off we went.

Taking control of the cooler, Dump Truck insisted that everyone have a beer for the road.

We all took a can, but no one drank a drop. We were all holding our breath every second of the twenty minutes to the hotel. Fortunately, Deacon kept it between the lines.

When we pulled up to the entrance at Harrah's, a sheriff was waiting for us with a couple of suits from the hotel. Apparently, the bus driver had called ahead.

However, as soon as the bus doors opened, Dump Truck fell out on his face, right at the sheriff's feet.

Looking disgusted, but relieved that everyone had made it back in one piece, and the bus was unscratched, the sheriff said to the hotel reps, "Gentlemen, I believe this is an internal hotel matter."

And with that, he marched to his patrol car and drove off.

Needless to say, the hotel never offered the shuttle bus again for softball games.

Cold Beer and Air Conditioning

A few weeks later, Willie and the Family were out touring the Midwest, doing state and county fairs. I hooked up with them again somewhere in southern Illinois, right after they finished a performance. While Willie signed autographs, I waited in his bus with Bobbie, Chris, and Snake. When Willie came aboard, he greeted me with a big smile, and we took off for Chicago, with Big Al at the wheel.

"Where we goin' tonight, Andrew?" Willie asked. "Humboldt or Mendocino?"

"Somewhere in the hills in-between, Will."

We all had a lot of laughs that night.

The next morning, I had breakfast with Poodie, Steve, and Kenny at a Holiday Inn outside Chicago.

"I've got a surprise for you, Andrew," Poodie said. "The Dead are playin' the same auditorium tonight that we play tomorrow night. We got an invitation from Rock Scully to go backstage for tonight's show."

"That's cool! I haven't seen Jerry or Billy for years."

We left for the concert in the crew bus around 8:00 P.M. Paul English wanted to see the drummers up close, even though he didn't know their names and had never seen them perform. Mickey Raphael, on the other hand, had been a Dead fan since he was a kid. Before Pigpen died, he had been one of Mickey's heroes on the harmonica.

I heard "Beulah" being played as Rock Scully took us to our assigned seating on cases and chairs at the side of the stage, just off the wing.

Paul seemed to feel a little like a fish out of water backstage, staying close to Steve, Kenny, and me. As he studied the drummers, he laughed and shook his head in disbelief at the whole spectacle. He loved it, becoming one of the faithful for the night.

Mickey Raphael Archives
Mickey Raphael

It was good to see Bill Kreutzmann again, my old Palo Alto buddy.

Although Dead concerts could go on for hours, Chicago had a curfew, so they finished up on time. As the band wandered offstage, Billy was beat, looking like he had just run a marathon. As he went up the rickety old staircase to his dressing room, I could see that Paul wanted to ask him some questions, or at least say "hi." But he was too respectful to ever bother Bill, or any musician, who had just played for hours.

"C'mon, Paul," I said, "let's go upstairs and say hello to the drummers."

"I cain't do that, Andrew. Them boys worked hard tonight."

"Paul, you may never get another chance. C'mon, let's go. You're Willie Nelson's drummer, for Chrissake!"

"Alright, but you go first."

Up the stairs we went, passing Rock Scully on the way down, who was carrying a big handful of tee shirts."

"Gimme some of them shirts, Rock!" Poodie shouted from the bottom of the stairs.

"That's my plan, Poodie. Hold your horses."

The door to Bill's dressing room was open.

"Go on, Paul. Go introduce yourself."

Paul quietly went up to Bill and introduced himself. Bill warmly shook his hand. As they began to talk, I backed up to the door to give them some space. Every few seconds, Bill looked over at me.

Finally, he excused himself and walked over.

"Don't I know you?" he asked. "You look familiar."

I replied, "Perhaps you remember my '63 Corvair Monza convertible..., the white one with aqua upholstery?"

He started laughing.

"Andy Bernstein! What the hell are *you* doing here?"

"I've been running with Willie's Family for a couple of years, off and on."

"No shit!"

Paul looked confused. He had no idea I knew Bill.

At that moment, Mickey appeared out of nowhere. I introduced him to Bill, and we all started yakking.

After a while, Mickey took me aside.

"Hey, Andrew," he whispered, "why don't you invite Bill to come to the bus to reminisce about the old days?"

I went up to Bill and said, "We got a bus outside. These guys would love to hear us 'talk story' about the old days in Buttholeville."

"That'd be great," he said. "Lemme finish up here, and we'll head out."

Once on the bus, with cold beer and air conditioning, Bill and I eased into a conversation about the Palo Alto we knew, and the characters we had grown up with: Tom McCarthy, Crazy George Hearst, and, of course, Pigpen, to name a few.

Poodie hooted at the funny parts, and Chris threw in some Gram Parson stories. We had a ball for three hours. Those Texas hippies couldn't get enough about San Francisco and the madness that was so much a part of Bill's life and mine.

Grifa

In the fall of 1978, after my old Cajun buddy René Comeaux moved to Maui, Peter Hays took over the house on Sierra Court in Palo Alto. The scene of so much madness when René lived there kept rolling right along. Dickie Jackson from La Honda, Uncle Glen and Red Headed Mike from Rockford, Illinois, and several others were constant characters in residence—not to mention Spencer Bornes, for whom Rollie and I had produced the Chuck Berry show.

One eventful night when I was in town, Peter tossed a big party just before Christmas. The whole gang was there, including many of René's old fishing buddies and the usual suspects from Palo Alto, La Honda, and Boulder Creek. However, one of the guests was a surprise for me, a bigger-than-life man around town, the now 300-pound Gordie Howe. This was the same Mr. Howe who in 1964 had made the front-page headlines in the *Palo Alto Times* as the face of drug dealing in town when he and his Foothill College pals got busted for one ounce of pot.

A Paly graduate in '61, Gordie had achieved local rock star status at a young age as a guitarist, along with Charles Haid, in a very early incarnation of The Legends, a starting point band for many Palo Alto musicians, including Bill Kreutzmann.

Gordie recognized me as soon as I came into the room. He had tried to fleece me for my grandmother's inheritance several years earlier on a pot deal, which I stayed away from. But he was an irresistible character, really a local icon, who could sell snow to an Eskimo under the worst of blizzard conditions. He had married his high school sweetheart, Judy Dawkins, and they had a young baby son named Roadie. An undoubted genius, Gordie had a way of drawing you into his most recent scheme as if your very life would change merely by agreeing with his sales pitch. But this time, he wasn't pushing pot or drugs of any kind—he had a screenplay and was trying to produce a movie.

Through the local grapevine, he had heard that I was spending time with Willie, and he was certain that Willie would want to sign on. Although I was suspicious, since I knew Gordie's penchant for hard living, he nevertheless dazzled me with his latest flavor of snake oil.

As it happened, just weeks before, I had read an interview in *Penthouse* with Thomas Pynchon, the author, who argued that marijuana should be made legal. He also briefly mentioned that he had worked on a project having to do with that very subject. Gordie was claiming to have partnership rights to a screenplay that had been at least in part written by Pynchon.

"Gordie," I said, "I've known you a long time, but this is a tall tale. I'll need far more than your word to ever approach Willie or any other musical friends…. But I'll think about it."

"Well, I understand, Andy. But I'd like you to meet my partners in this venture, who are both upright citizens and professionals in the local TV and literary fields. David's a producer for ABC-TV, and Paul's in publishing. We have a small production office south of Market in the city. You're welcome to stop by anytime."

"Have ya got any money?"

"Two hundred and fifty thousand in seed money. And we've got a second-unit Hollywood director named Glen Wilder onboard. He's currently working on a new movie called *Raging Bull*, about Jake LaMotta."

"The boxer?"

"Yeah. He was middleweight champ in the forties and fifties."

"Okay, but what's this Thomas Pynchon thing, Gordie? That's a big leap of faith. The guy's hot shit…, and a hermit by all accounts."

"Okay, I know. But just read the screenplay before you kiss it off. I'll get you a copy, then decide. It's a love story about pot smugglers…, an action adventure, very well crafted and thought out."

"Has it got a name?"

"*Grifa*."

"What the fuck does *that* mean?"

"It's Spanish slang for pot."

That got my attention.

A. Bernstein Archives

By the following Monday afternoon, I had a copy of the screenplay in my hands. I pored over it for the next three or four days, reading it five or six times. Every time I read it, I loved it more. A Cuban femme fatale seduces a Central American general and a South American dictator in a plot to smuggle thousands of pounds of pot into the U.S. It reminded me a bit of my own little escapade.

When I met the other partners, I found out that they were indeed responsible businessmen, who actually owned the rights to the thing. One of them was a distant cousin of Señor Gordo, who had conned these gentlemen with his gift of gab into bringing him in to market the screenplay—as it turned out, a fatal mistake. But for now, it was all engines full steam ahead. They even had a logo and tee shirts made up, a beautiful tricolor design featuring a marijuana leaf.

I told them that I felt there was a killer sound track dying to be made here, and that Willie might be the perfect one to make it.

"Do you really think he'd be interested?" David asked.

"Give me ten of those tee shirts, put that logo on the front of the screenplay, and I'm pretty sure he'll be interested. The story has to stand on its own, though. He's nobody's fool."

At that point, the Family was playing a series of gigs in L.A., so I called Snake, gave him a thumbnail sketch of the story, which he loved, and asked him to set up a meeting with Willie.

Gordie told me that he was eager to come along, so I booked two rooms at the Sheraton on Wilshire. However, when he kept drinking all morning, I figured Willie would be alarmed by a sweaty 300-pounder whose mouth never stopped. I loved Gordie, but he was an acquired taste.

In the end, I said, "Gordie, if you wanna know the truth, you're just too over the top. You'll kill the deal with your hyperenthusiasm. Nothing personal."

"Whaddaya mean by that?" he said, obviously pissed.

"You're gonna have to trust me on this one. I have a relationship with the man, and I need to run solo with this deal."

He didn't like it, but he didn't have any choice.

At that point in Willie's career, his default mode was skepticism, since he had offers coming at him from every direction and had been burned a couple of times.

But I think this one's gonna pique his interest.

I took an elevator up from the fourteenth to the eighteenth floor for the 2:00 o'clock meeting and knocked on the door to Room 1820.

Mickey Raphael opened the door, smiled when he saw me, and said, "Ah, the drug dealer's arrived."

"Fuck you, Mickey!"

Willie, who was sitting on a chair at the far end of the room, called to me, "C'mon in, Andrew. How are ya? Have a seat."

I sat down on the other side of the coffee table and pulled out a small Ziploc bag.

"I brought along a little somethin' special for ya, Willie."

"Ya always do." He laughed.

I rolled a fat one and handed it to him.

"I brought you somethin' else, too."

"So I hear."

I pulled a copy of the manuscript out of my shoulder bag and put it down on the coffee table. Willie was instantly taken by the marijuana logo.

"If the story's as good as that picture, Andrew, we just might have a deal…. What's the story about?"

"Marijuana smugglers, with a bit of love, intrigue, and a lotta pot."

"Somebody told me Thomas Pynchon had somethin' to do with this. Is that true?"

"That's what they tell me, Willie. All I know is that I've read it ten times, and I think you'll love it. I'm pretty sure this thing is gonna get made, and we'd sure as hell love to have you onboard."

"Well, there's one problem, Andrew. I just signed an exclusive contract with Warner Brothers. I don't fully understand what I can and can't do. But if I like this, I'll find a way to help you guys out."

"I've got one more thing for ya, Willie."

"What's that?"

I pulled one of the tee shirts out of my bag and held it up so he could see it."

"Holy shit! That's gorgeous!"

"I've got nine more, Willie. You're gonna have to decide who gets 'em."

"I might just keep 'em all."

"I want one!" Mickey said.

"Toss him one, Andrew."

When we finished the joint, Willie said, "You got a second copy of that script?"

"I sure do."

"Okay, give me both. I want some other people to read this, too. I'll be back in touch with you through Snake after we've all had a chance to look it over. In the meantime, keep my involvement under your hat."

That night, the concert was at the Greek Theatre in Griffith Park. When I showed up at the show on the crew bus, Willie was backstage, looking radiant in the tee shirt I had given him a few hours earlier. He wasn't the only one. I had mine on, and a few of the crew and band members were wearing them, too—Snake, Poodie, and Easter, as I recall—all of us with the colorful logo spread across our chests. Of course, everyone else wanted one in the worst way, and the word was out that they had come from me.

"Hell," I said with a laugh, "I don't know anything about it."

During the next month or so, I stayed in touch with Poodie over the phone.

"That script of yours," he said, "has drawn a lot of attention from some of Willie's Hollyweird pals…, like James Caan and Robert Redford. They apparently feel fairly confident that if Pynchon didn't do it, a damned good writer surely did. And Willie's been wearin' those tee shirts you gave us almost every night."

Not long after that, I got a call from Snake.

"Andrew, we're gonna be at Harrah's in Tahoe at the end of the month," he said. "Willie would like to talk to you further about how he might be able to help out with the movie."

"I'll be there!"

Meanwhile, money was flowing in for the project, thanks to Gordie, David, and Paul hustling friends and family. Glen Wilder, who was still working on *Raging Bull*, invited the four of us to come down to L.A. to watch some boxing scenes he was directing. The action was being shot in the musty old Memorial Auditorium, which soon after was torn down and replaced by the Staple Center.

As we took our seats, the crews were arranging the ring and the cameras for the shots. Soon, an overweight sixty-year-old man in an orange sport coat walked in with a couple of fifty-year-old bubble-haired bleached blondes, one on each arm, and sat down a few seats away to my right.

Gordie whispered to me, "That's Jake LaMotta."

"He looks like a dirty old man. Look at that puss on 'im…. Scary."

To my surprise, I didn't get to see any boxing that day. They were shooting a riot scene in which the crowd burst into the ring to protest the referee stopping the fight. I got to see that scene at least ten times. The most interesting part was watching the stunt chairs being cracked over people's heads and fake blood being splashed all over the ring.

"Clean up the blood!" the assistant director would call out between each take.

The next day, I flew back to San Francisco, picked up Lisa, left the kids with my mom, and drove to Tahoe. Aside from Maynard, Lisa didn't know any of the Family, since she had her hands full at home with the kids. But she was a big fan of Willie's.

"Do you really think this movie has a chance?" she asked. "I mean, it's a cutthroat business, and none of your guys has any real experience in it."

"That's true, and fucking Gordie has some issues that worry the hell out of me. But the script is golden, and Willie seems onboard. It's gotten a lot of attention around Tinsel Town since he's had it. Gary Busey and Jan Michael Vincent know all about it."

When we got to Harrah's, they told me at the desk that Willie was staying in the Star Suite on the top floor.

"He's expecting you, sir," the clerk said. "Your suite is right next to his. All the charges have been paid. Here's your key to the private elevator."

I had been in the Star Suite once before for a party. It was beautiful—two levels, with a spiral staircase and a white grand piano in the living room.

That night, Lisa and I hung out with Maynard. We had a quiet dinner, then took a long walk along the lake.

"Hey, Maynard," I said, "remember the time you sprang Lisa from college?"

"Ah, yes…, Reed Penitentiary. I remember it well. You had to hide in the bathroom, Lisa, then make a dash for it. Right?"

"Oh, my god, I did!" Lisa said. "And then I had to ride the whole way from Portland on the back of your Harley…, in the rain and snow yet!"

The next afternoon, Snake dropped by our room to tell us that Willie wanted to talk between the first and second show that night.

"Just knock on the door. He'll be expecting you."

I gave Snake a little weed that I'd brought along.

Lisa was excited to see Willie live for the first time. However, she wasn't a party animal, and had no interest in drinking or gambling.

"All I see in the casinos, Andy," she said, "is depressed people everywhere."

She also wasn't very impressed by Koepke and Poodie clashing over young cowgirls.

But she loved watching the show from backstage. I grabbed a couple of folding chairs, and we sat in the wings at stage right, ten feet from Bobbie's piano. Lisa was mesmerized by how Bobbie played—this little woman, twenty years older than her, with hair down to her waist.

After the performance, as we headed to the elevator, Lisa said, "Willie never just shows up, does he, Andrew? I bet every performance is just as heartfelt as that one."

"That's certainly been my reaction since the first time I saw him."

We freshened up in our room and then went one suite over.

"Hey, Willie," I said as he opened the door.

"Come on in, Andrew, good to see ya. This must be Lisa. Great to meet ya after all this time. Heard about you from Maynard and your husband."

"I love your music, Willie. So do my babies, Ode and Autumn."

"That's great…. I'm makin' some coffee. Ya want some?"

"Sure," Lisa said.

"Ya got a beer, Willie?" I asked.

"I'm sure I can find one for you in this refrigerator, Andrew. Make yourselves comfortable."

Lisa and I sat down on a big white overstuffed couch, which faced a billion-dollar view of the lake.

"I *love* that piano, Willie," Lisa said. "What a beauty!"

"Do you play, Lisa?"

She nodded.

"Well, feel free to use it. It's all yours!"

Lisa blushed. "I'd be too nervous, Willie."

"Just relax, guys!"

A minute later, Willie came over with the coffees and the beer, put them down on the glass coffee table, and sat down on a love seat across from us.

Pointing toward the lake, he said, "Beautiful place, isn't it? Phil built this suite for Sammy Davis Junior. That's why the piano's here."

"I bet these walls could tell some Rat Pack stories," I said.

He smiled.

"Andrew," he said, "I've shown this script to some pretty important people, and they all love it. Most think it has a real chance. Unfortunately, I can't make a commitment just now, but let me know what I can do to help you get this thing rollin'. You've been a good friend to all of us. Hell, you're like one of the family. What can I do?"

I thought about the songs he'd written for *Honeysuckle Rose*, especially "On the Road Again," and then it hit me!

"Willie, how about if you agree to write at least one song, like the theme song or somethin', and maybe volunteer to do a cameo? You could indicate that in a casual letter of intent, nothing like a contract."

"That's not a bad idea, Andrew. I think that can be arranged. If this helps you kick the can a little further down the road, I'll write ya the letter. I'll even make sure it's on my new stationery. The script's great. Some of my folks seem to think Pynchon did write it, under a pseudonym."

"I've suspected that myself."

"Be sure and give David Anderson the address where to send the letter to, and when we get back to Austin, I'll get it out to ya."

"Thanks, Willie, I'm sure it will go a long ways towards helping us.

And thanks for wearing the tee shirts. Man, that's the best publicity in the world!"

"Everybody wants one, Andrew. Got an extra hundred?"

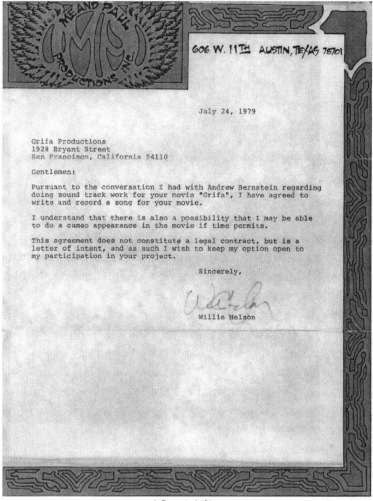

A. Bernstein Archives

We all cracked up.

"Well, guys, it's time to head down for the next show."

He grabbed a black cowboy hat off the piano, and we took the private elevator to the backstage area. On the way down, Lisa noticed something on his hat.

"That's a beautiful pin, Willie," she said.

"Well, thank you, Lisa. I like it, too. But I have no idea what the image on it represents."

"It's the Buddhist symbol for a loving heart. A very spiritual piece."

"A fan gave it to me. I loved it and put it on my hat so I wouldn't lose it. Now I know why. Thank you." He put his arm around Lisa and gave her a hug.

Willie's letter arrived at the production office in San Francisco two weeks later, which impressed Paul and David immensely. On the down side, I had assumed that they had exercised some control over Gordie's access to the production funds, since I had told them on at least a couple of occasions about his weakness for China white. They assured me that he had cleaned up his act, and they were keeping a watchful eye on him, as well as the production funds, now approaching three hundred thousand dollars.

Leaving the duties of storyboards, site trips, and interactions with the Hollywood folks to the production team, I set out to put together a group of musicians for a sound track that would rock this motion picture.

With Willie's letter in hand, I approached The New Riders of the Purple Sage, thinking that their hit song, Peter Rowan's "Panama Red," would be a perfect fit. I knew John "Marmaduke" Dawson from the late '60s. My girlfriend from those days rode horses with his sister, so I spent a good deal of time on the Dawsons' big country spread in the Palo Alto hills. John and I used to get stoned and talk about the Palo Alto music scene, including the Dead. I found out that he and Jerry knew each other from Dana Morgan's. John went on to co-write several Grateful Dead songs, and Jerry sat in on steel pedal guitar at many New Riders' concerts.

I got John's phone number from a mutual friend in San Francisco.

"John, its Andrew Bernstein."

"From the old horse days?"

"Yeah, long time. Hope you're well."

"How'd you get my number, Andrew?"

"Sally Mann gave it to me…. Anyway, I've got something I want to share with you…, a special project you may be interested in. Willie Nelson's a part of it."

"Cool. But listen, man, I'm exhausted. We just got off tour, so I can't do anything this week. How 'bout next week?"

Robert Altman Archives
John "Marmaduke" Dawson

"Fine."

He gave me his address.

On the evening we arranged, I drove up to Marin County and found his place in Corte Madera on the side of a gentle slope.

"Great to see ya, man!" John said as he opened the door and gave me a big hug. "C'mon in."

He introduced me to his wife, Alena, who was a documentary filmmaker.

"Are you still with Caroline?" he asked. "She was nice. And, oh, so beautiful!"

"It wasn't meant to be, John, but we're still friends."

"Those horse ladies are a handful, man."

I was eager to get down to business.

"Listen, John," I said, "this is new territory for me. I mean, you just never know when some crazy shit is gonna drop in your lap."

"What's up, man?"

"I've come across a hot screenplay that's gonna need a soundtrack. Willie's already made a commitment, and I think you would be perfect, too."

"You mean, a movie? Man, I grew up around that stuff. You know, with my dad being a producer and all. But we were never a Hollywood family. I've got great respect for the art, but the hustle always looked brutal to me. I'm a musician, and happily so."

"I hear ya, John. But Willie seems to be intrigued with Hollywood right now. He's got a major movie release coming out soon, and now he seems to be genuinely excited about this script. I don't know for sure who wrote this thing…, Thomas Pynchon's name's been mentioned…, but no one seems to know for sure. It's a helluva story, though. I mean, it's really hard not to like."

"Have you ever tried to put anything like this together before, Andrew? A movie soundtrack is a big job, man."

"It all starts with a good story, I hope."

"A good story's the easy part, Andrew," Alena said. "Most movies that get made are the worst scripts, but meet certain marketing models for the producers, and that's a fact. They're looking for properties that can target audiences all over the world and sell everything from Chevrolets to hamburgers. I suggest you do some more homework before you bet the farm on this thing. I mean it."

"Now, my dear," John said, "don't deflate his dream. You're such a realist. Us dreamers travel light. We don't much like stop signs. Besides, Willie's no slouch, and he likes it."

"Well, it might just sell a lot of records," she conceded.

At some point, I excused myself to go to the bathroom, which turned out to have the most unusual walls I had ever seen. They were covered with graffiti from every imaginable musician, artist, and gadfly in and around Marin County at the time. I picked out a blue pen from a basketful, searched for a square inch somewhere, and wrote, "Long live rock 'n' roll and marshmallows!" Then I signed it "California Slim."

"Nice work on the brag board in there, John," I said when I came out.

"Did you leave any words of wisdom for the ages, Andrew?"

"Of course, man. Squeezed in between Country Joe and Grace Slick."

"Well done!"

Alena had prepared a light meal for us, so we headed into the kitchen. At the end of the evening, I said, "John, I'm gonna leave a copy of the script for you and Alena to read. Please keep your minds open, and give me your honest opinions."

"If I like it," John said, "which I'm pretty sure I will, I'll probably sign on. Can I talk about this with anyone else?"

"Sure, but please keep the script to yourself."

"I will, I promise, but your phone may be ringing. Just about everybody I know would break a leg to work with Willie."

"Hey, man, let's go left foot, right foot, for the time being."

Within a few days, the phone did start ringing. First, it was Peter Rowan, from the old Homer's days with Old and in the Way. Back to Marin County to meet with Peter, only this time I brought Gordie, who Peter found a most intriguing figure. He wanted onboard, along with his rock band, The Free Mexican Air Force."

The guy who wrote Panama Red. Perfect!

I was batting 1,000 so far. Soon, I heard from Van Morrison's manager that Bonnie Raitt had gotten wind of it, and Marin County was buzzing about the project. But when John called me, he swore he had only told a couple of people, and the script never left his home. Whatever he did to spread the word, I forgave him, because he loved the story.

"This thing is real, boys," I said to Paul and David. "It's time to get some contracts in place. I know a music lawyer in town..., my classmate Jon, who's now working with Brian Rohan, a big shot music attorney in the city. I don't wanna go any further down this road without a legal plan. And, by the way, Gordie appears to be using again."

"Yeah, we know Andy," David said. "But we have no idea what to do about it."

Paul chimed in, "His latest plan is to rent a home in Hollywood to be closer to the action."

"What!? Gordie has access to *that* kinda money from the account?"

"At this point, his family's the biggest contributor to the bank account," David said.

"Well, for fuck sake!" I said. "That would've been nice to know before now!"

Things went quickly downhill from that point on.

We all tried in vain to get Gordie off his self-medication, but the movie money got pissed away on "pre-production" expenses—which meant lavish living in a big house in Hollywood, with lots of extracurricular activities.

I felt awful, since Willie had pitched the project to half of Hollywood, and I had half of Marin County talking about it. I truly believe it was one of the biggest creative casualties of the late 1970s.

White Limos and Red Carpets

For the premiere screening of Willie's film, which was now called *Honeysuckle Rose: A Song for You*, we all converged on LAX from Vegas, after a run of sold-out shows at Caesars Palace. Once again, a long line of white limos awaited us, this time courtesy of Warner Brothers. Everyone got his own limo, including me.

Poodie Locke Archives
Kenpeck, Tunin' Tom (who replaced Schroeder), Budrock, and Poodie, 1980

Off our caravan went to the Sheraton Universal Hotel for fun and sun a few days before the big night. As we drove up Sunset Boulevard, we passed a gigantic *Honeysuckle Rose* billboard with Willie, Dyan Cannon, and Amy Irving smiling down on our little caravan.

Surreal!

We spent the next couple of days hanging out at our hotel's bars and pools, or walking around the theme park at Universal Studios.

On a warm Saturday evening in June, the Family gathered in the lobby to go to Grauman's Chinese Theatre for the premiere. As the limos lined up, nobody was in a hurry, because a few well-known suspects had concocted a surprise for Willie.

Connie made sure that she and Willie got off the elevator at a prearranged time. All the rest of us had to do was act natural when they arrived in the lobby.

Stu Canall was a tall, thin man with white hair, whom Willie had nicknamed "Q-Tip." He and his band of merry men had found a fifteen-year-old Cadillac limo that looked as if it had been rolled out of an auto salvage yard. Deacon was in the driver's seat in a suit and tie, quite a contrast from his usual Hells Angels togs.

When Willie and Connie arrived right on time, a shiny monster of a white limo awaited them, on the other side of the foyer, with a tuxedoed driver holding open the back door. We all smiled as Willie and Connie greeted us on the way to the car. Just as they passed through the front doors, Stu gave the signal, and Deacon pulled up to the curb, with the old Cadillac spewing black smoke out the back. Then Stu rushed up to the car, opened the back door, pulled out a six-pack of Budweiser, handed it to Willie, and announced, "Your car is ready, sir!"

Willie was too distracted by this big night to notice that anything was wrong, and started to climb in. But then he saw that there was no back seat. At that point, Connie couldn't contain herself, and we all erupted.

Finally getting the joke, Willie laughed along with the rest of us, and Deacon pulled away in a cloud of smoke as a hubcap came spinning off across the driveway.

As I was about to get into my own limo, Kenny came up to me, looking miserable.

"Andrew," he said, "I'm feelin' sick. I think I've got some kinda stomach bug. Can I ride with you?"

"You look like you should be in bed, Kenpeck."

"I can't miss this."

"Well, lie down on the sofa and don't look out. It'll make you dizzy."

As our limo rolled up to the theatre, with its red carpet in front, a VIP usher opened the door for us, and Kenny and I got out to a sea of flashbulbs going off in our faces, as if we were somebody. It was a classic Hollywood opening with as much glitter and glam as Sydney Pollack could muster.

"Andrew," Kenny pleaded, "git me to a bathroom before I throw up all over this carpet."

We rushed to the lobby, and I grabbed the first person who had an official badge.

"Where's the nearest bathroom?" I asked.

The man took one look at Kenny and said, "Follow me, gentlemen."

He led us to a private office with a bathroom, where Kenny spent the next several minutes. When he finally emerged, he still looked green about the gills, but said he felt a bit better.

"Is there anything I can do for you, sir?" asked the tuxedo.

Pointing to some talent in the lobby, I asked, "Could you introduce us to those two blonds over there?"

The tuxedo smiled and left.

When Kenny and I returned to the lobby, there was Poodie in his element, giving interviews as if he were the producer of the movie. (In fact, after that night, we started calling him "the Producer.") In the background, we could hear him bellowing, "Cost of millions, cast of thousands" to anyone who would listen.

I spotted Steve outside, talking to two girls in the bleachers, so Kenny and I went out to listen to his pitch.

"So, y'all," he was saying to the cuties when we got there, "just gimme your names, and I'll git ya into the party after the movie."

He had those names in two seconds flat.

Inside the auditorium, there was a whole section set aside for the Willie Nelson Family, but there were only two seats left, right in the middle, so Kenny and I bumped knees with half the band.

"Where the fuck you assholes been?" one of the guys yelled.

We didn't bother telling him.

I sure hope Kenny doesn't puke in my lap!

When the audience quieted down, Sydney Pollack got up in front and gave a short speech.

"Making this movie," he said with some understatement, "was certainly a unique experience."

I could hear Dyan Cannon guffawing a few rows away.

Then the lights went down and the movie began. There were my friends on the silver screen, some with more face time than others, but everyone, including Kenny, with at least a bit part. Kenny sat stone-faced the whole time, just wanting to get back to the hotel. The concert scene with Willie and Emmylou was outstanding. Slim Pickens was especially great as Willie's manager, dispensing words of wisdom on all things important, from drinking to music to women. His affection for Willie was obvious.

After the movie, we all piled into our limos to make the drive from Hollywood to the party, which was held at Paramount's back lot western town, which had been used in hundreds of old TV and movie westerns, including *Gunsmoke*. Most of the buildings were just storefronts, but a few of them, like the saloon, had interiors as well. I'd seen that set in so many westerns that the place felt like home.

A stage had been set up at the main intersection of the little town for Willie and the band to perform. The buses were parked nearby, so we could relax with a little privacy. Of course, the band and crew had work to do, but everything was ready to go when we arrived.

The guests included film and studio people, and anyone lucky enough to "know someone." There were at least five hundred people there, many in western wear they had purchased for the occasion.

I can't tell the Jewish lawyers from the Jewish cowboys.

Since this was a celebration for a movie, something Hollywood does so well, the line between fantasy and reality seemed to blur. With the amps turned on and the sound adjusted, it was showtime. The western setting made a wonderful backdrop for the music. As usual, Willie opened with "Whiskey River," and also as usual, the audience went nuts. But this wasn't Cleveland, it was La-La Land, proving once again what a cross-section of Americans loved this man and his music.

Since I was allowed one guest for the party, I had invited Tom McCarthy, my old friend from elementary school days, who was a huge Slim Pickens fan. After my limo deposited Kenny and me at the party, I instructed the driver to pick Tom up at the Burbank airport. He arrived about midway through Willie's performance.

Dyan Cannon, who looked like a million bucks, was onstage with Willie, singing a few songs.

"Let's go onstage," I said to Tom. "This should be good."

Poodie saw us and waved us up with his pinlight.

Until that moment, I didn't know Dyan could sing. As freaked out as she had been on the set in San Antonio by Pee Hole's antics, she was equally relaxed and happy to be onstage with Willie that night. When she made a few comments about the unexpected journey she had embarked on with

Willie, it was quite touching. She had clearly come to love this man—like everyone else who gets to know him.

After a while, Tom whispered to me, "Andy, there's Slim Pickens down there. Let's go over and say hi."

Sure enough, Slim was drinking and laughing with some folks off to the side of the stage, near the old western bar. So down we went to engage with Mr. Pickens. He nodded to us as we approached, so we hung around until he had a chance to say hello.

"I've been a fan of yours all my life, Slim," Tom said. "My name's Tom."

Slim threw out his big paw and said, "Goddamn, good to meet you, Tom!"

I stood aside and let them talk and talk. Tom loved old western novels, especially Tom Mix, and it turned out that Slim did, too. Looking at the joy on Tom's face, I was so pleased for my old friend.

I was just about to leave the two to their chat, when Tom said to Slim, "You probably get asked this a hundred times a day, but would you mind saying 'shit' the way you did in *Dr. Strangelove?*"

"Actually, I haven't been asked for a long time," Slim replied. "I'd be happy to. Give me a little room here."

Tom backed up, and Slim, replete with cowboy hat, big belt buckle, and bolo tie, mimicked his famous missile-riding scene. He reared back, held his hat in place, with his other hand gripping imaginary reins, and let out the real deal: "Sheeeeeeeee-IT, Tom!" he bellowed.

Everyone within twenty feet broke out into applause and laughter.

Just about that time, Willie played the opening chords of "On the Road Again," and Slim started dancing and toasting everyone around us.

What a guy! He's having more fun than any other ten people here.

When the evening wound down, and people started to leave, Tom and I strolled around the old west. As Poodie's crew took down the amps and the drums, Tom and I sat on the wooden sidewalk in front of the Long Branch Saloon in *Gunsmoke's* Dodge City.

"Hey, Tom," I said, "remember when Chester limped up these stairs with his bad leg, looking for Marshall Dillon, always with a worried look on his face?"

"Yeah, I wonder how many times we watched that..., including the reruns. There was a lot of blood spilled on these stairs."

"Not to mention all the moves put on Ms. Kitty by outlaws inside this saloon," I said.

"Andy, we've seen it all, man. Remember Kreutzmann, the reborn cowboy, ready to walk away from his drums? And a year later, he and Jerry gave birth to the Grateful Dead."

"Shit, Tom, what about those crazy wonderful nights developing the light show, and your being the only jarhead at the first acid test in L.A.? Who could have guessed what would come out of those LSD-fueled experiments? I always loved it when you came to those shows at the Fillmore to help out, Tom. All of us Paly boys together, making the walls of that hallowed hall explode with color. And Jake's critters crawling around, changing colors and jumping off the screens."

"Remember the nights that Dan needed help at Homer's?" said Tom. "One night we had to teach a guy a lesson about slapping his girlfriend around in the parking lot!"

"Shit, I forgot about that one!" I howled. "Bloodied that fucker's nose up, probably broke it! Man, I'm so glad you came down tonight. You were reading westerns when we first met as nine-year-olds. And here we are, at thirty-three, still acting out our cowboy fantasies."

Just then, Poodie walked up. "Hey, Tom, the limo driver's waitin' to run ya back to Burbank. Time to go. We're sure glad to see ya. Come out anytime…. The bus is ready to roll, Andrew."

I walked over to the limo with Tom and gave him a big hug. It had been quite a night.

Tom laughed. "I'll take the sight of Slim Pickens dancing in the street to my grave," he said.

As the Lincoln pulled away with Tom's window down, I called out, "See ya, buddy! Be well!"

I walked over to the Silver Eagle, which had all its lights in emergency flasher mode. The words to "Somewhere Over the Rainbow," which Willie had recently started playing in his sets, filled my head. I took a whiff of the sweet diesel on the breeze just before Big Al opened the door for me. As we slowly pulled out of Dodge City, I grabbed a beer and took a seat on the couch. Budrock was rolling a joint at the table. Kopeck, Kenpeck, Easter, D.W., Pee Hole, and Garvey were onboard, milling around. Poodie was on his throne, overseeing his brood. These guys had become my family. I knew the bonds with some of them would last a lifetime.

Yes, Dorothy, you CAN go home again. Even if Kansas is in Los Angeles, and the Wizard has pigtails.

In loving memory of my mother...

Betty Grace Bernstein
(November 12, 1914–May 16, 2000)

Index

s/677/P